Coping with Stress
at Work

This work is dedicated to all those who are making it part of their jobs to reduce stress at work

Coping with Stress at Work

Case Studies from Industry

Edited by
Judi Marshall and
Cary L Cooper

Gower

Published by
Gower Publishing Company Limited
Aldershot, Hants, England

British Library Cataloguing in Publication Data

Coping with stress at work.
   1. Psychology, Industrial
   2. Stress (Psychology)
   3. Stress (Physiology)
   I. Marshall, Judi
  II. Cooper, Cary L.
  158.7   HF5548.8

ISBN 0-566-02338-5

Typeset in Great Britain by
Pintail Studios Ltd, Ringwood, Hants
Printed and bound in Great Britain by
Biddles Ltd, Guildford and King's Lynn

Contents

The Contributors

Judi Marshall Editor	Lecturer in Organisation Behaviour, School of Management, University of Bath, Bath, UK
Cary L. Cooper Editor	Professor of Organisational Psychology, Department of Management Sciences, University of Manchester Institute of Science and Technology, Manchester, UK
John D. Adams	Consultant, Washington, USA
Laurence E. Burns	Clinical Psychologist, Rochdale Area Health Authority, Rochdale, UK
Michael D. Cohen	Manager of Executive Fitness Programs, PepsiCo Inc Headquarters, New York State, USA
Dennis L. Colacino	Director of Fitness Programs, PepsiCo Inc Headquarters, New York State, USA
Nico van Dijkhuizen	Research Psychologist, Ministry of Defence – Navy, The Netherlands
Peggie Kellam	Member of MIND Executive, Northamptonshire Association for Mental Health, UK
John Lightbody	Counsellor, Shell Chemicals UK Ltd, Manchester, UK
Michael A. McDonald	Occupational Health Physician, London, UK

Andrew H. Melhuish   General   Practitioner,   Henley-on-Thames, UK

Thoralf Ulrik Qvale   Senior Research Officer, Work Research Institute, Oslo, Norway

Geoffrey N. Sworder   Training Officer, ICI Ltd, London, UK

Charles Vetter   Director, ACCEPT Services, London, UK

Introduction

The calls for companies to do something about stress have become common and often strident over the last few years, as we become more aware of its multiple ill-effects. This book was prompted by curiosity about what (if anything!) is being done in industry, and an interest in encouraging other companies to follow suit. Its chapters then have been written by practitioners for practitioners and many of the authors will describe the stress *they* experienced in trying to put 'practice' down readably and to a deadline. The emphasis throughout is on the realities of practical attempts to reduce and manage stress in organisations. Not the scheme as it looked on paper, but in action with all its difficulties, setbacks, compromises and triumphs. Initial guidelines from the editors suggested that authors include discussion of four key issues in their chapters. Whilst not all followed this format, a brief discussion of it will give the reader some idea of what to expect.

Firstly, what is being done? This speaks for itself as the main expected content of a chapter. Secondly, why? Where did the idea come from to do something about stress? Who had been involved? Had key people sponsored action? How had the critical decision been justified? Especially for people who must influence large, cost-conscious organisations, these are key issues in motivating and achieving change. It is interesting that in one case study the 'reasoning' behind their decision to go ahead was very obviously 'multi-stranded'. The company has become committed, but no simple explanation of why and how can be given. Thirdly, what problems were encountered in implementation? We did not want a glossy account, but one from which we can learn – 'warts and all'. How did people react? Were there 'suspicious' individuals or groups who tried to block the scheme's development? What things went wrong? How did the implementers deal with these difficulties? Have they, in fact, been able to do so? Fourthly, we asked for some evaluation of effects. Is there any data, however anecdotal, on the effects of the action? Given companies' reluctance to get involved in stress management, we expected particularly severe pressure on our authors to justify the value of their work. Positive evaluations might encourage others and help them take up the topics in their own companies. We were also curious to see how well practical experience supports academics' prophecies of the benefits of stress interventions, and to be able to compare in some way the usefulness of the various strategies. The authors have covered these topics well, and more besides. We do, however, have one regret – that a potentially highly instructive, but probably rather pessimistic, chapter was never written because of illness. Its title was to have been: 'A personal account of how I have never been allowed to tackle stress in organisations'!

What then can be done about stress? And how did we select our contributors? Elsewhere we have discussed the range of options available in theoretical terms (for example, Cooper and Marshall, 1978) and several chapters here elaborate them more practically (especially those by Melhuish and Dijkhuizen). Essentially, we can ask three questions in deciding on an *initial* strategy. Whose responsibility is it – the company's or the individual's? Is the initial action to be directed at changing the individual or the environment in which he or she operates? Are we trying to prevent stress or cure it once it has occurred?

In practice, and in the long term, the answer to all three questions is 'both'! There is little point in a company offering a counselling service if employees don't use it. Changes in individuals' attitudes to work will eventually help to change the company culture, or they will be extinguished. And whilst we may be able to prevent much stress, there will always be some which must be attended to 'after the event'. But here we are concerned with who can start and where.

The issue of whether companies should take an interest in reducing stress is vital to this book and so is left for separate consideration below. We firmly believe that the answer is 'yes', and shall do our best to persuade the uncommitted reader to this view. To move on to the second question, in practice it seems that most activities which are overtly anti-stress are directed at helping the individual cope better, rather than at changing the work environment, and this person-orientation is therefore reflected in this volume. This touches on two important points about doing things about stress, which help to explain this apparent lack of organisational change and are thus worthy of note here.

The first is that stress management is the implicit aim of many organisational maintenance and development activities not overtly labelled as such. For example, the clear demarcation of responsibilities between levels in the nursing hierarchy serves to reduce individual anxiety (Marshall, 1980). Most factors in the work environment have potential to cause stress to someone at some time and so many organisational activities which intentionally or unintentionally change the work situation have some power to increase or alleviate stress. Holidays, pleasant working conditions, and regular 'skills training' are some of the more routine stress reduction tactics. In many circumstances, for example in the introduction of a new appraisal system, it is more appropriate to take stress into account as one of several important factors than to focus attention on it as a separable dimension of working life (which it is not). In the UK at least, the concern about stress does not yet appear to have motivated substantial deliberate changes to the environment of jobs and organisations or, if it has, less emotive reasons are given for the resulting interventions. The Norwegian chapter particularly, and to a lesser extent the Dutch contribution, present a markedly different perspective. Their approach is to look for structural causes and solutions to stress. The cynic might say that organisations will never change 'substantially' or are too slow to do so or often change for the worse anyway, and that we must focus on the protection of the individual, to have any effect at all. We are less pessimistic and feel that with time, interventions that seek to change *both* the individual and his or her environment will become the norm.

The second point revealed by the current person-oriented focus of stress interventions is the extent to which solutions must be individually tailored to the organisation in which they are implemented, and to the society in which that organisation operates. The organisation's structure, size and resources, but most importantly its norms and values, will determine what are acceptable stress management strategies and how these can be implemented. The stage of acceptance of a new 'topic' is also an important influencing factor. Given current circumstances on all these dimensions, relatively low-risk interventions are understandably the 'order of the day'.

The third basic issue of whether action should be preventive or remedial is also significantly affected by the organisation's position and attitudes at a particular time. Both preventive and remedial possibilities are covered in this volume. Currently training is the main preventive and counselling the main remedial strategy employed.

Having set the scene of what we were looking for, how did we find our contributors? 'With difficulty', as the saying goes! We initially knew of a few companies or individuals who were doing something about stress, and extensive search revealed a few others. There was certainly no widespread knowledge of what is happening on which we could draw, although we have the impression that more and more companies are at least 'interested'. We discovered, however, that many are reluctant to publicise their experiences in this area. A few had shown interest in taking action, had perhaps even piloted some activity, but had let this initiative lapse, usually explaining that it had not been 'the right time' to do anything. Other companies who are currently actively involved felt that they did not want to attract publicity. Some were concerned about their company's public image – 'we don't want to give the impression we're a company with a big stress problem' – although reasonably sure they are not atypical in the incidence of stress amongst their workforce. Others were more concerned about the effects publicity might have internally. Having 'nursed' a project along, they did not want to disturb it at a sensitive stage by writing it up for the outside world.

This, then, was how we found our authors. They are some of the growing band who are taking stress, or more correctly its management, seriously, and are keen to share their triumphs, disappointments, lessons learnt and conclusions to date with a wider public.

Before detailing the book's contents, we should like to outline the reasons why companies should take an interest in and do something about stress. We shall do so by considering the three most common objections they raise when asked to do so. Firstly, at times executives do not see stress as their business, because they do not think it's 'a bad thing'. This is partly a matter of terminology. The word 'stress' has been used to refer to many things, some of which have obviously beneficial consequences; it is not surprising substantial numbers of people want to keep it. If, however, we distinguish between everyday *pressures* and *stress*, where individuals experiencing the latter are unable to cope and anxious, suffer symptoms of physical and mental ill health and perform badly in their tasks and interpersonal relationships, then the concept of stress becomes much less appealing! Given such a distinction, even hard-headed top executives can more easily be persuaded that improved employee health can contribute either directly or indirectly to efficiency, effectiveness and the organisation's ability to cope with change. Those with a quality of working life perspective will need even less persuading, for they will see improved employee health as a legitimate end in its own right. Anyway, we are not suggesting that organisations do away with stress altogether, but that they manage it to tolerable levels. A further possible reason for senior managers' belief in the value of stress is the obvious fact that they are survivors of organisational stress and so may be expected to approve of the 'survival of the fittest' management development 'policies' from which they have benefited. What evidence we have suggests that senior managers are markedly healthier than those lower down the hierarchy – particularly middle managers – and so should not judge others by themselves.

A second major obstacle to action is companies' arguments that stress is not their problem – it is the individual's responsibility and largely caused outside work anyway. Firstly, companies can hardly deny the significant impact they have on individuals' lives, and life-styles. They demand, at a minimum, approximately one-third of the individual's waking time, determine their standard of living and main non-voluntary relationships; they significantly influence where they live geographically and what the future holds. They are, in sum, a major source of demands and constraints on their employees. As stress is multi-causal, complex, interactive, highly individual and often self-reinforcing, it is artificial to ask whether it is caused by work *or* home (although two authors in this book do suggest that the final trigger to seek help often comes from developments in the latter). Typically, the two 'arenas' act in combination to reduce or foster potential stress initiated in either. Having failed to assign blame definitively, it can be said with far greater certainty that if an individual is suffering stress this will show up in effects at work. Early signs include being unable to make decisions or to think long term; poorer quality relationships; tiring more easily and the loss of a sense of perspective (and humour!). Obviously, effects on job performance vary, but for most people, most of the time these behavioural symptoms will lead to poorer performance. This will be especially detrimental for those in more creative, broadly-based and future-oriented jobs. This is why the organisation cannot be pedantic about assigning 'blame' precisely before it starts dealing with the effects and improving its employees', and therefore its own, performance.

The third argument we should like to tackle is that appropriate selection can screen out stress 'cases' and therefore this is the only action companies need to take. Whether or not it is ethical, it is certainly not practicable or desirable. Measurement would be extremely difficult. Could we do it, however, we would be robbing the company of much material which is very valuable in its place: the achievement-oriented performer, the perfectionist, and possibly 'nervous', but environmentally sensitive learner, for example. And we would still not account for stress which is less predictable because it is largely environmentally-caused or time-dependent.

These are some of the reasons why companies should pay attention to stress and try to manage it to tolerable levels. Pilot schemes in this area are especially high risk and we hope this volume will encourage those tempted to take action by: exploring some of the

options; providing 'tips' on how they can be put into practice; supplying some data by which the different strategies can be evaluated; and,
thus, reducing some of that risk.

The chapters in this book cover a range of approaches to stress
management. Most concentrate on changing the individual either by
equipping him or her with more skills or physical resilience to stress as
prevention, or helping him or her cope with stress once it has
occurred. Some approaches are currently aimed mainly at management levels, others are organisation-wide. As training is the most
common way of dealing with new organisational requirements (apart
from ignoring them) we start with this approach. Melhuish offers a
particularly comprehensive and wide-ranging discussion. He provides
a valuable background to the volume as a whole in an exploration of
stress as a concept and, more practically, as identifiable symptoms.
He also covers some of the many different forms training can take
before going on to describe his own work with managers from various
companies. This contribution emphasises the role a doctor can play,
particularly in influencing top management to take an interest. The
second chapter by Sworder is a more specific description of the initia-
tion and development of a tailor-made stress programme within ICI.
The third training contribution provides the views of an independent
consultant. Adams outlines the format he has developed during extensive consultancy work in both the United States and the United
Kingdom. He also provides some evaluation of the benefits of training
to participants.

A second obvious string to the preventive bow is the promotion of
good physical and mental health, and this is the focus of the book's
second main section. Some companies are now providing sports
facilities, for example, to encourage employees to take regular
exercise. In the United States many now offer integrated 'physical
fitness programmes', and we hear from Colacino and Cohen about
one currently being piloted by the headquarters of PepsiCo Inc. with a
view to extension to its divisions. Relaxation underpins many recommended 'anti-stress' strategies. In the fifth chapter, a highly
experienced consultant, Burns, looks at relaxation techniques and
what they have to offer.

The third part of the book deals with remedial action to help the
individual cope with stress and its symptoms. The first chapter in this
section describes the setting up and working of an occupational health
service in a company of approximately 1000 employees. This is a
particularly appropriate link between the preventive and remedial
themes as the service provides elements of both. McDonald's account
also shows a 'referral' system in action and so anticipates the remaining chapters in the section which essentially deal with such a system's

'output'. This 'investigation' provides, in addition, valuable data on the incidence and distribution of mental ill health in a work population. The next two contributions consider counselling as a service organisations can offer employees. Lightbody discusses counselling in theoretical terms before describing and evaluating the in-company system he has been operating in a large plant for the last six years. Kellam's chapter explores an alternative strategy of 'working from the outside'. She has been involved in the building up of a community-supported service which now offers help to local companies who might be unwilling or unable to set up such a resource for themselves. The fourth chapter of this section looks at one of the more severely disabling and job-threatening symptoms of stress – alcoholism. Vetter considers how employees can be helped to cope more successfully.

The book's final part moves away from individual-oriented action to illustrate ways in which environments can be changed to reduce stress. In Norway, legislation has stepped in to promote the quality of working life. Qvale describes the background to this legislation, and illustrates the effects it is already having with two case study examples of participative job re-design. Dijkhuizen takes a wider view of this area. Based on research work in the Dutch steel industry, he maps some of the possibilities open to organisations interested in change and improvement. He too discusses examples of stress management in action.

This, then, is the book's team of 'explorers' – an enthusiastic group who have volunteered to make public the wide variety of activities they are directing to managing stress in organisations more effectively. In conclusion let us summarise the hopes we and they have for this volume. Firstly, we hope that it will contribute to reappraisal of the criteria by which organisations measure themselves. Many of the more mechanistic indices of organisational performance are now being rejected as inadequate. Here, we have added to the growing body of evidence that taking care of our working population as people is not mere 'do-gooding', but makes financial good sense (a yardstick we can seldom escape) by improving efficiency, effectiveness and creativity. Secondly, we hope these chapters will be of direct practical value by providing a 'cafeteria' from which interested readers can not only select approaches suitable to their organisation's character and current state, but also formulate plans to convert grand ideas into sensible action. If we have contributed to concern about stress and enthusiasm for its better management we shall also consider these pages well-spent. Our final hope is that this book is a beginning rather than an end. We hope to see our work respected (please!) but copied, bettered and even superseded, so that the next few years will bring many similar stories to tell.

REFERENCES

C. L. Cooper and J. Marshall, *Understanding Executive Stress* (London, Macmillan, 1978)

J. Marshall, 'Stress Amongst Nurses', in C. L. Cooper and J. Marshall (eds), *White Collar and Professional Stress* (London, Wiley, 1980)

PART I

TRAINING

1 The Doctor's Role in Educating Managers about Stress

Andrew H. Melhuish
Henley-on-Thames, UK

The last twenty years have seen a steady accumulation of evidence from research and from work statistics to demonstrate the link between stress and impaired physical and mental health on the one hand, and decreased performance at work and individual quality of life on the other. There seems no doubt at all that stress can cause illness and impair performance. Knowledge of the factors which can cause stress, and ability to manage stress when it occurs should therefore be an essential part of management education. Senior management require this knowledge in order to utilise the human resources under their control to the best advantage, while the manager himself has a stake in both his own health and that of his staff.

The stakes involved in stress at work are indeed high. Impaired quality of life and performance at work are difficult to measure, although recent reports from the United States of the results of company rehabilitation programmes for alcoholic staff have shown the tremendous financial benefits which can accrue for the firm through the successful rehabilitation and return to full work of the alcoholic. An alcoholic employee represents the firm's investment in his training; firing him is a total loss of this investment, while rehabilitation recovers the investment and gives great personal benefit. The medical consequences of stress are more definite. It has been calculated that one in four managers will die before they reach their 65th birthday, the majority from coronary heart disease. Such figures refer only to death; they take no account of those managers forced into early retirement by illness. And retirement from work does not take away the medical risk of stress. The superannuation department of one large British firm calculated that in 1977 nearly one-half of all its managers retiring at 65 failed to reach their 66th birthday. These figures apply just to managers, who in fact enjoy much better health than their staff. At a staff level, it has been estimated that over the last twenty years in Britain, certificates for mental illness increased by nearly 200 per cent for men and by 370 per cent for women and that mental illness (mostly, it seems, related to stress) caused three times more time lost from work than did industrial action.

This gloomy picture is not, of course, the whole story. Annual statistics show that, in general, the health and quality of life of all social classes have improved considerably since 1945. Managers, in social class 1, do even better than 'average'. More detailed analysis of the figures for mortality and morbidity in 1978 showed clearly that better health was enjoyed by managers in comparison with other social classes. This better health probably reflects the greater satisfaction obtained by managers from the challenge of their work for, in simple terms, it can be assumed that stress at work occurs when pressures exceed satisfaction. Numerous surveys have shown that managers obtain far more satisfaction than stress from their work, while in a survey I carried out on young managers at Henley Staff College, 89 per cent reported that they obtained great satisfaction from their work. The physical and mental health of this sample was uniformly high.

The fact remains, however, that an understanding of health, and of the effects of stress on health, is of vital importance to the manager and that stress can intrude into three separate aspects of his life:

(i) *His own personal health* Many diverse factors contribute to good quality of life. Good health is one of the most important of these factors. Certainly, poor health can create for the manager great problems in coping at work and in sharing life fully with his family and friends.

(ii) *His value to the firm as a manager* Ill health can remove from the organisation, without warning and for an uncertain period, an important member of the management team. If this removal is permanent, the cost of replacement will be high. In addition. the effect of the illness of one manager on the morale of the others is considerable. In a recent management course at Henley a member died from a heart attack during the first week of the course. The overall performance of that course was significantly altered by this one tragic event.

(iii) *His ability to recognise stress in the staff whom he manages* Mention has already been made of the benefits which can be gained from the early recognition and treatment of staff with an alcohol problem. The established alcoholic, however, is a gross example of impaired health. How many more workers are performing at a reduced level of efficiency due to chronic stress or chronic ill health which are not sufficiently obvious to attract help? The manager is in an ideal situation to recognise poor performance and to offer help to the sufferer.

Why then do managers have so little knowledge about stress; and why is it that, even if they do recognise stress in themselves or their staff, they have very little idea how to manage it? The answer is complex and includes:

(a) The reluctance of senior management to admit that the work style they encourage may cause stress and damage health. Increasing pressure and challenge to staff may increase performance but, as will be discussed later, may exceed the individual's potential, and then cause stress and reduced quality of life. This conflict between responsibility for the firm's financial success, and responsibility for the quality of life of employees must be hard for senior management to resolve. At the same time, senior managers who may have achieved their exalted positions by working long and unsocial hours, travelling great distances and, as a result, seeing little of their families, may expect their subordinates to make similar sacrifices.

(b) The ambition and pride of so many managers which makes them reluctant to admit that they cannot cope with the job they have been given.

(c) The dependence of many managers on their job for the provision of most of their satisfaction in, and quality of, life. Such managers are often termed 'workaholics' and their commitment to their work can set off a vicious circle in which too little time with the family leads to family problems and often divorce, with the result that the 'workaholic' becomes totally dependent on his work for satisfaction.

(d) Reluctance of managers to learn about stress. Ignorance so often causes fear and fear may lead, like the ostrich burying its head, to a resistance to education.

(e) Lack of medical support when help is needed. Today's medical culture provides treatment rather than prevention and the six-minute general practice consultation, often resulting in the prescription of a tranquilliser, is of little value in treating stress.

The answer to these problems must lie in improving the ability of managers to cope with stress through better education. Senior management must be persuaded that such education is necessary and can be cost effective, and the manager himself must have the time and interest to learn. Educating managers about stress can be such a worthwhile exercise, for managers have the intelligence to learn about stress, the ability to alter their own work environment if necessary in order to reduce stress (unlike most factory workers), and the facility to influence the work environment of their staff if they feel that the latter need greater support and less pressure.

Who then is best qualified to explain stress to managers? Stress impairs health and reduces performance. Knowledge of stress at work is thus shared between such disciplines as doctors, psychologists and behavioural scientists, and all these disciplines have a contribution to make to education. The specialised skill which the doctor can bring to education is his awareness of the factors which can affect physical and mental health. In addition, the firm's doctor may have the opportunity to meet the manager during a consultation requested by the manager, or at regular medical checks arranged by the firm. These meetings should provide the opportunity for frank discussion of health and stress in the totally confidential atmosphere of the medical consultation.

This chapter will cover mainly the role of the doctor in educating groups of managers. The individual consultation is a personal experience and difficult to describe. Its success depends on the expectations and openness of the manager, and the medical skills and willingness to listen of the doctor. It will be mentioned therefore only when its content can contribute to education. The whole field of education about stress will first be considered. It is difficult to review the availability and content of education without knowing who is to be educated, where such education will take place and who will provide it. This review will come in the section entitled 'theoretical considerations'. This will be followed by a section on the practical content of education about stress, which must contain information appropriate to managers concerning their normal health and the effects which stress can exert on their health. The importance of preventing stress through an understanding of its effects, rather than treating it when it has occurred, will be emphasised. The third section will attempt to describe in detail some of the education taking place at present in Britain, and in the fourth and last section the prospects for education in the future will be discussed.

Throughout this chapter the assumption will be made that manager and staff are male. This is, of course, not always the case, and reduced discrimination and prejudice against women in management must mean that soon there will be even more women managers. The male manager is described because it is grammatically easier. The woman manager does, of course, have her own problems; these are outside the scope of this chapter but are mentioned in my book *Executive Health* (Melhuish, 1978).

1 Theoretical considerations

The aim of education about stress should be to make available appropriate information to the manager who most needs to receive this information, at a time and place which will suit both the manager and his employer. However education can only be made available through the goodwill of the employer, and so this section will start with ways in which doctors may attempt to increase the awareness among senior management of the benefits of educating their managers about stress. Once the decision to provide education has been made, then management (or in the case of larger firms, the department responsible for education) must select which managers have most to learn, where they can be taught, who best can provide the education and what sort of information should be provided.

A medical approach to senior management

The manifestations of stress are many and so the 'straws in the wind' which may alert senior management to the need for education about stress will be equally diverse. Often sudden illness acts as a trigger. In one firm, the deaths within a three-month period of two middle managers from heart attacks precipitated the decision, although the subject had been discussed at board level during the preceding two years. The research department of another company showed interest in education when two of its leading research workers suffered bizarre presentations of stress, namely periods of total amnesia (forget-fulness), at almost the same time. Several more firms have set up symposia on stress due to the realisation that their staff turnover, sickness absence and uncertified absenteeism were steadily increasing, and compared unfavourably with their competitors. The realisation that one of their board had a serious alcohol problem pushed two other firms into education. One last factor which may influence senior management is the increasing awareness (particularly in the United States, Canada and Sweden) of the financial consequences which can result from failure to manage stress. This awareness is based on research findings and informed discussion freely available in management journals.

A second stimulus towards education can be feedback from managers themselves, either directly to senior management or through the personnel department. Most managers want to learn more about stress, and the increasing emphasis on feedback in modern education gives full impact to these requests.

Another factor has been the realisation by senior management that many of their brighter staff are requesting early retirement, or are refusing promotion or relocation. Such attitudes reflect the greater awareness of many modern managers of the priorities in their lives. They may not see the financial, taxed rewards of promotion as adequate compensation for the added pressure and commitment to work. Similarly, relocation is, not surprisingly, being resisted on many more occasions; indeed it seems surprising that in the past so many managers have accepted without complaint the pressures of moving themselves and their families at regular intervals. They are perhaps taking notice of the wise words of Logan Pearsall Smith 'There are two things to aim at in life: first to get what you want; and after that to enjoy it. Only the wisest of mankind achieve the second.' Promotion and relocation. are well-known 'at risk' periods for stress; education about stress must help the manager to make well-balanced, rational decisions at these times, and will also enable senior management to receive helpful feedback concerning the attitudes of managers to these changes.

Lastly, the boards of many companies are looking at the industrial climate of the next few years with some trepidation, feeling that stress may become a more frequent occurrence in their employees. It seems that unemployment will continue to rise. Some managers may lose their jobs, while those that are secure still have the stressful task of making loyal and long-serving staff redundant. Competition for shrinking markets in Europe and the rest of the world must lead to increased demands on management. If stress among managers does not exist at present (and some companies seem still to believe that they are lucky enough to be exempt from it) it will certainly occur in the future. The sensible approach must be to prevent stress as much as possible through education. An additional benefit to senior management of early action should be the improved morale of their staff as they see that interest is being taken in their welfare – the so called 'Hawthorne effect'.

Which managers will benefit most from education?

Ideally, education about stress should be available to all managers. The newly-promoted young manager is particularly at risk, for example, as managing people and taking greater responsibility for decisions must provide pressures to which he is unaccustomed. This is an ideal time for education, for experience learned at an early age will provide benefit for the rest of his working life. Middle management may be under stress themselves, as they fight for promotion or reach their own particular career ceiling. In addition, they seem increasingly aware of how important it is to recognise stress in their staff, a simple guide to recognising stress being the most requested part of my talks. Senior management might be thought to have learned about stress by experience, yet managers attending senior management courses at Henley have proved to be my most receptive audience. Finally, for the older manager, retirement can be a major source of stress, and with more and more firms now offering early retirement, the opportunity to discuss this important decision is vital. Further education during the last two or three years at work should be available to prepare the manager satisfactorily for retirement.

It is to be hoped that senior management, having made the decision to provide education about stress, will do so for as many levels of management as possible. Unfortunately this is by no means always the case. Like regular medical checks, education is often only offered to the more senior manager. As will be mentioned later, all the available health statistics for managers show that the more senior the manager is, the better his health. To offer this successful, healthy senior manager regular medical checks and education about stress is splendid; but these should not be provided at the expense of his more junior colleagues, who are more likely to suffer stress and illness.

Where and when can education take place?

The educational policy of the individual firm will normally determine the site of education about stress. Some firms prefer to provide education in their own premises. For a topic such as stress they will provide symposia to bring together groups of interested managers and experts in the particular field. As a result, time lost from work and expense are reduced to a minimum. Such planned, live, education at work can be supplemented by audio-visual teaching which can be used to provide information for anyone interested. In the United States, information on topics such as stress and alcoholism are often available on videocassettes in public rooms. Other firms set aside a definite period of time each year, usually a week, for education. This week may be arranged at a convenient residential centre and run by the firm's own management and development staff. Some firms, such as the banks, are large and wealthy enough to run their own educational centres. Alternatively, firms may make use of management training colleges for a week's education, or for longer periods at certain stages of the working manager's life.

Firms using management training colleges cannot necessarily assume that courses at these colleges will include education about stress. Managers who have attended such courses are often critical retrospectively of the content of the course, feeling that they contain too much theory of management. They comment that most theoretical information can be provided by colleagues at work, while the manager should really be learning about himself, his strengths and weaknesses, the priorities in his life, managing stress – in fact, about how to manage himself. Education at management training colleges can itself provide problems for the manager. Regular meals, long sedentary hours of education, busy social life with alcohol and tobacco readily available are all unhealthy habits, and the manager may finish his spell of education intellectually sharp but physically flabby. These particular problems will be discussed in detail later.

In the context of where education can take place, mention must be made of the important role of the regular medical check. This check may be carried out by the firm's doctor or by an outside specialist, or by an organisation such as BUPA (the British United Provident Association Ltd). Most managers, and unfortunately many of the doctors carrying out the medical examinations, regard these checks as an exercise in diagnosing illness and initiating treatment when necessary. This would seem a very real waste of a marvellous opportunity for preventive medicine, for positive advice from doctor to manager on how to stay well, not how ill he has become, and for discussion on how to cope with stress.

Finally it should be pointed out that the manager must not assume that all the responsibility for providing education about stress lies with the firm. Individual managers can learn about stress for themselves. Courses are run at centres in large cities for example, and the manager can also take the initiative in approaching personnel officers and medical staff at work for discussion and advice.

Who best can provide education?

Education about stress must be carried out by doctors with an interest in the effects of stress on health, and a knowledge of the pressures involved in a manager's work and life-style. The doctor most suited to this role must be the industrial doctor who possesses the knowledge, and hopefully the interest, and is readily available to the manager. The firm's doctor is in an ideal situation to influence senior management, both to provide education about stress, and to make other changes in the firm which might improve work satisfaction and encourage good habits on the one hand, or reduce pressures and the risk of bad habits on the other. In larger firms he will have available a medical department staffed by nurses qualified in industrial medicine, who have great potential to educate staff about stress and recognise and treat stress in the patients they see. However, the close relationship of the firm's doctor with senior management can sometimes prove a greater disadvantage than benefit. Many managers are unwilling to discuss medical or personal problems with the firm's doctor for fear they will be reported back to senior management, and so influence future career prospects. Equally, the manager may simply be unwilling to admit to a friend and colleague that he is having difficulty in coping. In addition, part of the doctor's medical duties may be to carry out medical examinations on managers to see if they are fit for their work. The results of these examinations may be disclosed to the employer, but only with the knowledge and full agreement of the manager. So the concern of the manager over confidentiality is understandable, and may be difficult to resolve. In the United States this possible impasse is often avoided by retaining outside medical specialists to give advice to staff. The manager is then seen away from his place of work, which takes away any threat of loss of confidentiality. Education about stress requires time, enthusiasm, and personal understanding of the subject and lecturing skills as well as knowledge, and for this reason firms may invite outside doctors to help with education. The choice of contributor must be a personal one for every firm.

What sort of information should be provided?

The most important criteria in the selection of what information to pass on to the manager about stress must be the manager's own requirements. When asked what they want to know about stress, most managers reply that they would like to know more about the nature of stress, how it can be recognised and how best it can be managed, both in themselves and in their staff. However, other factors do influence the content of education about stress. Firstly, stress is immensely complex both in its origins and in its manifestations, and must always be seen in the full perspective of health and quality of life. Stress must be clearly defined − not an easy task, for it is difficult to persuade any two knowledgeable doctors to agree on a definition of stress. This definition should clearly differentiate between stress and pressure. Most managers are under pressure at work; not all are under stress. This brings us to the second point, which is that any approach to education about stress can thus be optimistic, for stress is not an unavoidable component of managerial life, but rather a manifestation of poor management of one's life-style. Many managers fear stress and are anxious about health; these unrealistic feelings must not be encouraged. Lastly, stress can impair health and so the manager must have some understanding of health and all the other factors which may influence it. The next section summarises my own views on what information is most appropriate to managers.

2 The practical content of education about stress

In the first half of this section an attempt will be made to paint the whole picture of stress and how it can affect health. First, a concept of health will be presented and this concept will be used to achieve a definition of stress. The basic facts of health will then be discussed, so those illnesses most relevant to managers can be identified and discussed in greater detail. Stress will then be discussed, first the theory of how it can affect health, and then the practical ways in which it may manifest itself. The evidence relating stress to impaired health will be reviewed and finally, prevention and treatment of stress considered. In the second half of the section, facts and research findings particularly applicable to managers will be dealt with in greater detail.

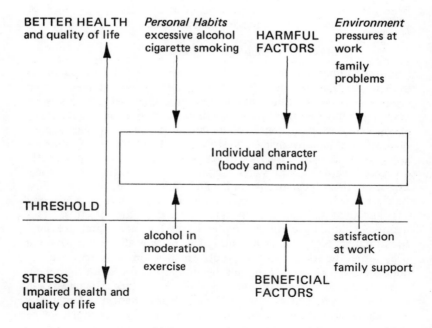

Figure 1.1 A concept of health and stress

A concept of health and definition of stress

Figure 1.1 provides a concept of stress and health. In the centre of the diagram is the individual, the product of heredity and environment, nature and nurture – a unique person. He floats in the 'sea of life', his buoyancy determining his health and his quality of life. The higher he floats, the healthier and happier he is; the more he sinks, the lower the quality of life and, if he sinks down below his threshold (different for everyone), then he is at risk from impaired mental or physical health. The factors acting upon him and determining his buoyancy can be split into two groups – his personal habits on the one side, and his environment on the other. In general, individual habits and specific factors in his environment can be labelled either beneficial or harmful, but there are no firm rules as to where they should go on the diagram – only guidelines. This is because each individual is unique, and so will respond to these different stimuli in different ways. An example of this concept is responsibility at work. The average worker would consider responsibility a beneficial factor and would rate lack of responsibility as harmful. The manual worker might respond quite differently, and find any responsibility harmful. The same rules apply to habits; alcohol in moderation seems a healthy habit, while excessive consumption is a real danger. One man's meat can thus be another man's poison.

The nature and complexity of stress are easily explained by considering the same diagram, for stress occurs when the balance of factors affecting the individual cause him to sink. It is very important to distinguish between stress and pressure. Nearly all managers work under pressure, their good salaries and status reflecting the demands made upon them. If the results of their work are satisfactory then the pleasure this provides will usually exceed the pressure, and so the manager will float up on the diagram, and feel well. But if the satisfaction is exceeded by the pressures (such as heavy workload or demanding deadlines) then the situation is reversed, down he sinks, and stress occurs. In this situation the heavy workload or demanding deadlines can be labelled stressors, but in fact the situation is obviously more complicated. If all factors are equal, an increase in workload may be the straw which breaks the manager's back and pushes him down into stress. More often, however, the workload remains the same, but stress occurs either because supportive factors are reduced, or because other potentially harmful factors are increased.

Stress can then be defined as the unhealthy response of the individual at a particular time to the wide variety of factors affecting him at this time. And stress, of course, does not only occur in individuals – it occurs in groups, companies and even at a national level.

The basic facts of health

The broad spectrum of modern disease, the details of individual
illnesses, the general distribution of disease by social class, and the
more specific distribution of illness within the various tiers of management are all of interest to managers. The modern manager is exposed
to a mass of detailed information on medical subjects through the
media. Unfortunately, this information is often inaccurate and biased,
for television and the newspapers often consider that sensation sells
better than education. A balanced, rational view of health is badly
needed by managers, and this can seldom be provided by the general
practitioner due to his heavy workload. Many managers consider that
their particular life-style puts them at high risk for stress – and to
some extent this is true. But the main risk to their health comes from
the sedentary nature of their jobs, rather than from the many pressures they face at work. For not only is the work sedentary, so is
much of their leisure (particularly if they relax watching television) and,
in addition, many spend a great deal of time sitting in aeroplanes and
cars. The manager may work long hours, carry heavy responsibility,
take work home and, as part of the social commitment of his job, eat
too much, drink too much and smoke too much. But despite these
undoubted facts, medical research has disproved the picture of the
anxious, ulcer-prone manager. Indeed the manager gets far fewer
peptic ulcers than do other social classes; the hazard he faces is
coronary heart disease and the origins of this modern killer lie in lack
of exercise, obesity, cigarette smoking and an inappropriate response
of the human body to mental pressures.

How then, and why, has the pattern of health changed in the last 60
years, and what illnesses must the manager understand in order to
look critically at the effects of stress on health? Between 1900 and
1960 health and quality of life in Britain improved considerably, due
to improvement in the standard of living, the discovery and refinement
of antibiotics, and better preventive medicine which has now almost
eliminated typhoid, smallpox and tuberculosis. But since 1960 health
has not improved much, nor are future prospects much more cheerful.
In place of infection have come the two modern epidemics – coronary
heart disease and carcinoma (particularly of the lung), which together
cause well over half of all deaths in 40–65 year old men. Not only is
coronary heart disease the most common cause of death; its incidence
in this same age group has increased steadily since 1940 and is still
rising.

That is the bad news; but it is tempered by a number of more cheerful considerations. First is the fact that coronary heart disease and
lung cancer have really only increased in incidence because the other

severe illnesses have been eliminated, and we are not all dying earlier. Which brings us to the second point, which is that coronary heart disease and lung cancer while difficult to treat, are eminently preventable. It seems that over half the deaths from these causes could be avoided through better medical supervision of health, and through a real effort by the individual to take more exercise, fight obesity and stop cigarette smoking. Karelia in Northern Finland had the highest incidence of coronary heart disease in the Western World (Salonen *et al.*, 1979). In 1972 a programme of positive health education and medical checks was introduced. The results over a five year period were a reduction of 38 per cent in the number of strokes, and 16 per cent in the number of heart attacks.

Many managers defend their cigarette smoking habit and their lack of exercise by saying that we must all die of something, and that a heart attack is preferable to severe arthritis or senile mental deterioration. This is quite true, but does not take into account the risk of dying at 45 from a heart attack. Comparing statistics in Sweden and Britain it is apparent that while the two countries have equal fatalities from heart attacks for the population as a whole, many more young people suffer heart attacks in Britain. The average Swede is much fitter physically than the average Briton and does have much healthier habits. (But despite these enviable characteristics he also has the highest suicide rate in Europe, which proves how difficult it is to see the whole picture from one – statistical – viewpoint!) One cheering fact is that the manager, as a member of social class 1, enjoys better health than the members of other social classes – to such an extent that the 60 year-old manager has a 40 per cent better chance of reaching 65 than his social class 5 colleague. Within the managerial hierarchy it seems that success brings not only material rewards but also better health. The two biggest studies of occupational health in the United States were in the Du Pont company (Pell and D'Alonzo, 1958) and the Bell Telephone company (Lee and Schneider, 1958) and both showed that senior management had fewer heart attacks and less sickness absence than their more junior colleagues. Finally the use of modern techniques to photograph the amount of blockage in the coronary arteries is demonstrating that the fatty deposits (atheroma) which block the coronary arteries can be 'melted away' by positive efforts to adopt more healthy habits.

Managers frequently request more information about heart disease and hypertension (raised blood pressure), and about the role of diet, and in particular fats, in contributing to heart disease. Such details are beyond the scope of this chapter and are summarised in my book *Executive Health* (Melhuish, 1978). What must always be stressed is the fact that no single factor causes coronary heart disease but that many factors contribute; the risk coming from a 'profile' of 'risk factors'. This profile consists of three parts; the first, the physical and mental characteristics of each individual which are not easy to change; the second those physical characteristics which can be altered by medical intervention, and the third, the characteristics most susceptible to alteration, namely the personal habits. In the first group come family history of heart disease, sugar diabetes and some types of personality. In the second group the greatest risk factors are the blood lipid profile and hypertension – easily identified in the routine medical – while the pill in women over thirty-five has also been identified as a risk factor. The third group includes lack of exercise, cigarette smoking and obesity. The point about the profile is that if more than one factor is present, then the risk is multiplied by each additional factor, and by the degree to which each is harmful. Equally, a good habit such as physical exercise will divide into the total risk factor, and so reduce the score. Unfortunately, many risk factors tend to occur together. Thus lack of exercise, obesity, high blood pressure and high serum lipids tend to go together and multiply up to a very high risk factor.

The physiological, physical and mental effects of stress

The effects of stress on the human body have been researched in great detail over the last fifty years by physiologists and physicians, and scientific evidence can now provide the basis of an understanding of the link between pressure, stress and impaired health. Two basic concepts underlie this understanding. The first is the work on the physiological response of animals and humans to threat or challenge. Professor Hans Selye, at Montreal, showed that every animal had a common response to potentially harmful pressures – a response mediated by the adrenal glands (Selye, 1974). The purpose of this response was to enable the animal to perform significantly better for a short period in order to cope with the threat – a sort of supercharge or booster effect. The adrenals were found to release adrenalin and noradrenalin, together with the steroid hormones in response to stress and these hormones stimulated the body to peak performance. The animal which produced the best performance was more likely to survive in the hard physical world in which it lived and so, by Darwinian principles of survival of the fittest, this response to stress was perpetuated and increased. This natural response is not, however, just a response to harmful pressures (or stressors); it is also the means by which the body obtains greater awareness and pleasure from challenging and pleasurable stimuli.

The body thus responds to challenging stimuli with a physiological response which is a healthy response and, if employed appropriately, does not cause illness. Great care must be taken to distinguish between this healthy physiological response and the harmful effects that can result from stress. The distinction is illustrated by the second physiological concept, typically expressed as the Yerkes-Dodson Law, which states that the response of the individual to increased pressure shows a steady improvement of performance up to a peak, but that more pressure beyond this point actually diminishes performance, first slowly and then dramatically. So in terms of performance, increasing pressure produces better performance up to the potential of that particular individual. The same principles apply to health. Pressures within the potential of the individual improve health; he floats high in Figure 1.1. But pressure beyond his capabilities becomes dangerous or stressful and down he sinks. This concept is summarised in Figure 1.2.

The application of these two principles affects managers in particular. It is that the natural response of the body to challenge is a heightened physical response. Our predecessors lived in caves and survived by fighting or fleeing. Faced by a sabre toothed tiger they did not hold a group meeting to discuss and define policy, or indulge in a rational discussion with the tiger as to the relative tastiness of man or monkey. Evolution is long-term and the physiological response to challenge was evolved over hundreds of thousands of years. The manager, however, has existed only for 30 to 40 years. His challenge comes in the boardroom, or with a difficult client or colleague. He cannot expect to modify evolution in those 40 years; it would take far longer than that. So he responds to the mental challenge of his work with a physical response totally inappropriate to his needs, and the relevance of this in terms of illness in general, and coronary heart disease in particular, will become apparent when the nature of the physiological response is discussed.

The improved physical performance in response to challenge comes from a readjustment of the blood supply to various parts of the body, together with a heightened nervous tone mediated through the brain. The muscles must receive more blood, fuel and oxygen, and to satisfy this extra demand the heart must pump the blood more effectively, the lungs must work harder to push more oxygen into the bloodstream, and fuel, in the form of glucose and fats, must be liberated into the blood. The extra blood needed by the muscles must be diverted away from 'unimportant organs' – in this context the stomach, bowels, skin and sexual organs. All managers will have been aware of the symptoms of this normal, natural, physiological response: the increased pulse, feeling of sweatiness and apprehension, the hollow feeling in the pit of the stomach (hollow because short of blood), the looseness of the bowels and the frequency of passing urine.

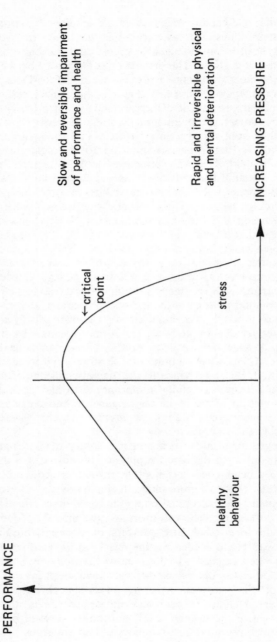

Figure 1.2 The effects of increasing pressure on performance

However, if pressure should continue for a long period, then the capabilities of the body will be exceeded and impairment of health will occur. Such impairment may be mental – constant arousal of the nervous system producing exhaustion – or physical, from the continued alteration of the natural balance of the circulation. It is easy to see how the heart can be a prime target for such physical change, both from its role as pump and from the possibility that the fats released into the bloodstream but not used up by exercise will form a sludge, and so block the arteries supplying the heart. The other varied stress-related diseases can also be explained on the basis of the over-use of the physiological response, as can the mental symptoms of anxiety, sleeplessness and depression.

Pressures in managerial life can thus become stress if they are excessive or if they are long-term. Examples of long-term or chronic stress are the fear, frustration and anger which may be produced by an unhappy relationship with one's boss or with a difficult customer, and the unhappiness of an unsuitable job. Stress also occurs at times of change and uncertainty and at specific times, such as relocation, promotion and, just as relevant, failure to be promoted. There are 'at risk jobs' and 'at risk' periods of life, and those which apply particularly to the manager will be discussed later in the chapter in more detail. In addition, the sedentary nature of the manager's life can make even the natural, healthy physiological response to pressure potentially dangerous, since the response is not used up or sublimated by physical activity. It is, therefore, quite understandable that stress can produce impaired performance and impaired health, and that the manager would be particularly at risk to heart disease.

An understanding of the ways in which stress can cause impaired health must benefit the manager in recognising stress in himself, for it helps him to differentiate between the natural physiological response to pressure and real illness. Failure to recognise this difference can itself cause illness. The raised pulse and the diarrhoea occurring naturally at times of pressure can be interpreted by the manager as evidence of heart disease or bowel cancer – so more worry occurs and the symptoms get worse and worse. Such a vicious circle is only broken by competent medical intervention, which must exclude physical illness and educate the manager to recognise those particular symptoms as his own natural response to stress. Then, if in the future he again has the symptoms, he will be able to recognise their origin and adjust his life-style, rather than worry unnecessarily about illness.

The relationship between stress and impaired health is, of course, highly complex, for stress may precipitate changes of habits which in themselves can cause ill health. Thus cigarette smoking is often increased at times of stress, and many alcoholics drink to forget their worries. The nicotine in tobacco and the caffeine in coffee stimulate the heart so that the manager worried about his raised pulse may accelerate it even more by increasing his smoking or by drinking a lot of coffee.

To recognise stress in his staff the manager does not need much information about illness; he can start looking directly at behaviour. One major predictor is taking more time off work due to certified sickness. He should particularly be alert for uncharacteristic or inappropriate behaviour. Basically, stress can be spotted in staff by an awareness of changes in their health, changes in their habits and changes in their performance. Changes in their habits can only be spotted if the normal behaviour of the individual is known – hence the need for the good manager to know his staff well. Thus a salesman smoking twenty cigarettes per day is not necessarily under stress; the salesman whose smoking *increases* from ten to thirty cigarettes per day almost certainly is. Accident proneness is another very frequent presentation of stress, along with irritability, loss of sense of humour and forgetfulness. The manager is the best person situated to identify these changes in performance and so instigate helpful intervention if he can. As can be seen in Figure 1.2, the earlier stress (or alcoholism as one presentation of stress) can be recognised, the easier it is to reverse the unhealthy situation, by personal encouragement, the arrangement of more support and, on occasions, the organisation of a temporary reduction of pressure. The manager must realise though that the member of staff under stress may, in fact, need his work and the status his work gives to keep him going during a stressful period, and too much sympathy and offers of support may harm rather than help.

Finally the possible number of potential sources of stress in the individual's life must again be emphasised. The variety of factors involved in Figure 1.1 should have clarified the point that the member of staff performing poorly at work due to stress may not be demonstrating that the job is beyond them, or is even contributing to his stress, but rather that his wife may be having a baby or that his mother may be seriously ill. Fifty-five per cent of the managers at Henley Staff College identified work as the main cause of bad periods of stress they had experienced in the past, while 41 per cent identified their families as the most important cause of stress.

The scientific evidence relating stress to impaired health

None of the above considerations have any relevance to the manager unless there is acceptable scientific evidence to support the association between stress and impaired health. This evidence comes from many sources. Most figures from general practice and casualty departments suggest that some 50 per cent of all consultations can be ascribed to stress, but of course it is very difficult to be precise in this diagnosis. At a more scientific level, the exact way in which experimental animals react to stress, and the way this reaction can impair health, is known, and similar physiological mechanisms have been demonstrated in man. Studies of population have shown how, for instance, Japanese workers develop the increased Western risk of heart disease when they leave the social support of their own country and go to work in Honolulu or in the United States – even when their diet remains unaltered.

Other research is of greater interest in that in addition to relating stress to poor health it points out areas of managerial behaviour and life-style where stress could be anticipated and prevented. Thus Rosenman and Friedman (1975) in San Francisco observed that heart attacks occurred more frequently in managers with a hard driving, tense, time conscious, ambitious personality and termed this 'Type A behaviour pattern'. It contrasted with the relaxed, easy going 'Type B' manager. They enrolled over 3000 managers in a long term trial, split them into Types A and B, and watched their future cardiac health. At the end of the trial, evidence of heart disease had been observed nearly twice as often in Type A managers. The authors are now working on ways of helping Type A managers to modify their behaviour in order to see if this will reduce their risk of heart disease.

Of particular relevance to the manager is the work of Holmes and Masuda (1973) who postulated that stress occurred at periods of change, and selected what they felt were the 43 most important life changes in an individual's life. The relative magnitudes of these changes were rated by a large number of Americans, and this produced a 'Life Event Rating Scale'. The authors then successfully correlated the amount of change in a person's life with the number of mental and physical illnesses he suffered. This work has supported the idea that change within the family is just as important as pressure at work as a cause of stress. The scoring methods also make the point that relocation, often a standard three-year feature of the British manager's life, actually scores more adverse points than the loss of a spouse. This conclusion may sound far-fetched, but it is backed up by my own clinical experience that many bad illnesses and accidents occur during the three months following relocation. Buying and selling a house, arrangement of mortgage and bridging loans, the challenge of a new job, and the disruption of the whole family unit add up to a very stressful period.

A final depressing feature is that the incidence of stress in Britain does seem to be increasing. Figures for the prescriptions of tranquillisers suggest that one in ten adult men and one in five adult women take tranquillisers in any one year, and the number of prescriptions continues to increase each year. The incidence of alcoholism among managers, and particularly among their wives, also seems to be steadily rising although the habit is so secretive that figures are difficult to obtain.

Prevention of stress

The most important part of any talk about stress must be the identification of areas where the manager can take steps to prevent stress occurring, both in himself and in his staff. Prevention can be approached in various ways. One important area is that of personal habits and an up-to-date summary of the effects of personal habits on health is always well received. Sources of stress at work are well summarised by Cooper and Marshall (1978) in their book *Understanding Executive Stress*. The prevention of problems at work lies in the hands of both senior management and the manager himself. The doctor can only bring these facts to the notice of the listeners and stress the importance of reducing uncertainty for staff by planning future prospects for personnel as well as possible, and making such plans readily available. The doctor, however, does have much more information about the factors affecting the health of the manager and providing increased risk of stress, at various periods during working life and after retirement. Identification of these problems can lead to prevention, and so this approach will be dealt with in some detail.

The importance of understanding the effects of habits on health is apparent in Figure 1.1. Good habits provide the manager with buoyancy in the diagram, and habits are completely under his own control. Changes in environment are not. There will be times when parents are ill or the workload hard, and at these times the more positive factors which are working *for* the manager, the better he is able to cope. The feedback from managers who have become physically fitter through increased exercise, or who have learned a method of relaxation has been striking; they all claim to be much better able to cope with periods of stress.

Habits, however, are very personal and are very difficult to change. As Mark Twain says 'A habit cannot be tossed out of the window, it must be coaxed down the stairs a step at a time.' Habits should always be discussed within the context of the quality of life. Eating, smoking and drinking provide great pleasure; they may also harm health. The manager should understand the risks in order to make a balanced judgement of whether it is worth attempting to alter his own personal habits. Medical experience shows that it is much easier to adopt good habits than to give up bad ones, and so emphasis on exercise, learning to relax and eating bran as good habits to adopt are part of my own approach to this subject. The doctor must beware of too critical an approach to habits, for as George Bernard Shaw says 'By giving up everything we like we can live to be 100; or at any rate it will seem like it.' In general, the right approach must be a counselling, adult one; the habit has benefits and risks; here are the medical risks; the choice is yours; above all, practise moderation in all habits.

(i) *Cigarette smoking*   The four big surveys of the risks of cigarette smoking carried out since the war, one in England and three in the United States, leave no doubt that smoking is dangerous. Smoking in public is also anti-social. A working party of the Royal College of Physicians (1977) has calculated that each cigarette smoked takes five minutes off one's life. But to balance this, cigarette smoking does relax the tense manager and does also keep down weight; and pipe smoking can be absolved from most of the medical risks of cigarette smoking. One point not always appreciated by managers is that cigarette smoking is more likely to cause death from coronary heart disease than from lung cancer.

The good news about smoking is that managers are smoking less. In 1955, 60 per cent of men in social classes 1 and 5 smoked cigarettes. But while this percentage has stayed stationary in social class 5 men, by 1975 social class 1 men were down to only 30 per cent cigarette smokers. And further good news is that many managers could find giving up cigarette smoking easier than they think, for their smoking is just a habit. For others it seems an addiction, and withdrawal symptoms such as irritability and sleeplessness make everyone's life a misery for two or three months when they give up. In small-group discussions each group will usually have a reformed smoker who can pass on his own experiences in giving up smoking.

(ii) *Alcoholism*   While the manager who smokes heavily may be running an increased risk of future illness, his performance at work is unaltered by his habit. The manager who drinks heavily, however, is endangering the lives of other people and is destroying his own. Police statistics in one recent survey showed that over 50 per cent of drivers killed in road traffic accidents had blood alcohol levels over the legal limit of 80mg per cent. An American survey suggests that the same proportion of fatal accidents at work are due to excessive drinking of alcohol. In addition, the manager who drinks heavily will become devious and difficult, and his work performance will fall disastrously.

Any discussion of alcoholism must cover both the increased risk of alcoholism which results from the manager's life style, and the role of the manager in spotting the alcoholic worker under his supervision. In

Britain, one in a hundred adults is an alcoholic, and it does seem that alcoholism is more common in managers than in other social classes, so the risk to the manager is very real. His supervision of work performance gives the manager the opportunity to help any of his staff with a drink problem. The importance of early advice to the alcoholic, or potential alcoholic, must be stressed. Considerable help can be given by Alcoholics Anonymous, the general practitioner and specialist psychiatric units, but this successful intervention requires early diagnosis of the problem and encouragement of the individual to admit that he has a problem. So the potential alcoholic must be made to face his problem honestly, and the manager must insist that he obtains help, backing this up with the threat that his job will be in jeopardy if he won't accept this advice. Many firms now have a definite company policy concerning drinking at work and the management of any known alcoholic on the staff, and this seems an excellent idea.

(iii) *Diet*   As with drinking alcohol, the social entertaining which is part of many managers' working lives must, together with their sedentary lives, put them at risk for obesity. Moderation must be encouraged – never eating between meals, for example, and eating the main course from a dessert plate, rather than a large plate; together with full communication with the provider of food at home so a large evening meal is not awaiting the returning manager bloated by his business lunch. Emphasis must also be placed on the value of roughage, particularly bran, in the diet. Mention is made of ways of losing weight – weight-loss must be slow but sustained – and for those interested, further reading in books by Professor John Yudkin (1958) and Dr Malcolm Spira (1978) is recommended.

(iv) *Exercise*   Although the value of exercise both in improving quality of life and in preventing heart disease seems now proven, the manager must be encouraged not to rush straight into vigorous exercise. Moderation must again be adopted, with a steady increase in the amount of exercise taken and the choice of exercise should be matched to age, interests and facilities available to the manager. Ideally, exercise should be taken three to four times weekly, and for many managers the Canadian Air Force Exercises satisfy these criteria (The Royal Canadian Air Force, 1971). Management may also be able to help with the provision of sports facilities. Swimming provides the ideal exercise but is not readily available, and many managers enjoy playing squash. Some British firms do provide facilities for both these sports on the premises, but they do take up valuable space. We certainly lag far behind Japan in this context. One opportunity for the provision of such valuable resources is the decision to decentralise, when the facilities can be planned into a new building in a smaller town where space is less costly. A gymnasium is another medical investment; modern circuit training apparatus offers the manager the chance to keep fit without physical risk or supervision, and the employment of a trained physiotherapist allows injuries to be treated, and convalescence from major illness to be supervised, with little time lost from work.

(v) *Other personal factors* Managers frequently wish to discuss methods of relaxation, modern views on sleep, the use of tranquillisers and sedatives, the advisability of regular medical checks and the medical risks of sex. Methods of relaxation are of particular interest to doctors themselves, for the teaching of relaxation to individuals and groups in general practice and hospital seems to be of great value in reducing raised blood pressure, blood cholesterol and other risk factors for heart disease.

Another way of looking at stress in the manager's life – both for work and home – is the identification of pressures which occur at different stages in his life. The young manager is ambitious, work is a great challenge, but at the same time he will probably be newly-married and must find time for his wife and young family. Education and personal advice from the more experienced manager will help him to see his future in perspective. Uncertainty over priorities at this stage can lead to marital problems – wives are quick to spot work as a competitor for their husband's time. The increasing rate of divorce among managers as well as other social classes in Britain reflects this problem and is a source of unhappiness and stress. Another factor predisposing to divorce is early marriage. The wife of a student at university or technical college has little idea of the demands which her husband's future career as a manager will make on herself and her family. In addition the future manager marrying early is more likely to marry below his own social class – another potential hazard to marriage. Young people can be obstinate and headstrong and require firm but tactful counselling at this stage.

The middle-aged manager faces the problems of middle age – the slow but steady deterioration in physical health and sexual interest, the loss of goals and attractive future prospects at work, increasing worries about the health of parents, and perhaps the worries of bringing up adolescent children. Many of these problems cannot be avoided but the knowledge that they affect everyone, and the opportunity to discuss them, should help the manager to cope with them better.

The older manager may face the threat of early retirement and redundancy, and the chance to discuss fully the medical aspects of early retirement is valuable. There seem many medical arguments to support the view that early retirement, properly anticipated and explained, will benefit health. This view seems to be supported by the early findings of Professor Cary Cooper's current research into early retirement (personal communication).

Throughout his working life the manager's relationship with his family can provide an all important source of support or, unfortunately, adverse pressure. The way in which the manager arranges his family and social life must be his own responsibility; the doctor can simply emphasise the importance of priorities in balancing work and family life. Firms vary considerably in their policies concerning the manager and his family. Some encourage blurring of the barrier between work and family by providing sporting and social facilities for the manager and his family near the place of work, by arranging annual conferences to which wives are invited, and by a sympathetic approach to taking wives on occasional business trips. Others have decided that their employees' families are their own responsibility. The doctor is in no position to comment on the commercial implications of these attitudes. He can only point out that the provision of support from facilities for the wives and families of the manager should pay dividends in the manager's health, quality of life and loyalty to his firm.

Treatment of stress

As was discussed earlier and demonstrated in Figure 1.2, stress may become apparent in individuals either as change in their performance and habits, or as change in their health. These changes occur at first slowly and insidiously, but if the situation is left unaltered deterioration into real and often severe physical and mental ill health can occur. The important principle of treatment is therefore that it should be early.

How can stress at work be treated? First, the firm must decide on its policy for the treatment of staff suffering from stress. Then the manager must know how he can help members of his staff whom he recognises to be under stress or who ask him for help. Finally, if the manager is able to recognise stress in himself, he must know how to help himself.

(i) *The role of the firm in treating stress*   Firms should define their policy for treatment of staff with a stress problem, and should make this policy as straightforward and well-publicised as possible. A number of firms have well thought-out policies for the treatment of one manifestation of stress – namely alcoholism – but have less clear-cut ideas as to how they should be treating stress generally. Others have clear policies stating that if their staff develop any manifestation of stress they should seek help outside the firm. Few have clearly defined internal channels through which help can be provided.

Within those firms that are prepared to provide help, such help can come either from the personnel or from the medical department. Personnel departments are more likely to recognise the employee under stress, while the medical department is probably more skilled in providing help, particularly if there is any evidence of actual physical or mental illness. The latter department is also probably less threatening to the employee who may fear that his job will be put at risk by a request for help and the implicit admission that he is unable to cope. Close cooperation between personnel and medical departments is thus essential for their separate roles to be combined to the greatest benefit of the employee under stress.

(ii) *How the manager can help staff under stress* The individual manager can provide the greatest benefit for his staff by being aware of the ways in which stress may affect them, and so being able to recognise those under stress. One way in which firms can give managers the opportunity to spot stress in their staff is the organisation of once or twice yearly 'appraisal and counselling sessions'. Such sessions enable and should provide an opportunity for the employee to raise problems without having to take the initiative to approach his senior colleague. To recognise stress, however, is unfortunately to win only half the battle. The employee under stress must be tactfully encouraged to admit his problem and accept help.

The best way to help anyone under stress is to give them the chance to talk about it. In general, such counselling should be non-directive, and consist of patient and sympathetic listening rather than the provision of slick answers. It is probably best carried out over a mug of coffee or a pint of beer rather than across a desk. One of the earliest mental symptoms of stress is the loss of perspective; just the opportunity to talk is the most helpful answer to this. As has been mentioned before, the manager must remember that most men wish to keep their self-respect, so the more the employee can be encouraged to help himself and the less the manager needs to interfere (by altering workload or responsibility) the better. The manager must never lose sight of the fact that early intervention reduces the risk of any resultant illness and lasting stigma of stress, for even in today's more educated world senior management and colleagues tend to be suspicious of the potential of any manager who has suffered stress symptoms in the past.

(iii) *How the manager can help himself* The manager can help himself by facing up to the fact that he is just as likely as the next person to develop stress symptoms at some time, and by seeking help quickly and honestly when this occurs. He must try to remember that stress may take away the individual's insight into his state of mind. The best person he can turn to for help and discussion is probably his wife. Seventy-three per cent of Henley managers discussed serious stress problems with their wives, 33 per cent with colleagues of equal status, 19 per cent with senior colleagues, and 4.5 per cent with their doctors. One positive way in which the manager can reduce stress at times when pressures are high is to develop a positive method of relaxation. Such methods do now appear to have scientific support. Methods of relaxation are discussed sensibly and in great detail by Benson in his book *The Relaxation Response* (Benson, 1976). Exercise is another positive way in which the manager can improve his resistance to stress at difficult times.

In the first half of this section an attempt has been made to suggest the whole range of information about stress which a doctor can make available to senior management and to managers. Some facts, however, will appeal particularly to management and others to the managers themselves. Management should be able to see some practical return for the time and expense involved in the education of managers about stress. The manager himself should feel better able to justify his efforts to modify his life-style and habits. He should also see some practical improvement in performance as a result of his attempts to prevent and, if necessary, treat stress in the departments for which he is responsible.

Information of particular interest to senior management

(i) *The beneficial effects of exercise on health* While most managers who have become physically fitter claim that they feel better and work more efficiently, such subjective claims are obviously difficult to substantiate. However, a recent large-scale study in Canada did investigate very carefully possible benefits which could result from the provision of a fitness programme at work. The two companies involved in this research were the Canada Life Assurance Company, whose employees were given a fitness programme, and the North American Life Insurance Company whose employees were not, and so acted as controls. A total of 1125 employees took part, both male and female. Evaluation at both companies took place between September and December 1977 (before introduction of the experimental programme) and from January to June 1978 (after introduction of the programme at the Canada Life Assurance Company).

Fitness levels, absenteeism, worker turnover, worker satisfaction and health costs were measured. Canada Life showed remarkable gains in measures of fitness, with individuals' improvement being proportional to their level of participation in the programme. The important benefits lay in a 22 per cent reduction in absenteeism (when compared with the control company) and a decrease in labour turnover – 1.5 per cent per annum in the group which received the fitness programme compared with 15 per cent in the control group. The turnover figures would seem to show the benefit in morale produced by evidence that the firm cared enough for its employees to provide the programme.

In Russia, research carried out in industry in Leningrad suggested that workers who have five minutes organised exercise once or twice daily are 2.5 per cent more productive than their colleagues who take no exercise. Other research showed that people taking part in sport activities consulted doctors four times less than those not engaged in physical training or sport.

(ii) *The cost of alcoholism to industry* Very little information is available in Britain regarding the cost of alcoholism to industry; a cost which must take into account the investment made by the firm in every trained member of staff, together with the increased risks of accidents and the poor performance of the alcoholic worker. Figures however are available from the States, where the problem is much more in the open, and where some 2400 firms run alcohol treatment and rehabilitation programmes, often led by reformed alcoholics. One large firm reported that 6 per cent of its work force had a serious drinking problem, while another claimed that 80 per cent of 450 referrals to its rehabilitation programme were restored to full work. The estimated financial benefits were even more impressive. Caterpillar reported 414 employees completely rehabilitated out of 990 who requested help. Follow-up study of these 414 reformed alcoholics showed that, compared with their previous behaviour, there was a reduction of 50 per cent in hours lost at work, a reduction of 31 per cent in accidents on the job, and a reduction of 74 per cent in disciplinary action. The point here is that the loss of performance at work and the increased risk produced by alcoholism had only become apparent *after* the problem was removed. How much might British work performance be increased by similar help?

In the last two years two divisions of a major British firm have set up counselling services for alcoholics, but a disappointingly small number of employees have taken advantage of these services. This would seem a reflection of the secrecy exhibited by the British alcoholic. But at least an attempt has been made. It is difficult to compare the incidence of alcoholism in Britain and the States as so many alcoholics hide their problem, but there is no reason to suppose that it differs greatly.

(iii) *The place of self-help in the firm in the treatment of mental illness*   One reason why the manager or worker who develops symptoms of anxiety or depression due to stress is unwilling to seek help for his problems is the punitive nature of treatment. Referral for psychiatric help involves the loss of the support given by work itself, and the persisting label of someone who cannot cope with the job and who suffers mental illness. An exciting approach to this problem was made by a social work expert, Hyman Weiner and his colleagues in a clothing firm in the States between 1964 and 1968 (Weiner, 1973). They noted that many workers in the firm lost time from work due to emotional problems. Rather than refer them outside the firm for psychiatric help, Weiner argued that it would be much better for management and union to join together in identifying workers with emotional problems and then offer them support while they continued to work. In most cases it was thought that work did not cause the problem but was in fact a form of helpful supportive therapy. Help for the anxious or depressed worker was offered at the place of work by skilled medical personnel, management, union and fellow workers. The results were impressive: time lost at work due to mental illness was dramatically reduced and 43 per cent of mentally-ill workers made a complete recovery within three months. This concept of self-help in industry could surely be used with benefit in Britain, particularly in smaller firms or divisions of large firms in which group support might be expected to be maximal.

(iv) *Reducing the risks of relocation*   The work of Holmes and Rahe identified relocation as one of the most stressful events which the manager can face, and application of this principle produced practical benefit in a North American lumber firm. Professor Holmes was invited to study causes of stress in a number of lumber camps run by this firm (personal communication). By assessing stressful changes in the lives of workers in these camps he was able to predict the camps with the best health and productivity records. The firm, encouraged by this success, invited him to suggest improvements in the organisation of the firm to reduce stress in their workers. Professor Holmes selected relocation as an important cause of stress, and the problems involved were reduced by providing, at the firm's expense, legal services to take over the buying and selling of the manager's house and total financial cover for the worker during his move. As a result, workers were guaranteed they would move into suitable houses with their families before they started their new job. The result was a dramatic reduction in the amount of illness suffered by the manager in the first six months of his new job. This practical application of theoretical considerations seems a sensible way in which to use research to help reduce stress at work. Similar links between research and management decisions exist in Sweden, but are rare in Britain.

Information of particular interest to the manager himself

(i) *The recognition of stressful managerial behaviour at work*   Many successful managers achieve success at work by devoting as much of their life as they can to it – they become 'workaholics'. Such disregard of the other priorities in life such as family and recreation may suit the workaholic himself – although in general it seems that the workaholic is Type A and more liable to heart disease – but will not be shared by his staff. Unreasonable demands for work in the evening or at weekends must create stress in staff who enjoy their family life and spare time. The workaholic must also beware of retirement, when his life style will leave him nothing to enjoy and available evidence suggests that the workaholic fares badly after retirement. This problem may apply especially at a very senior level of management for it does often seem that the very successful executive has a built-in survival system which enables him to flout the usual health rules. History is full of examples, one of the best being Sir Winston Churchill who lived to a fine age with undiminished performance and the maximum of cigars, alcohol and good food, together with a minimum of exercise and sleep. Lesser mortals should admire, but not try to emulate, such achievements!

(ii) *Identification of the worker under stress*   The manager must use his personal knowledge of those under his supervision to help him recognise when they are under stress, and his knowledge of the causation of stress to help him identify that part of their life style from which the stress emanates. He should look for change – in behaviour, performance and habits – and should be aware of at-risk factors and at-risk periods. Some jobs carry a high risk for stress – the foreman under pressure from management and workers, and the salesman who may be expected to achieve unrealistic sales targets being good examples. Rosenman and Friedman (1959) in the United States demonstrated clearly the physiological changes occurring in accountants as they approached their annual tax deadlines, and the increased illnesses they suffered at these times. A change of job is a well known 'at-risk' period, particularly when associated with relocation. The timing of relocation with regard to the ages of the member of staff and his family will also give clues as to how stressful the move will be. Ideally, relocation should be avoided when his wife is pregnant and when his children are between six and eighteen, while the time when children have left home will be one when most people would welcome the opportunity and challenge of a move. Middle age creates stress as does the realisation of reaching one's ceiling of promotion. In general the manager can assume change equals stress.

The manager must also remember that one feature of the mental changes which may occur under stress, is a total lack of insight by the individual concerned into his condition. Poor performance and change in behaviour may be strenuously denied, and suggestions of help turned down flat. In order to help such an individual, the manager must be well equipped with concrete evidence of poor performance, and must try to adopt a firm, but sympathetic and warm, approach.

(iii) *The importance of making time available to listen* Although the manager may be very busy and a request for help may come at an inconvenient time, time spent listening to a subordinate or colleague who is under stress and is willing to talk will never be regretted. It often takes an enormous act of courage for the individual under stress to pour out his problems to his boss or colleague, and the circumstances necessary for such an act may not occur often. Should the opportunity be missed it may never recur.

Hopefully the preceding discussion will convince management and managers that there is a body of research knowledge about stress which is available to doctors and which can be communicated to managers. Certainly, from the feedback I receive from managers, they welcome the opportunity to listen to and to discuss the subject. Looking to the future, there is no reason to suppose that pressures on British managers in the next twenty years will be any less than they have been in the last twenty years; on the contrary, they may be expected to increase with the current economic uncertainty. Nor is there any evidence to suggest that, without education, managers will cope better with stress in the future than they have in the past. So what is the present situation concerning education, and is there any suggestion that there will be any change in the future?

3   The present situation

It is not possible to provide detailed information about the availability of medical education about stress in British industry today because the position is constantly changing, and because not all such details are made available or published. This summary is based on my own knowledge, correspondence with management consultancy firms, study of published information, and my contacts with medical colleagues in industry, many of whom belong to the International Committee on Occupational Mental Health.

Use of medical services

The main body of education about stress will occur within those individual firms which provide medical services, and it will be part of the everyday care provided by doctors and nurses. The firm's doctor can provide preventive advice to the manager during the routine health check – hopefully each year. Regular checks of weight and blood pressure, less frequent but more detailed medical checks, and the opportunity these give to discuss habits such as smoking, alcohol consumption and exercise will provide valuable information as to the present state of the manager's health, and the opportunity to counsel him concerning the future. Strong positive advice at these meetings, together with the offer of regular follow-up by doctor or nursing staff to sustain motivation if needed, can provide most rewarding results. The time taken for these routine checks is small and can be shared between doctor and nurse; ideally they should be made available to every manager and to as many staff as possible. It must be emphasised that the objective of these checks is to prevent rather than to diagnose illness. The diagnosis of chronic bronchitis or coronary heart disease may give satisfaction to the doctor and may be beneficial to the patient, but they do mean that the disease is established and cannot be reversed. It is obviously preferable that these diseases should be prevented by simple advice on smoking, eating, drinking and exercise.

Much of this preventive medicine can be done by industrial nurses who have the time, training and enthusiasm. Indeed, several firms' nurses do run preventive medicine clinics, and literature on prevention is available in the medical departments. This approach should be extended as much as possible. The nurse, in close contact with the managers and staff, is also the ideal person to spot early symptoms of stress, such as frequent minor illnesses and minor accidents, and to encourage the manager or worker with such symptoms to seek medical help from the doctor at once. Finally the provision of gymnasia staffed by qualified physiotherapists and with medical cover offers another excellent method of encouraging prevention of stress in industry, and at least three major British firms now provide these.

My own involvement in education about stress lies in a number of areas. These divide conveniently into discussion with senior management or boards, invitations from firms to talk to large and small groups and to individual managers and teaching at management training colleges.

Boards and senior management

My own optimism concerning the future of the education of managers about stress stems from the fact that in the last two years I myself have been invited by the boards of two large companies, two smaller companies and a division of a major company to sit down with them and discuss the possibility of such education. Not all meetings resulted in the provision of education, but at least interest in the subject does exist. Change of attitudes occurs very slowly and much seems to depend on the personal involvement and enthusiasm of the managing director.

Involvement with individual firms

Firms have shown an interest in education of all grades of managers and for groups of all sizes. Large groups are usually drawn together at the firm's headquarters and a panel of experts is invited to discuss stress in general or some particular aspect of preventing stress. Details of exercise, methods of relaxation and diet are perhaps the most requested individual items. These large groups have the advantage of providing a wide variety of information and excellent speakers, but lack any personal involvement of the managers. Discussion with smaller groups can be much more rewarding and fifteen to twenty managers make up an ideally sized group. The presentation usually lasts about two hours; half of this is usually a presentation of facts about stress and half a discussion within the group about application of these facts. A number of firms organise education at management training or residential centres for this size of group, the course lasting for about a week and having the objective of teaching management skills. Sometimes a film is shown: 'Run Dick, Run Jane' providing a positive American approach to the value of exercise, particularly jogging; 'Managing Time' demonstrating the senior manager whose work style is unproductive to the firm and frankly harmful to his junior colleagues; or 'Managing Stress' (Training Films International) giving a well balanced account of this subject.

Involvement with individual managers

As a result of a multidisciplinary presentation at Henley Staff College extolling the benefits of physical fitness to health and performance, a colleague, Tom McNab (a physical fitness expert and recently coach to the Olympic field events and bobsleigh teams), and myself were invited to talk to the senior management of one large firm. Our brief was to see if we could motivate volunteers towards improved health and physical fitness, and to assess whether the resulting increased fitness provided personal benefit to the managers in terms of enjoyment of life and quality of work. An initial presentation to the whole group was well received and ten senior managers joined a trial six-month programme. Full cooperation and help were received from the medical department of the firm and each volunteer was seen four times. The first visit included a full medical assessment and an exercise test, following which suitable exercise was prescribed. At two months and four months the exercise test was repeated and progress discussed. At six months the full medical assessment was repeated to see if there was any objective evidence of benefit, and each volunteer rated the value of the programme subjectively.

The results of the six months have been most rewarding. All the volunteers improved their physical fitness (measured by the Harvard Step Test) considerably. Four volunteers were significantly overweight at the start of the programme and all lost weight dramatically. Blood pressure was reduced and bad habits modified. Subjectively all the volunteers rated the programme a success. Regular follow-up is planned to sustain motivation and the programme is now being extended to include more managers.

Teaching at management training colleges

My experience of this form of teaching is based on invitations to talk at Henley Staff College and at the Oxford Management Centre. Such teaching can take three forms:

(i) Formal and informal lectures about stress followed by discussion with groups of between fifteen and seventy managers.

(ii) A formal lecture to a large group of about sixty managers followed, two or three days later, by half-hour sessions with the same managers but in syndicates of about ten. This has proved most exciting. The managers having listened to my views at length can then discuss the particular items which interest them within their own small supportive groups.

(iii) Discussion on a voluntary basis with members attending the ten-week long General Management Course at Henley Staff College in the first week of the course in order to stress the benefits and risks provided by the course. The risks – increased exposure to bad habits such as smoking, overeating and drinking – have already been discussed. There are, however, also benefits – any manager wishing to embrace healthy activity such as exercise, or to stop bad habits, has the opportunity, the support of his colleagues, and the time to assess the benefits of change. During the last two years most members have attended these talks and the response has been dramatic. Many have stopped smoking, alcohol has been drunk in moderation and members have actually missed meals in order to go swimming. Hopefully both body and mind are now educated at Henley.

Other approaches

What other approaches to the task of educating managers about stress have been tried during the last two or three years? My own knowledge is of two; the first, in Northern Ireland, being preventive, and the second, at the BUPA Medical Centre in London, more oriented towards the treatment of established stress.

The preventive programmes are a series of one-week courses entitled 'Stress, Strain and Management Performance' run in Northern Ireland for the Public Service Training Committee. Several colleges in England such as Loughborough and Cranfield run pure fitness programmes. The Northern Ireland programme, however, has gathered together a whole team specialising in different aspects of coping with stress to provide education for groups of managers. The courses are run by Jim Maguire, Bill Hurst and a psychologist, Dr Andrew Stewart, with the help of a physician, Dr Michael Scott, an athlete, Gerry Hannon, and a resource team including a dietitian and experts on relaxation techniques. Physical examinations are carried out by Dr Scott to assess fitness, psychological tests are administered by Dr Stewart to assess the existing stress level, and a wide choice of sports is made available in the country setting at Enniskillen. Seminars, films and practical sessions involving exercise fill up the week; the objective being to assess needs and then provide practical solutions. The courses have been running since 1977, five having been completed up to the end of 1979. Follow-up is thorough and has shown that changes in behaviour achieved during the course have largely been maintained in the long term. It is hoped that some of these findings will be published shortly. The whole concept seems quite excellent and hopefully similar courses may soon become available in England.

Finally, BUPA have recently opened their Behavioural Science Unit at the BUPA Medical Centre in London. This unit is managed by a psychologist, Dr David Burns, who was a successful businessman before he studied psychology, and so is fully conversant with the stresses of managerial life. The unit provides two services. The first is preventive, providing seminars, education and training programmes in the management of stress. In such courses David Burns and his colleagues discuss what they believe stress to be, and teach members how to analyse its occurrence and how to derive from this analysis ways of coping. Tips such as 'positive thinking' are given, along with advice on what the manager can do for his subordinate to pre-empt stress ('do as you would be done by'). The second facility provided by the unit is an individual counselling service for the manager under stress, with the objective of restoring his confidence and ability to cope with his environment without his exhibiting the harmful signs and symptoms of stress. Referral to this unit can come through a doctor, or the manager himself can make an appointment direct. Initial discussion helps to identify the manager's problem, which is then discussed in more detail with one of Dr Burns' colleagues. These include a psychiatrist who deals with the more medical problems, and three psychologists who provide counselling and psychotherapy. This usually involves six to eight appointments at weekly intervals and quite routinely can involve the manager's family, if it is helpful to do so. The whole concept seems most helpful, matching the needs of the manager with skilled therapy in a way which has not been available before.

Developments in the United States

Fashions in health care in the United States often precede those in Britain by several years, so it is interesting to note the availability of education about stress in the United States at this time. Apparently stress management programmes exist by the hundreds. Some are designed to teach various forms of meditation and relaxation; others provide a fair amount of didactic material. Still others focus on individual bio-feedback sessions. Commenting on these programmes, Dr Alan McLean, Eastern Area Medical Director of IBM, points out that the popularity of the concept of stress in the United States has caused many such training programmes to appear under somewhat dubious sponsorship and of questionable merit. Along with other American physicians, he feels that serious stress reactions cannot be prevented just by learning how to meditate or by attending an occasional seminar. In IBM in the United States specific techniques are not taught, but sessions about stress in general are provided from a more academic position – providing, for example, details of how to recognise a stress reaction in an employee or in oneself. These sessions are often taught by physicians and last from about an hour to half a day. They are under the control of division and location management training staff. More detailed information about education to manage stress available in the United States is provided in Leon Warshaw's book *Stress Management* (1979).

4   The future

What then of the future? It must be hoped that future economic uncertainty will not prevent management from providing resources for education. The budget for education is often the first to suffer at times of financial constraint, but since it must be expected that the same uncertainty will increase managerial stress this would seem a false, and self-defeating, economy.

An optimist looking into the future would hope to see:

Greater involvement of wives in education

The importance of wives in helping the manager to cope with stress has already been mentioned in this chapter. As well as sharing responsibility with her husband for the support and happiness provided by the family, the wife is also her husband's counsellor at times of stress and is deeply involved in his personal habits. She is in a position to motivate, and indeed share, any beneficial change of habits with the manager. It must make sense then to involve wives with their husbands in education about stress. Wives are equal partners in their husband's lives, and would seem to have the right to receive information and to share discussion of priorities with their husbands. Most education of managers takes place in one-week courses, and a practical solution would be for any discussion of stress to take place on the last day so that the wives could attend, if they were free to do so, and go home with their husbands when the course had finished.

Provision of medical care within the firm

Short annual medical checks should be made available at the place of work for as many staff as possible. These checks should concentrate on prevention rather than treatment. In those firms with a medical department, the work can be shared between the doctor and the industrial nurse, who must also be encouraged to provide every service she can to educate all levels of worker in matters of health and stress. Smaller firms with no medical department can use centres such as BUPA, or employ an outside doctor, with an interest in preventive medicine, to come in to the firm to carry out these examinations.

The future role of the doctor

The doctor most likely to influence senior management to provide more education for managers about stress is the firm's doctor. This objective could perhaps best be achieved if industrial doctors decided to join together to pool information and ideas on how to influence management. Management must be persuaded that stress at work is a real problem and that education can reduce this problem. Scientific facts and well reasoned arguments will be needed to achieve this objective. Management, however, will not be impressed by the fact that most of the available scientific facts originate in the United States,

Canada and Sweden. Carefully-planned original research to assess the incidence and effects of stress in British industry – both at managerial and shop-floor levels – is desperately needed. For the last five years I have been involved with Professor Cary Cooper and Dr Judi Marshall in research into the prevention and treatment of managerial stress, which is already starting to provide more (British!) facts to persuade management of the need for education.

Educational escalation

One final hopeful factor lies in the self-perpetuating nature of education. Decisions to provide education for managers are made at board or senior management level. Hopefully, the increasing number of middle and senior managers now receiving education about stress will mean that soon a number of influential decision-makers will have received such education and be committed to providing similar education for a further generation of managers.

REFERENCES

H. Benson, *The Relaxation Response* (New York: Wm Morrow & Co., 1976)

C. L. Cooper and J. Marshall, *Understanding Executive Stress* (London: Macmillan, 1978)

T. H. Holmes and M. Masuda, 'Life Change and Illness Susceptibility', *Separation and Depression AAAS* (1973) pp. 161–86

R. E. Lee and R. F. Schneider, 'Hypertension and Arteriosclerosis in Executive and Non-executive Personnel', *Journal of the American Medical Association*, 167 (1958) pp. 1447–50

A. H. Melhuish, *Executive Health* (London: Business Books, 1978)

S. Pell and C. A. D'Alonzo, 'Myocardial Infarction in a One Year Industrial Study', *Journal of the American Medical Association*, 166 (1958) pp. 332–7

R. H. Rosenman and M. Friedman, 'Association of Specific Overt Behaviour Pattern with Blood and Cardiovascular Findings', *Journal of the American Medical Association*, 169 (1959) pp. 1286–96

R. H. Rosenman and M. Friedman, 'Coronary Heart Disease in the Western Collaborative Group Study', *Journal of the American Medical Association*, 233 (1975) pp. 872–7

Royal Canadian Air Force, *Physical Exercise* (Harmondsworth: Penguin Books, 1971)

Royal College of Physicians, *Smoking or Health* (London: Pitman Medical, 1977)

J. T. Salonen, P. Puska and H. Mustaniemi, 'Changes in Morbidity and Mortality during Comprehensive Community Programme to Control Cardiovascular Diseases during 1972–7 in North Karelia', *British Medical Journal*, 2 (1979) pp. 1178–83

H. Selye, *Stress Without Distress* (New York: J. B. Lippincott, 1974)

M. Spira, *How to Lose Weight without Really Dieting* (Harmondsworth: Penguin Books, 1978)

L. Warshaw, *Stress Management* (Reading, Mass: Addison-Wesley, 1979)

H. Weiner *et al.*, *Mental Health Care in the World at Work* (New York: Associated Press, 1973)

J. Yudkin, *This Slimming Business* (Harmondsworth: Penguin Books, 1958)

2 Stress Training in ICI Ltd

Geoffrey N. Sworder
ICI Ltd, London

This chapter describes how research into stress and, subsequently, management training about stress came to happen in ICI. Details of the research and training are given, and the results of the training (so far as they can be ascertained) are shown.

Introduction

The origins of stress training in Imperial Chemical Industries Ltd. (ICI) go back to two separate research projects carried out by Ph.D. students from the University of Manchester Institute of Science and Technology (UMIST), both of which were supervised by Professor Cary Cooper. Both of these projects were started in the mid-1970s, and I was not involved in (nor even aware of) them at that time. They took place in different divisions of the company, and were initiated by UMIST through the normal processes by which Ph.D. students are found places for project work. The Personnel Directors of the ICI Divisions concerned gave their permission for work to be done, and therefore remained responsible for any subsequent action that might be contemplated, although it is doubtful whether there was then any clear idea of what that might be. It is probable that the projects were seen as interesting and reasonably safe investigations of a fairly academic kind. ICI has hosted many pieces of research in its time, and is therefore not unfamiliar with managing such activities. The fact that there was no fee for this work must also have been an inducement.

The results of these research projects fed into my own growing interest in stress, which I had been pursuing independently via several 'common interest' groups. The information my own activities generated is summarised briefly below. Together all these developments led up to the training programmes, a description of which forms the main part of this chapter.

The research projects

The first of these projects was carried out by Judi Marshall. The work was done in one ICI Division which had a number of sites spread over England and Scotland, and the initial area of interest was to examine the effect of geographical mobility on the manager and his family. The first part of Judi's study was therefore to interview a large number of managers (and some of their wives), to find out how they had coped with moves in the past. The population that was chosen for interview consisted of 'senior staff', which in ICI terms is a category defined by salary level. It includes middle and senior managers and senior specialists of various kinds. The number involved was about 200, out of a total Divisional staff of around 10 000. This initial work was published as a Bradford Monograph called *The Mobile Manager and his Wife* (Marshall and Cooper, 1976) and provides some useful models of the different crises faced by manager and family during a move. Subsequently, the work was expanded to cover a survey of the variety of stresses and satisfactions affecting these managers in their day-to-day work. The details of these are described in *Executives Under Pressure* (Marshall and Cooper, 1979) and in Judi Marshall's Ph.D. thesis, available from the UMIST library (Marshall, 1977).

The second research project was carried out, somewhat later, in another two Divisions of ICI, by David Burns. The approach here was from a totally different angle, as David Burns began from the assumption that the causes of stress are complex and vary greatly from person to person and from occasion to occasion. He therefore decided to investigate the methods by which people believed they coped with stress, irrespective of its nature or causes. His sample population was the whole of the 'management and professional' and 'senior' staff, which is roughly all those who are in grades normally filled by graduate recruitment. This numbered approximately 3400 in the two Divisions concerned (total staff about 27 000). He arranged for a random sample of 200 to be extracted from the computerised personnel record system, and despatched questionnaires to them (their names were not known to ICI). These questionnaires were in three parts:

(a) A question asking whether the recipient regarded himself as 'vulnerable' or 'largely immune' to stress.
(b) A series of questions asking whether a variety of methods of coping with stress were used by the recipient and how important each was considered to be.
(c) A series of questions asking whether the recipient experienced a variety of symptoms of stress – physical, behavioural and psychological.

From the 200 recipients of the questionnaire, there were 120 replies, which is quite a high response rate for this kind of survey. Of the 120 who answered, 53 per cent regarded themselves as 'vulnerable' to stress, which is an interesting result and probably represents an honest majority who are prepared to admit to a problem. The true figure is likely to be greater. David Burns analysed the completed responses in order to discover which of the coping methods were most commonly reported by those reporting less stress symptoms. The details of his methodology and findings are described in his Ph.D thesis, available from the UMIST library (Burns, 1979). My version of his list of more 'successful' coping methods is shown in Table 2.1 below, with my own headings added. When the questionnaires were sent out, David Burns offered all those who answered the opportunity to have some training in coping skills. He then intended to use his questionnaire again to see whether people's perceptions changed after training. We shall see later in the chapter how this worked out in practice.

The common interest group

While these research projects were still in progress, a group of ICI staff started to meet to discuss the subject of stress. They were the Personnel Manager of part of Head Office, the Principal Medical Officer and myself. We had been hearing about work done, and reading articles and books on the subject. In particular, we wanted to make effective use of the results of the research projects.

Some of the items of interest to this ICI group included:

(1) Dr Andrew Melhuish, a general practitioner in Henley, who was beginning his longitudinal study of the physical and mental characteristics of members of the Administrative Staff College's General Management Course (Henley) and their subsequent

TABLE 2.1   More 'successful' coping methods used by the managers

1 *Understanding self*
   Understand causes of depression
   Accurate appraisal of one's personal capacities
   Having realistic objectives

2 *Ability to behave flexibly*
   Limit one's pre-occupation with stressful situations
   Capacity for emotional detachment
   Cope with being disliked
   Ability to relax deliberately
   Ability to behave appropriately in public despite private feelings
   Ability to modify one's behaviour

3 *Understanding situations and others*
   Systematic observation of difficult interpersonal relations
   Ability to recognise cues indicating tension build-up

4 *Ability to control situations*
   Ability to control the pace of potentially difficult situations
   Practice in pre-empting potential crisis

5 *Attitudes*
   Confidence in the essential tractability of stressful situations
   Confidence in ability to modify personal stress
   Acceptance of responsibility for self-help

experience of stress. As this population is similar to ICI management (and each course usually contained at least one person from ICI), the study was obviously relevant, and there was a reasonable expectation that useful data about executive health would emerge in due course, although this would be several years away (see Melhuish 1975, 1977 and 1978).

(2) The author became a member of a group, based in London, consisting mostly of doctors from industry concerned with the subject of occupational mental health. This group met monthly for evening sessions, to listen to visiting speakers discussing practical experience of industrial situations. It was evident from these sessions, both from the speakers' input and from the members of the group, that more was known about stress in industry than had been published. (A notable exception to this was the publication of Dr J. L. Kearns, then working for J. Lyons & Co. and now an independent consultant (Kearns, 1973).)

(3) Later Dr Ann Hollingworth (then a Regional Medical Officer for the Post Office and now at Yorkshire Water Authority) who had

been one of the originators of the above London discussion group initiated a companion North of England group which the author also joined. This group, centred on Manchester and Leeds, had a more varied membership, with a much smaller proportion of medical doctors, but dealt with a similar range of subjects.

(4) Two varieties of training for handling stress became available – one from Roy Payne, of the Medical Research Council's Applied Psychology Research Unit at Sheffield, and the other from Valerie Stewart, of MacMillan Stewart & Partners. The latter led to the one-week courses sponsored by the Public Services Training Committee in Northern Ireland, which were described at the 1978 conference of the Institute of Personnel Management in Harrogate.

(5) The subject of counselling was becoming widely discussed, mainly under the auspices of the Standing Conference for the Advancement of Counselling (later to become the British Association for Counselling) and its Counselling at Work Division. A book *Counselling at Work* (Watts, 1977) was written, which had much to say about counselling as one way of dealing with stress. Another useful book to appear was *Transitions and Life Stress* (Adams, Hayes and Hopson, 1976), in which Barrie Hopson and his co-authors extended the original concepts of Steve Fink, Elizabeth Kübler-Ross, Holmes and Rahe, Murray Parkes and others to produce an extensive analysis of stress arising from change.

Training programmes

When David Burns administered his questionnaires he indicated that training in coping with stress would subsequently be offered to anyone interested. There was therefore an obligation on the company to provide this training in due course, and in any case it seemed useful to build on the interest that had been created in the subject and the support that had been obtained from the Personnel Directors of the two Divisions concerned. It also seemed sensible to capitalise on the work done by Judi Marshall. A group was therefore formed to design and run a series of events, and this included (as well as myself) a training officer and a medical officer from each of the two Divisions concerned. This was done so that a local team would be created, capable of running its own events subsequently in its own patch. Involvement of the medical function was seen to be important, both to provide someone who could give an input to the courses of medical aspects, and to demonstrate that the whole approach to the subject was approved in principle by the medical function.

Invitations were sent (as promised) to all those who had completed

David Burns' questionnaire. A small number of managers refused, and
for the remaining vast majority the only problem about attendance
was their availability on the dates proposed. There was therefore strong
interest in spending time on the subject. When David Burns checked
his records to see what proportion of participants had answered the
questionnaire as 'vulnerable' rather than 'largely immune' to stress, he
found (not surprisingly) that the former were in the majority, but the
latter were also represented. Twelve to fifteen managers attended each
course.

The design of the first three-day programme is described in detail
below. Input sessions were balanced by many opportunities for
participants to evaluate the material presented, to generate their own
ideas and to try out the various techniques on offer. The sessions
which made up the programme can be grouped under three broad
overlapping headings: the nature of stress, its potential causes (including those relating to conflicts between work and home lives) and
possible coping strategies. Subsequent courses (of which there were
several) were somewhat shortened but the content was much the
same.

The nature of stress

The programme started with an introduction to the nature of stress
and its symptoms, with some information on its extent, provided by
one of the Division Medical Officers. This session was intended to give
the participants an understanding of stress, what it looks like in others
and feels like in oneself, so that it can be recognised when it occurs.
The information about its extent was in order to get stress into proportion with other problems of life in organisations.

Potential causes of stress

Next, managers were given an overview of the stress field as it relates
to their jobs. Judi Marshall presented this session. She started with a
relatively comprehensive list of sources of stress in organisational life
derived from her own initial studies and a review of the literature. She
then talked specifically about the extent to which these sources were
strongly experienced by those she interviewed in ICI. The list of
possible sources of stress is given in Table 2.2. It was more interesting
and useful however (for ICI people at least) to study the results
(shown in Table 2.3) of one of the questionnaires used during the
research. This analysis revealed which job factors were most significant contributors to stress and also which were the main sources of
job satisfaction. It is important to note that certain items are typically
both stressful and satisfying.

After this input, participants separated into groups from each of the two Divisions represented, with the task of examining their own experience, and their own Divisional culture, in order to identify the main sources of stress in their part of ICI. The results were shared in plenary, and there was (not surprisingly) considerable similarity to the data collected by Judi Marshall in her research.

As a complement to the possibly detached view of stress so far achieved, a later session presented an individual case study of its causes and effects. Bill Hurst, a training consultant from Industrial Training Service Ltd. in Northern Ireland, described graphically to the course his experience of a severe heart attack, and how he believed his life-style had been largely responsible (overwork, smoking, no exercise etc.). He also described how he had planned, while off work, to change this style to a healthier one which should preclude a further attack, and how far he had been able to implement these plans. This session, although dispassionately presented, was a salutary experience for the course members, and created a lot of interest and discussion.

The final formal input to discussion of causes of stress broadened the topic under consideration still further and led into several aspects of coping. Its aim was to bring managers' home lives 'into' the training course. Judi Marshall's research (mentioned earlier) into the effects of geographical mobility on the manager and his family was felt to be particularly relevant, as it demonstrated the importance of the family, and especially the wife, as a support system for the husband at times of stress. A group of wives of ICI managers, who had taken part in the research, were invited to a discussion session where they shared their experiences of being married to ICI managers, what stress they themselves experienced, and how they saw their contribution to coping with their husbands' stress. They remained anonymous to the managerial course members (as their husbands were from a different Division). The session started with a discussion among themselves, facilitated by Judi, and was then thrown open to all participants. A number of insights were gained from this session, which had not been acquired by managers from their own wives. One example was the message – to which several managers responded enthusiastically – 'try and put off feeling tired, even if only for half-an-hour, when you come home, and spend it working at being a father'.

Methods of coping with stress

The treatment of possible methods of coping with stress followed a similar progression to that for causes above. A relatively theoretical introduction preceded participants' own discussions of the relevance of the material to them, and opportunities to put the topics into practice.

TABLE 2.2   An overview of potential sources of managerial stress

1 *Intrinsic to job*
      Too much work Qualitative
                            Quantitative
      Too little work
      Time pressure/deadlines
      Poor physical working conditions
      Mistakes
      Too many decisions

2 *Role in organisation*
      Role ambiguity
      Role conflict
      Too little responsibility
      No participation in decision-making
      Responsibility for people
      Responsibility for things
      Lack of managerial support
      Increasing standards of acceptable performance
      Organisational boundaries (internal and external)

3 *Relations within organisation*
      Poor relations with boss
      Poor relations with colleagues and subordinates
      Difficulties in delegating responsibility
      Personality conflicts

David Burns first gave a description of his research study. The course participants had been amongst his sample and so were extremely interested to hear of its conclusions. The coping skills ICI managers identified as used by themselves in stressful situations (listed earlier) were emphasised. After this input, participant groups discussed this list of coping skills and identified:

(a)   those most useful to ICI managers and
(b)   those least possessed and therefore needing to be acquired.

Their conclusions were then shared in a plenary session.

A series of three inputs were then given, each of which was an attempt to offer a technique for helping to cope with stress.

(a) Dr Reg Beech, from Withington Hospital near Manchester, described the process of Progressive Desensitisation which he uses for

TABLE 2.2 continued

4 *Career development*
    Over-promotion
    Under-promotion
    Lack of job security
    Fear of redundancy/retirement
    Fear of obsolescence
    Thwarted ambition
    Sense of being trapped

5 *Organisational structure and climate*
    Restrictions on behaviour (e.g. budgets)
    Lack of effective consultation and communication
    Uncertainty about what is happening
    No sense of belonging
    Loss of identity
    Office politics

6 *Organisation interface with outside*
    Divided loyalties (Company vs. own interests)
    Conflicts with family demands

7 *Intrinsic to individual*
    Personality (tolerance for ambiguity, stable self-concept, etc.)
    Inability to cope with change
    Declining abilities
    Lack of insight into own motivation and stress
    Ill-equipped to deal with interpersonal problems
    Fear of moving out of area of expertise

patients with phobias, but which has potential value for self-administration in dealing with stress. This method involves constructing a hierarchy of stressful situations along one particular dimension (for example – speaking in public could range from 'speaking out in a small group', as minimum stress, to 'speaking on television', as maximum) with about seven or eight intermediate stages. Each level of stress in the hierarchy is then explored in the imagination, starting from the lowest, with intervals of relaxation between these levels. In practice, most people find it possible to diminish, by this method, the stressful effects of imagining each higher level of stress, and find that this helps with the real situation when it happens. The concept of constructing a hierarchy and then arranging to work up it gradually *in practice* is also found useful by some people, as an alternative to 'jumping in at the deep end'.

(b) Dr Laurence Burns, from Birch Hill Hospital, Rochdale,

TABLE 2.3   Categorisation of job factors into pressures or satisfactions

1 Those reported mainly as satisfactions:
       communications,
       relationships.

2 Those reported mainly as pressures:
       overload,
       ambiguity,
       career prospect worries,
       decisions,
       being in a large organisation.

3 Those reported as pressures by some people and satisfactions by
   others:
       job security,
       having a taxing job,
       interpersonal conflict,
       time management.

4 Those reported as both pressures and satisfactions by the same
   people:
       people-management,
       responsibility,
       challenging job.

introduced participants to the subject of relaxation, its origins and
some of the techniques used today. He led them through a session of
deep muscle relaxation, so that everyone understood how this works,
and had some experience of its effects. He left each person with a
sound cassette for use subsequently, containing his instructions for
carrying out the method. (Dr Burns' methods are described in more
detail in Chapter 5.)

(c) Dr Brian Sheffield, now of Manchester University, described
the history of bio-feedback and the various forms in which it has been
used. He demonstrated a variety of equipment, both portable and
static, covering several parameters, and in particular described the
work done relating skin resistance and skin temperature to stress.
Costs and availability of equipment were discussed. A lot of interest
was generated in the, predominantly scientific, audience.

A further coping-related opportunity offered to participants
encouraged valuable practice in 'mutual aid'. As expected, two things
which were strongly expressed in the preceding sessions were stress
caused by the frustration of insufficient advancement, and the need for
some kind of counselling facility which would allow people an
opportunity to talk to someone about a stressful situation and thereby

get personal help. A session had therefore been planned in advance, for participants to get some insight into the career problem and to practice the skills of counselling, believing that the latter needed to be present in most people as part of a mutual self-help process. This session consisted of the 'Planning for Living' process designed by Herb Shepard. This is a questionnaire framework taking the user through an analysis of their life to date, their skills, their uncompleted ambitions, and leading on to a definition of their needs for the future and plans to meet these needs. It is done in pairs by a process of reciprocal counselling in which each person takes turns to be the client.

The final session of the course was attended by the Personnel Director of one of the Divisions. In this participants related their experiences of the course, played back some of their material about the stress factors at work, and discussed with him what might be done to help.

The design described above was a compromise between various possibilities. It was structured firmly around the ICI research, in order to demonstrate that it was grounded on data derived from participants' own organisation, rather than on data from elsewhere or solely on concepts. It concentrated on providing usable skills, such as relaxation and counselling, rather than purveying philosophies or psychological methods. It aimed to relate the subject of stress directly to business needs and to be relevant to business effectiveness, rather than to be concerned only with personal needs and personal growth.

Effects of the training

Most participants said that they found the course helpful, the common ground being:

(1) Understanding the nature of stress and its symptoms makes it easier to cope with.
(2) Each person found something different which was useful among the techniques displayed – for several this was relaxation, for some it was desensitisation, for others life-planning and so on.
(3) It was valuable for the subject to have been aired – helping to reduce the 'tabu' effect – and for a group of people to exist with whom one could talk about stress.
(4) Resources were now known to exist (trainers and doctors) who could help with difficult cases.
(5) It was now clear (through the attendance of the Personnel Director) that the organisation cared enough to spend some money and time on the subject.

Subsequent events

After this series of programmes had been completed, and the obligation to provide training to those answering David Burns' questionnaire
thereby discharged, it was necessary to decide what should be done in
future about this kind of training. In discussion with the staff group
who had run the programmes, it was then agreed that 'training for
stress' should become a part of the basic training courses for
managers which are run from time to time in the two divisions concerned, rather than continue to have a separate module on stress. This
was felt to be in keeping with maintaining a fairly low profile on a
subject which was not, and did not need to be, seen as a major
problem.

For example, one division has found two main avenues particularly
suited to incorporating 'coping with stress' aspects into training. Their
emphasis is not on stress explicitly, but on offering coping skills as
valuable job skills anyway. Interpersonal coping skills have been
easily introduced into courses on negotiating and influencing skills,
and personal communication. Role-play exercises (a form of
desensitisation?) are often used. Planning aspects have received attention in course inputs which cover procedures for setting objectives,
appropriate standards and priorities, pruning inessential activities and
general time-management. The main benefits from training appear to
be that managers increase their personal competence, and therefore
confidence, and by dealing with others and the work environment
more effectively, incite less pressure in return.

Some time later, a request was received, from another division of
ICI, to provide a half-day 'appreciation programme' for the board of
directors, who wished to be made aware of the present state of
knowledge on stress. This was provided, with the help of Laurence
Burns, Andrew Melhuish (of Henley) and Ronald Markillie (a psychiatrist from Leeds) each of whom, plus myself, spoke about their
knowledge and experience of stress, its effects and ways of dealing
with it. At the end of the session, a list of possible actions was arrived
at:

Diagnose the stress-raisers in the organisation.
Open up the subject by discussion groups.
Educate management about stress and how to get help.
Provide some simple tools, such as relaxation.
Support those who are in need, by counselling and medical advice.
Change some of the things which are causing stress.

(These are obviously not mutually exclusive.) The directors were left
to consider which, if any, of these possibilities they wished to pursue.
In due course, they decided to collect together whatever information

could be found about the incidence of stress in the division, by drawing on the knowledge of staff in the medical, personnel and training functions, and then to take a view about whether there was a sufficient problem to justify taking action from the list above. This work is now in progress.

Conclusions

My conclusions from this experience, covering about five years in all, are:

(1) Stress is a real problem for managers, and is also seen by them to be so.
(2) Most managers have difficulty in articulating the problem, and are helped in doing this by being provided with concepts and a language.
(3) We have a long way to go in making it possible for managers, in our culture, to discuss their own experiences of stress.
(4) Stress is not a high-key issue, and needs to take its place among other items managers learn about in training.
(5) More needs to be done to provide support for those in need, ranging from 'someone to talk with' up to psychiatric help when in serious difficulty.

REFERENCES

J. D. Adams, D. Hayes and B. Hopson, *Transitions and Life Stress* (London: Martin Robertson, 1977)

D. Burns, The identification of potentially transferable psychoprophylactic phenomena (Unpublished Ph.D. thesis, University of Manchester, 1979)

T. H. Holmes and R. H. Rae, 'The Social Readjustment Rating Scale', *Journal of Psychosomatic Research* (1967) pp. 213–18

J. L. Kearns, *Stress in Industry* (London: Priory Press, 1973)

J. Marshall, Job Pressures and Satisfactions at Managerial Levels (Unpublished Ph.D. thesis, University of Manchester, 1977)

J. Marshall and C. L. Cooper, *The Mobile Manager and his Wife* (Bradford: MCB Monograph, 1976)

J. Marshall and C. L. Cooper, *Executives under Pressure* (London: Macmillan, 1979)

A. H. Melhuish, 'Executive Health', *BIM Management Review and Digest*, 2, 4 (December, 1975) pp. 6–7

A. H. Melhuish, 'Executive Health', *BIM Management Review and Digest*, 3, 4 (January, 1977) pp. 6–8

A. H. Melhuish, *Executive Health* (London: Business Books, 1978)

A. G. Watts (ed.), *Counselling at Work* (London: National Council of Social Services, 1977)

3 Planning for Comprehensive Stress Management

John D. Adams
Washington, USA

This chapter begins with a brief description of my basic model for understanding what stress is and how it operates in an organisational context. This is followed by a section which describes the sources of stress experienced as 'most stressful' in a wide variety of organisations. Next, in section III, a framework is introduced which serves as a guide for comprehensive stress management planning. Then, section IV describes a three-day training programme based on the basic model for understanding stress, and summarises the results of pre- and post-evaluation studies carried out on two of these programmes. Section V concludes the chapter with a discussion of a major source of organisational stress which is relatively unaffected by training programmes – stressor norms – and concludes that many norms must be changed if training recommendations are to be implemented on the job.

I Understanding stress

I use the model developed in this section in my stress management practice, which includes consulting, training, counselling and research efforts. Although it is not remarkably different from other models contained in this volume, an understanding of the specific model I use will be helpful in understanding the rest of this chapter.

Stress arises as a result of the interaction of an individual with his/her environment. Stressors are either episodic disruptions or chronic conditions which cause one's autonomic nervous system and endocrine gland system to disrupt one's normal biophysical equilibrium in preparing one to 'fight or take flight'. This biological response to external stimuli (sometimes triggered by an individual's internal psychological state as well) is non-specific in that it is always the same, regardless of what kind of stress is causing it. Good news may set it off (although somewhat less intensely) as easily as does bad news. It is a primitive biological response which helped earlier humans escape or repel real physical dangers. Fighting or running away are seldom appropriate responses in today's world. As a result, this stress response energy is turned inward, eventually creating 'strain responses' such as irritability, depression, sleep problems, high blood pressure, indigestion and so on. (See Figure 3.1.)

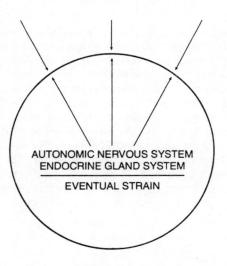

STRESSORS

AUTONOMIC NERVOUS SYSTEM
ENDOCRINE GLAND SYSTEM

EVENTUAL STRAIN

Figure 3.1

These behavioural and physical strain responses are important warnings to us that our stress levels are getting too high. While quite a lot of stress is needed to stimulate us to do our best work, we need to know when we are reaching our 'burn out' threshold. If we do not pay attention to the strain signals, our health, productivity and psychological sense of well-being all will begin to suffer. Figure 3.2 graphically illustrates that we need stress to function well, but that functioning falls off quite quickly beyond an individually unique threshold.

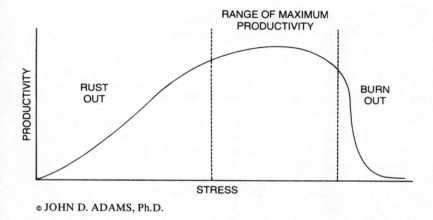

© JOHN D. ADAMS, Ph.D.

Figure 3.2

Most approaches to stress management spend little time identifying where the stress is coming from in one's environment. I believe that an understanding of the sources of stress in one's life is an important prelude to developing a plan for effective stress management. Further, understanding the organisational sources of stress is basic to developing processes for reducing or removing unnecessary stress. Where most stress programmes focus only on the individual and his/her ability to withstand stress better (e.g. through meditation or 'bodywork'), a complete approach must *also* consider altering stressful organisational norms and management practices. Therefore, I ask clients to identify their primary stressors in each of four sectors as illustrated in Table 3.1.

Stress Types I and II are derived principally from the work of Drs Thomas Holmes and Richard Rahe (1967) and their colleagues at the University of Washington. They were instrumental in developing the now widely known Social Readjustment Rating Scale, which predicts a growing likelihood of illness following periods of high change in one's life.

TABLE 3.1   Sources of stress

	On-the-job	Away from work
Recent Events	Type I	Type II
On-going Conditions	Type III	Type IV

Stress Type I

Recent events on the job include changes such as:

1. major changes in instructions, policies or procedures;
2. requirement to work more hours per week than normal;
3. sudden significant increase in the activity level or pace of work;
4. major reorganisation.

A 31-item list of such events has been developed by Douglas Naismith (1975). Each event has a point value reflecting the average amount of readjustment required for one to feel 'back-to-normal' following the experience of that change event. In a research project (Adams, 1978), I found the number of readjustment points accumulated by managers during a 12-month period to be correlated significantly with the number of ill-health conditions they were experiencing.

Stress Type II

Recent events away from work include changes such as:

1. restriction of social life;
2. marriage;
3. death of family member;
4. serious illness.

Following Holmes and Rahe, a list of change events such as this was developed by Cochrane and Robertson (1973). Here again, each change event has a certain number of points associated with it, reflecting the average amount of readjustment required to get back to normal. In my project, the number of readjustment points accumulated by managers was again correlated with the numbers of ill-health conditions they reported.

To summarise, events (both on and off the job) cause disruptions.

Whether or not we are conscious of it, these events have triggered a chain-reaction intended to restore our biophysical equilibrium, as a certain amount of readjustment is always necessary. The more often we trigger the stress response, the more likely it is that we will become ill. While specific kinds of stress cannot be linked to specific illnesses in most cases, with too much stress our inherent tendencies to become ill or psychologically distressed, whatever they are, are more likely to come to the surface.

Stress Types III and IV (Table 3.1) are derived principally from the work of Drs John R. P. French and Robert D. Caplan (1972) and their colleagues at the Institute for Social Research at the University of Michigan. This group of professionals has worked extensively with NASA, (National Aeronautics and Space Administration), in the study of day-to-day or chronic stress and its effects on health and well-being.

Stress Type III

On-the-job conditions include daily pressures such as:

1. too much work, too little time;
2. feedback only when performance is unsatisfactory;
3. conflicts between my unit and others it must work with;
4. unclear standards and responsibilities.

Stressors such as these are similar to the primary sources of stress identified by French and his colleagues: work overload, role ambiguity and conflict, responsibility level, poor interpersonal relationships and lack of participation. It is safe to say that most people in most large organisations today can readily identify with these conditions – and few are surprised that too much of them can be debilitating. In my research study, I found the frequency with which managers were experiencing these conditions to be correlated with the number of *chronic health conditions* they reported; and correlated negatively with their felt *work effectiveness* and their felt *satisfaction and growth*. It already has been pointed out that this type of stressor is frequently normative in nature. Thus, changing negative norms, to the extent this is possible, can lead to lower levels of chronic stress at work.

Stress Type IV

Away from work, chronic conditions include pressures such as:

1. pollution;
2. noise;

3. concern over the economy;
4. anxiety about children's activities.

Here again, the frequency with which managers experience conditions such as these as stressful is correlated (though less strongly) with the number of chronic health conditions they report. This type of stress has had much less attention from researchers than the other three.

In summary, daily conditions cause pressures which, even after one becomes accustomed to them, can cause illness and lower feelings of satisfaction, growth and work effectiveness. When on-the-job change *events* occur in large numbers to people already working under highly stressful *conditions*, the incidence of sick leave, accidents and inattention to work increases rapidly.

The overall format I have devised to guide my work on stress is portrayed by Figure 3.3. The above paragraphs have described the sources of stress (first level) on the diagram. The context, or the 'givens' inherent in any situation may serve to diffuse or to intensify stress depending on their nature. These givens include: (1) the personal characteristics and background of the individual; (2) organisational factors; and (3) quality of support. We inherit strengths and weaknesses or develop them through good or bad personal habits, accidents or abuses. Further, our behavioural orientations both predispose us to certain types of stress (e.g., needing close direction but working in an ambiguous role) and influence how we might break down (e.g. more driven, competitive, deadline and achievement oriented people – Type A behaviour – are more likely to have heart attacks). With awareness of one's orientations and idiosyncracies, one has more choices available relative to avoiding overly stressful situations. Secondly, the nature of the organisation one works in can either heighten or reduce stress levels. Factors such as the number of deadlines, manner of facing crises, or the frequency and nature of client demands all need to be considered as to their role in increasing or decreasing stress. Thirdly, people working in an environment lacking in social support are likely to have more health and emotional problems than people working in more supportive settings. Usually we cannot change these three factors much (personality, nature of organisation, quality of support) but the manager needs to develop an understanding of how they affect stress levels in order to promote effective stress management.

A different sort of mediating variable has to do with how well the individual *manages* his/her own stress in each of these same three areas: self, in relations with others and within the organisational context. Training in this area, first in mixed groups of managers and

THE EXPERIENCE OF STRESS

STRESSORS

	ON THE JOB	OFF THE JOB
EVENTS	Type I	Type II
CONDITIONS	Type III	Type IV

STRESS MEDIATORS

Situational Givens	**Stress Management**
• Personal Characteristics and Background	• Self Management
• Quality and Amount of Support	• Creation and Use of Support Systems
• Organizational Factors	• Organizational Improvement

STRAIN

Physiological and Psychological Strain Examples	
Hypertension	Depression
Elevated Cholesterol	Insomnia
Elevated Heart Rate	Irritability

OUTCOMES

Work Effectiveness	Health	Satisfaction and Growth

© JOHN D. ADAMS, Ph.D.   Figure 3.3

then in face to face work groups, seems to be the most promising approach to managing the high levels of stress in contemporary organisations. Both long-term (preventive) and immediate (responsive) stress management techniques are needed to protect the organisation's human resources from the effects of stress. The stress management techniques which are described in Section III have been shown repeatedly to be effective. While most stress management training focuses on one basic technique (e.g. progressive relaxation or meditation), I think it is important to cover a variety of techniques and encourage individuals to develop stress management plans suited to their own situations and preferences.

II Major sources of organisational stress

Over the past few years, I have been asking my clients to identify which Type I and Type III stressors they have experienced as being most stressful to them. They select these from lists which I provide and rank-order them in terms of intensity. I have accumulated data of this sort from 446 people. These 446 have been managers and administrators, lawyers, educators, medical doctors and engineers. They are working in a variety of kinds of organisations: government agencies, industrial firms, school systems, a medical school, research laboratories and law firms. These organisations are all located in the United States, although comparisons of data I have collected in the UK suggest that the same kinds of things are experienced as most stressful by British managers. One of the surprising features of these data, to me, has been the similarity of selections regardless of organisational type. I had expected that the major sources of stress in a school system, for example, would be different from those in a government research department. They are very much the same! Tables 3.2 and 3.3 provide composites of all of the selections made by the 446 people. In Table 3.2 are Type I stressors – change-events or episodes – which occur on the job and which were felt to be the most stressful, subjectively, of all the change events which the respondents had experienced during the previous year. Table 3.3 contains Type III stressors – chronic daily conditions – which were felt to be the most stressful, again subjectively, of all the stressful daily conditions experienced by the respondents during the previous year.

Keeping in mind that these change events are those most widely experienced as being most stressful, one can develop a picture of organisations in continuous flux. This picture is accurate more often than it is not, as most organisations today seem to be continually reorganising, moving people around, introducing new procedures, and

TABLE 3.2   Type I stressors – organisational change events (rank ordered by intensity of experienced stress)

1 Major or frequent changes in instructions, policies or procedures.
2 Major reorganisation (at least Department-wide).
3 Sudden significant change in the nature of your work.
4 Sudden significant increase in the activity level or pace of your work.
5 New boss or supervisor.
6 Required to work more hours per week than normal, due to crises, deadlines, etc.
7 Gave major briefing or formal presentation.
8 Decrease in status, either actual or in relation to peers.

asking for more output from their members. All of this change exacts a toll. Each individual change requires, to a greater or lesser extent, some readjustment by those affected. It has been shown (Adams, 1978; Cochrane and Robertson, 1973; Holmes and Rahe, 1967) that the more readjusting one has to do, the more one's resistance is lowered and the more one is likely to become ill. It seems that we may be reaching the point of diminishing returns when all of the change embodied in Table 3.1 is accompanied by a real decline in per capita productivity (as was the case in the US in 1979) when these changes are, by and large, introduced to improve work effectiveness. It is my contention that these changes are not inherently stressful! Rather, the stressfulness is embodied in the degree to which any given change: (1) takes the individual by surprise; and/or (2) creates a novel or unfamiliar situation for the person to cope with. To the extent that those creating or implementing changes in organisations can develop mechanisms for informing members of the need for and nature of impending changes and provide direct support for helping them become familiar with the new situation, they will be able to help reduce the stressful impact of necessary organisational changes. It is clear that the amount of time a given procedure or organisational structure is viable decreases as system complexity increases. The 'stress task' is to learn to make these necessary changes in less unilateral ways, so that the people affected are not so taken by surprise and are not left on their own to cope with the unknowns created by the new situations.

While it has been found that readjusting to changes increases the likelihood of illness, there are indications (e.g. Adams, 1978; French and Caplan, 1964) that the effects of chronic, everyday stress are more pervasive, adversely affecting productivity and satisfaction as well as health. Table 3.3 contains a rank-order list of which stressors of this type have been experienced most intensely. As can readily be seen, items 3 and 4 in Table 3.3 support the contentions made earlier that organisations are making frequent wide-scale changes without helping their members with needed adjustments. These two items are reflective of the everyday tension created by such changes. The picture embodied in these eight top daily sources of stress is one of being overloaded and not at all in control of one's daily working pace. It should be noted here that senior management identifies with these stressors as much as do non-supervisory people!

TABLE 3.3   Type III stressors — stressful daily work conditions (rank ordered by intensity of experienced stress)

1   I have too much to do and too little time to do it.
2   Others' demands for my time at work are in conflict with each other.
3   I spend my time 'fighting fires' rather than working to a plan.
4   Decisions or changes which affect me are made 'above', without my
      knowledge or involvement.
5   I must attend meetings to get my job done.
6   There is conflict between my unit and others it must work with.
7   Management expects me to interrupt my work for new priorities.
8   I lack confidence in management.

It is rare that any of the items included in Table 3.3 are mandated by policy. They are for the most part conditions which have arisen and become habitual with people in the organisation – norms. Anyone who has ever tried to change an organisational norm will be the first to admit how difficult (some will say impossible) a task that is. For example, if one learns a series of time management techniques for getting one's work under control, one will often be confronted by those who resist the new ways of doing things (such as being unavailable at certain periods or making telephone calls only at certain hours). If one learns to manage one's job well within an eight-hour period while everyone else in the area is appearing rushed and working 10–12 hours each day, the *best* thing that will happen is that one will be given *more work* to do by one's supervisor. As a second example, let us consider meetings. In many (most?) organisations, meetings actually get started 10–15 minutes after the designated starting time. If, in such cases, one begins to agitate for getting started exactly at the appointed hour, one is most often told to have patience and wait for the rest of the people to arrive. On the other hand, a person arriving 30 minutes after the scheduled start must make apologies and is viewed as being late by others. There is an acceptable amount of lateness in this example which people have learned to expect and accept. Demanding too much punctuality and arriving 'too late' are noticed and commented upon. These two examples are intended to illustrate the ways in which stressor norms operate in organisations. It is difficult or impossible for a single individual to effect changes in norms. Further, they are not often removed by mandate. *All* the members of a work group need to be involved in bringing stressor norms into common awareness and in making commitments to each other to make desirable changes in behaviour. There are few, if any, effective group training techniques available for changing norms, other than bringing the group together and asking its members to identify these troublesome shared habits and then to devise ways of changing those habits. We will return to this issue in the final section of this paper.

There are now many training courses and books available in the area of stress management. Most miss the mark in that they suggest simple techniques that individuals can use to *withstand* stress, but do not address the issue of how to *remove or prevent* unnecessary stressors when they accumulate to the point of reducing productivity, satisfaction and health. The root problem here is that a paradigm shift is needed in the way health (including work effectiveness and satisfaction) is viewed in Western society. We have been thoroughly socialised in the view that after a 'symptom' appears, a 'doctor' can be found who will prescribe a 'pill' to remove the 'symptom'. In organisations, this 'allopathic' paradigm does not encourage one to explore consequences in advance of acting, nor does it emphasise acting in ways that will avoid problems encountered by others who have made similar changes. Instead, we are socialised to make a further change to correct the adverse, unanticipated effects of a previous change. In order to remove or prevent unwarranted stress in organisations, a new paradigm is necessary which is 'preventive' in nature. This paradigm would encourage and even require more emphasis on the anticipation of problems prior to making changes, and on acting in ways to minimise these problems or prevent them from occurring at all. While the present allopathic paradigm considers the organisation's human resources to be rational and renewable or replaceable, the preventive paradigm views human resources as being non-renewable, costly to replace and having to pay a price for extreme levels of stress. Finally, the allopathic paradigm is short-sighted, focusing on expedients and short-term goals, while the preventive paradigm requires a broad perspective and concern for long-range goals. These two paradigms are summarised in Table 3.4. Section III develops a framework for comprehensive stress management planning which is based on the preventive paradigm.

TABLE 3.4 Comparison of allopathic and preventive paradigms in organisations

	Allopathic	*Preventive*
React to	Symptoms	Anticipated consequences
Nature of Response	Further changes	Active efforts to prevent undesirable anticipated consequences
View of Stress Management	Survival of the fittest	Individual and organisation jointly responsible
View of Human Resources	Casualties are renewable or easily replaceable	People are non-renewable, costly to replace
Time Perspective	Short term, expedient	Long range, relativistic

III A framework for stress management planning

The framework presented in Figure 3.4 provides a comprehensive way to assess the stress management practices present in an organisation. It contains a set of responsibilities for the management of stress for both the individual in the organisation (self-management) and for the organisation itself. It also can be used as a device to aid in planning for a comprehensive approach to improved stress management within an organisation.

The framework contains three levels of response to stress. On the first level are suggestions for removing stressors or avoiding them altogether. Often it is either undesirable or impossible to avoid or remove stressors, which makes the second level of response, the immediate response to stressors, necessary. That is, if a person *must* experience unduly high levels of stress, what can he/she and the organisation do to cope effectively with those stressors? And finally, some stressors keep up steady pressure in spite of good coping responses, necessitating a repertoire of habits which will protect the individual, over the long term, from the adverse consequences often arising from living for too long with too much stress. It is my contention that an organisation must exhibit good stress management habits in all six cells of the framework for it to be considered to have a comprehensive, effective stress management programme.

The items in each of the six cells are given as examples only and are not meant to be exhaustive or applicable to every situation. Each organisation would have to develop its own responses, as would the

STRESS MANAGEMENT RESPONSIBILITY

TYPE OF RESPONSE		Individual	Organisation

	Removal or Avoidance	• Self Awareness
		• Personal planning
		  Time management
		  Life/career planning
		• Supportive Relationships
			• Full two way information flow
			• Identify and change stressor norms
			• Decision making, policy formulation, etc.
			• Reassignments

	Immediate Response	• Conflict skills
		• Influencing skills
		• Assertiveness skills
		• Problem solving skills
		• Alter expectations
		• Supportive relationships
			• Problem identification
			  ↓
			  Diagnosis
			  ↓
			  Problem solving
			• Employee education
			• Employee assistance programmes

	Long Term Protective	• Effective self management
		  Nutrition
		  Exercise
		  Relaxation
		• Supportive relationships
			• Actively support/ encourage good self management practices by organisation members
			• Integrative support groups, task forces, etc.

© JOHN D. ADAMS, Ph.D.

Figure 3.4 Framework for stress management planning

individuals within the organisation, to reflect the specific situation within that organisation. For the sake of clarity, the suggestions contained in the six cells of Figure 3.4 are described briefly in the paragraphs which follow.

Level I

Removal or Avoidance of Stressor

Individual Responsibilities There are three general ways in which individuals can remove or avoid stressors. With high levels of self-awareness, one can choose to avoid or get out of some situations which one knows are/will be stressful. Second, one often can remove much stress from one's life by good personal planning, including good daily time-management practices and thoughtful long-term career and life planning. Third, if one maintains good quality relationships, one often can remove or avoid stressful problems through explorations with friends.

Organisational Responsibilities As discussed in the previous section, the organisation can help to avoid creating a lot of episodic stress for its members by providing good communications and taking other steps to reduce the 'surprise' and 'unfamiliarity' ordinarily associated with necessary changes. Second, the organisation can encourage face-to-face work groups to identify the stressful habits or norms influencing their work and to take steps to change these norms. Third, different styles of decision-making and policy formulation may be necessary. Last, organisations can often make it easier for people to be reassigned periodically to less stressful jobs.

Level II

Immediate Responses to Stress

Individual Responsibilities The basic individual responsibilities for coping with unavoidable stressors lie in the area of interpersonal skills. In order to handle stressors effectively, one needs a fairly high degree of competence in such skills as: influencing and negotiating with others, being assertive, and solving problems and managing conflict effectively. Sometimes one's expectations are unrealistically high or low (i.e. self defeating) and need to be altered in the light of reality. As on Level I, if one has good quality relationships, one can often resolve stress problems more easily as they arise.

Organisational Responsibilities The organisation can help its members cope with stressors on a day-to-day basis if it encourages the use of good problem solving models, rather than letting expedience or internal political dynamics solve problems. Second, employee education is necessary. In addition to educating employees about what stress is and what it can do, the organisation should identify the specific interpersonal skills needed by its members and make training in these skills available. Third, rather than removing the stress 'casualties' from the organisation *after* they have burned out, organisations should be providing competent, confidential counselling and referral services (called employee assistance programmes in the United States) for those with alcohol, drug, psychological or medical problems to go to *before* these problems become overwhelming.

Level III

Long Term Protection from Stress

Individual Responsibilities. When stress levels are high and unavoidable over a long period of time, as is the case in many, if not most, large organisations today, effective Level II responses are not enough to prevent eventual physical and/or mental breakdown. All of the major diseases we are 'concerned' with these days – cancers, heart diseases, ulcers, etc. – definitely have a stress component. None of them has a single cause, but prolonged stress creates internal conditions of lowered resistance making some sort of chronic illness more likely to develop. People can protect themselves, to a greater or lesser degree, by good self-management practices; including especially good *balanced* nutritional habits, *regular vigorous* exercise programmes and *regular* relaxation habits. As with the other two levels, good quality relationships, over the long term, have been shown in some studies of occupational stress to be a protective factor.

Organisational Responsibilities Organisations can help their members protect themselves by encouraging and supporting good individual self-management practices. This support needs to be made *manifest* through such things as quiet rooms and relaxation instruction; exercise facilities and instruction; and the kinds of foods offered in the cafeteria and vending machines. Verbal support without these manifestations are merely platitudes. Finally, by creating task forces and other integrating types of groups in the organisation (with real tasks and authority!), organisations can further develop long-term protection against the kinds of stress which arise when organisational units are overly differentiated from each other and/or often in conflict with each other. These can serve as informal mechanisms for resolving problems at an early stage as they carry out their assigned duties, *if* they have full authority to do so.

In summary, a good, comprehensive, preventive approach to stress management requires that both individuals and the organisation at large assume specific responsibilities. Neither must be allowed to abdicate these responsibilities. The illustrations given in this section apply to most organisations. However, any organisation needs to develop its own unique responses in each of the six cells of the framework.

IV Training results

I have been conducting training programmes based on the ideas contained in this chapter for several years. As a way of illustrating the effects of these training programmes, the results of two before-and-after studies (one in a law firm, the other in a government agency) are described in this section. These training programmes are typically run with the senior management of an organisation and subsequently with organisational units or teams. The programmes are also followed up with consultations on specific problems. In the studies described in this section, the pre-test was carried out two weeks before the training and the post-test was given six weeks after the training, before any follow-up consultations.

The training programme, called 'Understanding and Managing Stress' is typically three days long and consists of five modules, as described in the following paragraphs. Modules I–IV are approximately equal in length, Module V is shorter.

Module I is an overview of what stress is, where it comes from and what it can do. It utilises audio-visual presentations, lecture, discussion, group activities, self-assessments and feedback of pre-work diagnostic data.

Module II focuses on self-management and provides information, self-assessment and discussion on topics which include: time-management, life-planning, nutrition and exercise. Relaxation techniques, a logical part of this module, are used to begin and end each of the three days of the workshop.

Module III focuses on the creation and use of high-quality supportive relationships, which we saw in the previous section are critical to so many aspects of stress management. Participants are asked to develop a 'map' of their present 'support network'. They then engage in a variety of discussions focused on improving support in their lives — particularly on the job.

Module IV is a review of stressors present in the organisation and provides further input on how organisational stress operates. Groups are asked to develop recommendations for organisational actions which need to be taken. Some resolution of these recommendations is reached and responsibilities for follow-up are identified.

Module V closes the workshop with the development of personal plans for improved stress management. (A model for self-directed change is provided and individuals have the opportunity to check out their plans with others in the workshop.)

The twenty-four items included on the pre- and post-training questionnaire are given in Table 3.4. Participants are asked two weeks before, and again six weeks after, the training programme to rate themselves from 'one' to 'five' on each item. A 'one' means the statement is totally untrue of the respondent, and 'five' means the statement is totally true. Thus, lower scores indicated lower stress awareness and poorer stress management, and higher scores indicate higher stress awareness and better stress management. Two comparisons are made: (1) specific questionnaire items on which people

TABLE 3.5   Indications of significant stress management changes

Questionnaire Item	Workshop A n = 11	Workshop B n = 19	Total	
1 Meet or beat deadlines	−+	−	2−,	1+
2 Work as *much* as expected		−	1−	
3 Work as *well* as expected				
4 Satisfaction with job		−	1−	
5 Learning and growing on the job	−	++	1−,	2+
6 Sense of fulfilment and accomplishment	+	+		2+
7 Smoking (tobacco)	+			1+
8 Moderate use of alcohol	++	+++		4+
9 Maintain recommended weight	+++	−+	1−,	4+
10 Three balanced meals per day		−++	1−,	2+
11 Regular breakfast	−	−	2−	
12 Sufficient sleep	++	++		4+
13 Sufficient physical exercise	−+++	++++	1−,	7+
14 Self responsible for own well being	+			1+
15 Assertive about needs and preferences	+	+	,	2+
16 Striving for self awareness				
17 Regular relaxation practice	++++	+++		7+
18 Use time well	+	+++		4+
19 Sufficient personal friends	+	−+++	1−,	4+
20 Adequately supported at work		−−−−−++	5−,	2+
21 Aware of sources of stress	+			1+
22 Self responsible for removing stressors		−++++	1−,	4+
23 Awareness of consequences of stress	++	−+++++	1−,	7+
24 Overall stress management skills	+++	+++++		8+
			18−,	67+

NOTE
Changes of 2 or more
+ = improvement
− = decline

scored themselves differently on the two questionnaires by two or
more points (e.g. a '2' on the pre-test and a '4' on the post-test); and
(2) total scores for the pre-test and post-test (adding all twenty-four
responses) are compared to indicate overall change.

TABLE 3.6 Pre-post comparison by individual

	Individual Scores					No. items improved 2 or more	No. items declined 2 or more
	Pretest Total (x)	Post test Total (y)	Improvement (y − x)	Decline (x − y)			
	67	83	16	0		5	0
	70	75	5	0		0	0
	72	85	13	0		4	0
	78	85	7	0		1	0
	80	87	7	0		0	0
Workshop A	84	103	19	0		6	1
	86	91	5	0		1	0
	88	98	10	0		3	0
	92	92	0	0		3	1
	92	101	9	0		1	1
	93	98	5	0		3	1
Average	82	90.7	8.7	0		2.5	0.4

TABLE 3.6 continued

61	74	13	0	3	1
74	88	14	0	5	0
76	94	18	0	5	0
78	94	16	0	5	1
79	91	12	0	4	1
81	99	18	4	2	0
82	78	0	0	2	2
82	86	4	0	3	0
82	87	5	0	0	0
Workshop B					
83	84	1	0	3	1
85	87	2	11	0	0
87	76	0	6	0	3
87	81	0	0	0	0
91	91	0	0	1	2
93	104	11	0	4	0
98	101	3	5	0	0
100	95	0	0	1	3
101	103	2	0	0	0
102	109	7	2	0	0
Average					
85.4	90.6	6.6	1.4	2.1	0.7

Workshop A involved 11 administrators in a major government agency. Workshop B involved 19 attorneys and support staff from a legal-aid office in a large city. In neither case are the numbers large enough to warrant sophisticated statistics. As a 'rule of thumb' however, I consider an improvement or a decline of two points or more on a given item to be significant (see Table 3.5). I also consider changes in total scores of 10 or more points to be significant (see Table 3.6). Table 3.5 shows the before/after changes of two or more points on each item for each workshop. As can be seen, the post-test does not indicate much significant change on the job (items 1–6) for either group. However, the various stress-management techniques explored in the workshop do seem, by and large, to have led to quite a number of significant general life-style improvements. Only one item, 'adequately supported at work', received more than one significant decline. In the legal aid workshop, the top management of the organisation refused to make any commitments to follow up on the recommendations made by participants during the workshop. This led to some bitter feelings and at least in part accounts for this result. By adding up all of an individual's scores on the pre-test and comparing this total with the equivalent total on the post-test, we can get a measure of the total amount of changes in 'life/work style' made by the individual. Once again, I have been considering an overall change of 10 or more to be significant. Using this rule, we see that 4 of 11 participants in workshop A and 7 of 19 participants in workshop B have made significant improvements in their life/work styles. One participant in the legal aid group (B) made a significant decline in his or her life/work style. An examination of the last two columns of Table 3.6 indicates that, on average, each participant made 2.5 (A) and 2.1 (B) significant life/work style improvements and experienced 0.4 (A) and 0.7 (B) life-work style deteriorations during the pre-test to post-test period.

Overall, it is reasonably safe to say that the training programme has a positive effect on participants' stress management – particularly Level III stress management (see Figure 3.4). I have concluded that the matters of individual responsibility from Figure 3.4 can be adequately addressed in a training setting. However, it is not clear that these training programmes have had any effects on the ways in which the organisations operate. Certainly, the data do not indicate that the participants feel they are working any more effectively or with any improved satisfaction. In one case (A), organisational recommendations were never followed up subsequent to the workshop; and in the other case (B), the top management announced that they would not follow up, upon hearing the recommendations (in contradiction to the agreement we had made prior to the workshop).

V The necessity for direct organisational follow up

The primary reason that no organisational changes took place in the organisations reviewed in the previous section is that no follow up occurred. This phenomenon *is not* peculiar to these training sessions, or even to stress training generally. The failure to follow up on the job in implementing action plans is one of the most frequent reasons why team building and other training interventions so often fail. On the job application is necessary. It also is necessary for people to enter organisational training programmes with the expectation that they will be doing some things differently following the programme. The more usual expectation, however, is that by some inexplicable means 'things' will be different back on the job as a result of a training programme which takes place away from the job.

This brings us back to the topic of norms. The way things *really* work in an organisation is largely governed by the unwritten expectations members have about how to behave. Unless these norms are clearly upset or articulated and explicitly altered, they will overpower good intentions. The resolutions arising from a training programme will be forgotten or 'put off until tomorrow', as the pressures for 'getting the job done' build up. Individuals and task forces need to be assigned specific responsibilities and given authority to carry them out. The people following up need to be given working time to accomplish their tasks and they need to have deadlines clearly spelled out. Finally, there need to be clear accountabilities – rewards and punishments – associated with the follow-up tasks. It also helps to have an outside consultant working actively with the participants as they engage in their follow up tasks. In the vast majority of cases, few of these conditions are met and the recommendations generated in training are never implemented. Eventually, people resist taking part in subsequent training sessions as a result, since they never seem to lead to any improvements in the working situation.

This point represents the crucial difference between the allopathic and the preventive paradigms. Those who hold the former viewpoint see stress management as 'survival of the fittest' and do not seriously consider the need for following up on organisational recommendations; they thus reinforce the prevailing norms. Those who hold the latter viewpoint, that *stress management is the joint responsibility of the individual and the organisation*, must assert themselves here and provide leadership during the follow-up phase. When this happens, the cells in the organisational column of Figure 3.4 can be filled with action items and a comprehensive stress management programme becomes possible. Without the follow up, stress management really does boil down to 'survival of the fittest'.

REFERENCES

J. D. Adams, 'Improving Stress Management: An Action Research Based OD Intervention,' in *The Cutting Edge*, W. W. Burke (ed.), University Associates, La Jolla, 1978

R. Cochrane and A. Robertson, 'The Life Events Inventory', *Journal of Psychosomatic Research* (1973) pp. 135–9

J. R. P. French and R. P. Caplan, 'Organizational Stress and Individual Strain', in *The Failure of Success*, A. Marrow (ed.), AMACOM (New York, 1972)

T. H. Holmes and R. H. Rahe, 'The Social Readjustment Rating Scale', *Journal of Psychosomatic Research* (1967) pp. 213–18

D. Naismith, *Stress among Managers as a Function of Organizational Change.* (unpublished doctoral dissertation, The George Washington University, Washington, D.C., 1975)

PART II

PROMOTING GOOD PHYSICAL AND MENTAL HEALTH

4 The PepsiCo Approach to a Total Health and Fitness Programme

Dennis L. Colacino and Michael D. Cohen
PepsiCo, Incorporated, USA

The rationale for fitness programmes

Today the occupation of man differs greatly from prehistoric man. We earn our 'bread' by sitting behind a desk, using our computers and other advanced technology. This is markedly different from our ancestors, who obtained their food from hunting. History depicts a man on the move, not a sedentary person. The swivel chair and the telephone, claimed by many as the downfall of man, symbolise the busy executive in today's modern society: physically inactive. It really is not too surprising when we read that coronary disease and smoking are the diseases of choice. This is not to say we have not made remarkable gains in life expectancy. In fact, a child born in 1900 could expect to live 47.3 years, compared with the child born in 1974, who had a life expectancy of 71.9 years. The difference of 25 years reflects a decline in infant and childhood mortality resulting from immunisation and infectious disease control. Infectious disease plummeted during the first three-quarters of the twentieth century and should, therefore, have positively affected the length of a child's life. Although the newborn of the 1970s had greatly increased his life expectancy, the 45-year-old male had only a three-year increase in longevity. Why? The proportion of mortality from heart disease, stroke and cancer increased 250 per cent. There is no question that negative individual health norms (behaviours) such as smoking, poor nutrition, and a stress-related work place, among others, have a dramatic impact on the morbidity and mortality of the individual. Where does our potential lie in abetting longevity? Basically in three areas: lifestyle, the environs and the health-care system.

Lifestyle is reflective of the way people live; the ladder to success rings strongly with the 'workaholic' (new twentieth-century term). No longer do we mow our lawn but call in the 'lawn doctor'. We turn on the air-conditioners in our houses, cars and offices, only to travel to our clubs to relax in the sauna or steam room. We are automated, and our bodies show it. The environment also adds to this fast-paced mode of living. Those accepted, expected and shared behaviours of our society depict the subtle changes witnessed by an acceptance of violence. The frustrations, the search for ways to relax and relieve anxiety become increasingly apparent. Within the corporate structure, this has been seen for years by the martini lunch and the chain-smoking manager, who needs a vacation but never seems to take one. The environment also reflects this posture of society. The fast-food restaurants depict a man on the run; the violence in sports reflects our frustration and our competitive nature; and the ever-increasing people who in the prime of their careers suddenly 'step away', give us evidence of our stress related society. Granted competition is needed, but we need to provide a system of health awareness and a health-care system which is based on prevention rather than the traditional sickcare model (one only goes to the doctor when one is sick).

In addition, since the early 1950s, the public expenditure for health care in the United States has consumed approximately 11 cents of every federal tax dollar. This alarming cost is directed towards detection and treatment of disease, rather than the service and counselling of the well and practising of the preventive approach to health care.

With the rise of stress, increasing daily tension and the need for a remodelling of the American health-care system, many corporations are wisely assuming an active role towards health and fitness. National statistics, when related to business and industry, are alarming. Heart disease's direct cost is $3 billion and indirectly it costs more like $29 billion. The estimated loss of production from disability and death due to coronary heart disease has now reached $30 billion per year. These numbers are further inflated by the expense of recruiting and training replacements, which are additional liabilities to industry at $700 million yearly. The prosaic backache, due to weak musculature in a majority of cases, costs industry $225 million yearly in treatment; and another $1 billion yearly in workman's compensation. Absenteeism costs are up $1.34 billion, and $2.5 million in workdays lost per annum in industry. These figures reflect almost exclusively the common enemy – inactivity.

There are many other burdens of expenditure industry must consider besides the direct ones; direct benefits are those which can be measured with precision – for instance, diagnostic costs, such as an electrocardiogram. On the other hand, there are the indirect costs and the intangible expenses. Indirect costs are benefits or earnings lost due to premature death or disability; intangible costs are due to pain, discomfort and grief. These hidden costs are more difficult to measure. For example, corporations pay when employees lack enthusiasm and, therefore, call it a day hours before quitting-time, or when they are obsessed with minor aches and pains, which result in lost work-time or unnecessary absenteeism. There is no doubt that absenteeism is very costly; in fact, in Canada the cost incurred is eleven times the cost due to labour disputes. However, the real position is disguised by the fact that less than one-quarter of the companies in North America keep adequate records on absenteeism, let alone adequate cost data on those absent.

Intuitively, one would believe fitness improves productivity, yet empirical data does not conclusively support this notion. Productivity is difficult to measure; for example, when considering executives towards whom the majority of 'fitness programmes' in the United States are directed, we find they are rarely absent. By the nature of their positions, executives must be in attendance, therefore this measure of productivity becomes meaningless in this particular situation. Another difficulty with productivity is how does one look at it. Over a short term, the work cycle of an individual's productivity due to lack of health may be insignificant, but the long-term effect and cost-ratio become very significant when a 'star' dies suddenly at the age of 45. Not only is the company's investment lost but a replacement is needed. Therefore, fitness may be taking on new meaning for the leaders in industry. Fitness implies more than freedom from disease or not 'being sick', it challenges the concept of the 'sick model' and alludes to the upsurge of preventive medicine, it meshes and helps form the groundwork for a productive life. This has been noted by an increase in stamina and positive life-style behaviours as well as a more positive attitude towards work. When one is healthy and fit, one's self-concept improves, as well as one's stability and feelings of self-sufficiency.

This is supported by the data recently reported in the *New England Journal of Medicine*, which states that one-half of hospital costs in the United States are incurred by 1.3 per cent of the population. It also states that this high-cost patient is far more likely to smoke, be overweight, abuse alcohol and possess an adverse life-style. This reaffirms PepsiCo's commitment for a total health and fitness programme. The trends are strong enough for more than 300 companies to employ full-time 'fitness directors' and when totalled with recreation-based programmes, to spend more than $2 billion every year on fitness for their employees.

Regardless of the present justification or rationale, the first acknowledged fitness interest by a firm actually began in 1894 by the National Cash Register Company in Dayton, Ohio. However, many of the first company programmes emphasised athletic teams with formal schedules, coaches and recruitment. Today thousands of companies have some level of organised recreational programme. Recreation covers a wide spectrum of activities for companies, ranging from organised teams and theatre trips to discount opportunities. The intent here is to enhance the opportunities for the non-work related interest of the employees. The National Industrial Recreation Association (NIRA), which began in 1941 has been developed to assist in planning, updating and organising company recreation programmes. NIRA is international in scope and is divided into nine regions including the United States, Canada and other foreign locations.

In 1974, with the explosion of interest in employee fitness programmes taking hold throughout the nation, a professional organisation was formed called the American Association of Fitness Directors in Business and Industry (AAFDBI), which is an affiliate of the President's Council on Physical Fitness and Sports (PCPFS). This organisation was formed to carry out the following objectives:

(a) To form lines of communication and transmit new information among fitness directors throughout the United States and other countries.
(b) To form professional standards for health fitness programmes.
(c) To encourage and standardise research procedures in a corporate setting.
(d) To disseminate research information, such as research concerning productivity, absenteeism, psychological benefits and programme cost effectiveness.
(e) To develop operational, administrative, and educational material for corporate health fitness organisations.

As of December 1979, the AAFDBI has grown from 27 members to over 1200 people. This represents approximately 300 professional members, representing some 300 different companies; 700 general members, either those who work as consultants in fitness, have a strong interest in the fitness field, or are in allied professions, such as nurses, doctors, etc., but are not employed by a corporation; and 200 university and college student members, who would like to enter the fitness profession.

At present, companies of all sizes have an ideal channel to make an impact upon society, by helping to obtain the data needed to convince our society whether, on the whole, the subjective beliefs of those who are fit are actually true or not. The ideal large epidemiological study would be possible, because the majority of the entire population can be reached through the work force today. In spite of increased job mobility, the majority of the work force is very stable, providing the opportunity to apply long term interventions for health improvements. This situation sets forth the opportunity for employer and employee to engage in mutually beneficial activities. This has yet to happen, but the common elements that have made PepsiCo one of the most successful fitness and health programmes in business and industry are:

1. The programme begins with a certain philosophy in mind; benefits for employees and the company are considered.
2. Proper upper-level management support is obtained for promotion and continued success.
3. The objectives and goals meet the needs of the employees as well as of the corporation.
4. Proper educational tools, counselling and screening procedures are implemented for appropriate motivation and continued participation.
5. Long term commitment from the company has been received.
6. A functional, convenient facility, and accommodation have been provided.
7. A personal, but professional, approach by staff in working with employees is used.
8. Built-in measures for short, intermediate and long-term evaluation of the programme are set.

PepsiCo fitness programme: A model programme for business and industry in North America

PepsiCo's World Headquarters in Purchase, New York, was planned from its conception to include fitness facilities and a varied programme of exercise, athletics and recreation to be made available to all employees.

When the programme was first initiated, over a quarter of a century ago, by the then Pepsi-Cola Company, it was limited to top executives

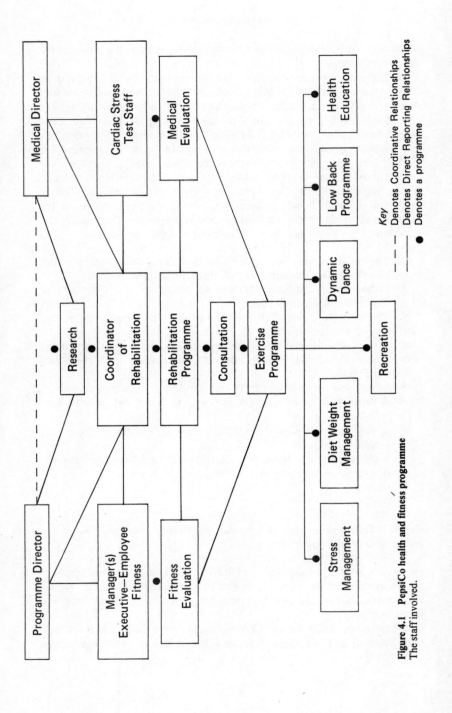

Figure 4.1 PepsiCo health and fitness programme
The staff involved.

and had only limited facilities. Today, continuing with the tradition, and consistent with the theme of the Pepsi Generation and 'Catch That Pepsi Spirit', the programme and the facilities have both been enhanced. Remodelled training facilities have been expanded for executive usage as well as employee participation. In the spring of 1981 a new exercise facility was completed.

The scope and services provided by a full-time professional staff has expanded to include four major types of programmes.

1. The Executive Programme.
2. The Employee Programme.
3. The Rehabilitation Programme.
4. The Recreation Programme.

Figure 4.1 shows the reporting relationships between staff involved in the services and activities of the total PepsiCo programme. The individual programmes offered are also indicated.

The Executive Programme is more *structured* than the Employee Programme and deals with approximately 150 key personnel. Because of the small number of executives (10 per cent of the population), and their importance to the company, the rigorous examination and comprehensive screening procedures becomes cost effective. The design, which is a total preventive medicine approach, is shown schematically in Figure 4.2. It begins with a physical examination provided by the continuing services of a staff physician. This clinical evaluation (Stage I), includes the following:

1. Medical History.
2. Resting 12-Lead Electrocardiogram (EKG).
3. Chest X-Ray.
4. Blood Chemistry Profile.
5. Pulmonary Function Test.
6. Vision and Hearing Test.
7. Urine Analysis.
8. Pap Smear.
9. Proctoscopic Examination (over 40 years of age).
10. Review of Clinical Findings.

The next area of the evaluation for the executives is called a Fitness Profile (Stage II). At this stage the measurements taken include the following:

1. Cardiac Stress Test (CST) with VO_2 Analysis.
2. Anthropometric Data.

3. Body Composition.
4. Flexibility, Muscular Strength and Endurance.

The results of the above Fitness Profile assessments are used to determine the individual's present health/fitness status and exercise prescription. This baseline data, in particular the Cardiac Stress Test (CST), provide a means of monitoring physiological change, which is used diagnostically as well as for information and motivation for the participant.

Stage III of the Executive Fitness Programme consists of a private consultation, which interprets the individual's CST and fitness profile, compared with their appropriate age group classification and sex. Additionally, cardiac risk identification/risk reduction counselling is given and a specific exercise programme prescription is outlined. This outline, based on the individual's CST, includes the type of exercise, intensity, duration and frequency.

Stage IV is the individual's actual exercise regime. The exercises are recommended based on the individual's need/desire, and each selected activity is discussed and demonstrated for safety and proper techniques before implementation. Daily fitness parameters and exercise activities are monitored and recorded. After 75 visits or one year (Stage V), the individual is re-evaluated and compared to his initial data and subsequent measurements.

The components of the PepsiCo programme are, therefore, broken down into five major divisions which are:

1. Pre-screening: Medical/Physical Examination.
2. Screening: Fitness Profile.
3. Education: Consultations/Counselling.
4. Intervention–Implementation: Exercise Programme.
5. Follow-Up-Phase: Re-evaluation.

Since the Employee Programme has a larger population, 1200 employees, than the Executive Programme, the same screening pattern, with a cardiac stress test, is not feasible. The same five divisions still hold but have certain modifications which are:

1. The physical examinations are given with the intent of risk identification. If the employee shows signs of high risk, further screening takes place. For example, a person with an abnormal resting EKG detected in the routine physical examination would undergo a CST before proceeding to the next stage.
2. In lieu of the CST, unless an individual is classified as a high risk, which would warrant the CST or further examination, the

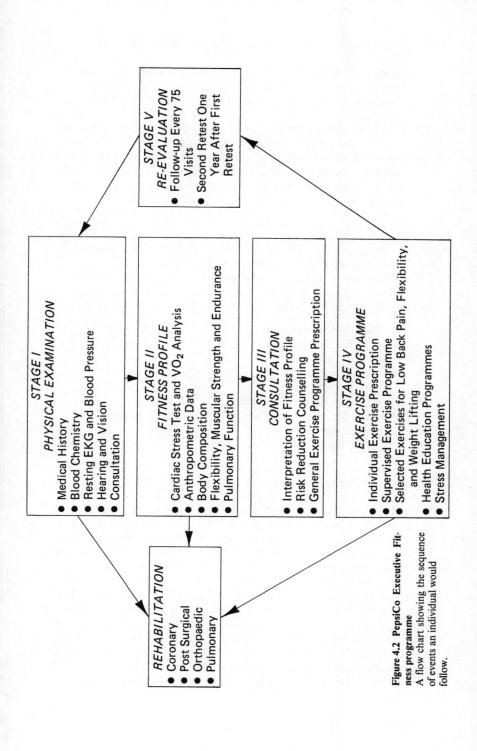

**STAGE V
RE-EVALUATION**
● Follow-up Every 75 Visits
● Second Retest One Year After First Retest

**STAGE I
PHYSICAL EXAMINATION**
● Medical History
● Blood Chemistry
● Resting EKG and Blood Pressure
● Hearing and Vision
● Consultation

**STAGE II
FITNESS PROFILE**
● Cardiac Stress Test and VO_2 Analysis
● Anthropometric Data
● Body Composition
● Flexibility, Muscular Strength and Endurance
● Pulmonary Function

**STAGE III
CONSULTATION**
● Interpretation of Fitness Profile
● Risk Reduction Counselling
● General Exercise Programme Prescription

**STAGE IV
EXERCISE PROGRAMME**
● Individual Exercise Prescription
● Supervised Exercise Programme
● Selected Exercises for Low Back Pain, Flexibility, and Weight Lifting
● Health Education Programmes
● Stress Management

REHABILITATION
● Coronary
● Post Surgical
● Orthopaedic
● Pulmonary

Figure 4.2 PepsiCo Executive Fitness programme
A flow chart showing the sequence of events an individual would follow.

Cooper 12-minute Walk/Jog/Run Field Test is administered. This does not represent a medical screening of one's electro-physiological response to a workload, but only one's predicted aerobic capacity.

3. The individual's fitness profile and exercise prescription are discussed in a group setting rather than individually. All data is still based on each person's records compared to their age-group and sex. The three main areas of concentration in both programmes are aerobic conditioning, flexibility, and muscular strength.

Although there are differences between the Executive and Employee Programmes (the main one being the CST), the same opportunity exists for exercise and re-evaluation. Re-evaluation in both programmes is a major factor for high adherence.

The population of both programmes includes a wide range of ages. For this reason, an emphasis on positive life-style is stressed. Seminars, clinics and ongoing programmes consist of the following:

1. Diet/Weight Management.
2. Smoking Termination.
3. Stress Management.
4. Low Back Programmes.
5. Dynamic Dance.
6. Employee Assistance Programmes.
7. Topical Subjects e.g. Hypertension, High Risk Factors.
8. Running Groups.
9. Weight Lifting Programmes.

Philosophy of implementation

In both the Executive and Employee Fitness Programmes, a great deal of sensitivity is needed when prescribing exercise. For starters, a successful exercise programme must meet the needs of the individual. It must not be too time-consuming where it will conflict with an individual's working schedule. Another consideration of PepsiCo when prescribing exercise is to realise that some individuals enjoy and require a set programme with an exercise regime tailored for their specific needs, while others prefer to be given their weaknesses and strong points in terms of their health and fitness, but want to feel free to explore and accomplish these goals in their own way. For these reasons, much flexibility is required to meet the different needs and personality types when counselling employees on fitness.

Figure 4.3 depicts the PepsiCo philosophy on the position of exercise as it relates to the numerous health risk factors such as smoking, dieting etc. We believe that exercise represents the 'hub of the wheel' with the spokes consisting of the high-risk intervention programmes, which when taken in total, signify our total health/fitness philosophy. If a person becomes involved in something they like, such as exercise, and find positive feedback and enjoyment, we feel that they will be more inclined to terminate or modify some of the 'spokes' in their quest for better health and fitness. To stop smoking or drinking without reason or cause lacks meaning, but when getting involved in fitness (running), it becomes difficult to run and smoke at the same time!

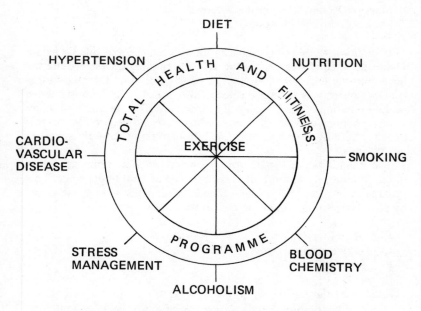

Figure 4.3   The place of exercise in the PepsiCo philosophy

At PepsiCo, we have the ability to put an individual on a strictly tailored programme, such as circuit training, or one where they select the activity and/or exercises they prefer. Most employees who are classified as high-risk individuals, or who are part of our rehabilitation programme, would more likely follow a pre-set designed programme with areas of muscular strength, endurance, cardio-vascular endurance, flexibility, coordination and balance already considered. However, at PepsiCo, we have seen a very low drop-out rate. We believe this is partly because of the many different types of equipment and facilities available for selecting different modes of activity. In both the Executive and Employee Programmes the centres are equipped with the following:

Treadmills
Bicycle Ergometers
Universal and Nautilus Weight Equipment
Dumbells – Free Weights
Ample Room for Stretching and Flexibility
Saunas
Whirlpools
Massage Rooms (Relaxation Rooms)
Showers and Locker Rooms

In addition to these two separate fitness centres and one Dynamic Dance area, employees utilise the 1.1 mile running course around the headquarters, the 440 yard track, and the adjacent 1.4 mile fitness trail, which travels through a peaceful wooded area. The attractive park-like setting of the complex, its garden areas, sculptures and many pathways also encourage many who have no desire for formal physical activity to spend their lunch hours taking leisurely strolls in the grounds.

The Rehabilitation Programme is supervised at all times, and day-to-day monitoring and progress records are of vital importance. This programme is used much of the time by employees who are referrals by physicians for the following concerns:

High Risk Individuals
Coronary Patients
Post Surgical
Pulmonary
Muscular Injury

Therapeutic exercises, treatment and individual attention is utilised to help the employee return to a normal daily routine. This service is made by appointment and provided from 8.00 a.m. to 7.00 p.m., Monday through Friday, as are the Employee and Executive Fitness Programmes.

The Recreation Programme is another alternative for employees at PepsiCo to stay active. For those who have no interest in formal exercise programmes, and prefer competitive team sports, facilities are available for a wide variety of activities. Both at an intramural and interleague level, PepsiCo offers tennis, basketball, volleyball, flag football, softball, bowling and a runners' club. These activities, with the exception of bowling, take place at the PepsiCo Headquarters. Also available and adjacent to the PepsiCo complex are swimming, racquetball and squash, which are part of the morning Recreation Programme. This part of the Recreation Programme includes instruction and supervision by staff.

Evaluation of fitness programmes

Over the years, PepsiCo has been a forerunner in the field of health and fitness programming for business and industry. The long term commitment by upper level management and, in particular, the active support by board chairman Donald M. Kendall, set the tone for progressive and innovative programmes. However, since these programmes are not viewed as goodwill fringe operations, and contribute to corporate success, they too must meet the same criteria for support and continued existence that all other budgeted departments are obligated to satisfy. Therefore, measures for evaluating departmental success are necessary for appropriate management attention and funding. At PepsiCo, built-in measures for evaluating the programme are used to indicate direction and/or trends for important administrative decisions and effective planning. These measures are broken down into two areas: short-term evaluation and long-term evaluation.

Short-term measures are primarily evaluating techniques, which take place after an individual has visited the fitness centre 75 times or one year. Measurements taken, to be compared, are physiological variables such as VO_2, heart-rate, blood pressure, as well as fitness parameters such as flexibility and strength measurements, medical reports, coronary risk factors and psychological changes. Using the variables for these individuals, trends such as absenteeism and personality parameters, morale camaraderie, self-confidence, and self-image emerge to provide staff with checks and balances to verify adequate utilisation of the programme. However, the primary importance for short-term measurements is for feedback and motivation of the participants. Long-term measures are primarily for corporate progress, which looks at the long-term impact of the programme based on productivity, organisational effectiveness and cost-effective analysis.

It is our hope that this total health/fitness concept will be broadened in the near future to the divisions of PepsiCo, Incorporated, and that a strong data base will enable us to pursue the eluding questions on health cost containment, such as questions concerning absenteeism and productivity when related to fitness. For example, does the lean, fit, early-to-bed, early-to-rise person make a better employee?

Suffice to say at PepsiCo the opportunity to make a large company small, to help be the leading edge of Pepsi's focus on a fit, active generation, and to feel our programme might help somewhere to protect our employee from the ever-alarming condition reflected in this poem may be enough.

> He spent his health
> To get his wealth
> And then with might and main,
> He turned about
> And spent his wealth
> To get his health again

REFERENCES

F. Heinzelmann and R. Bagley, 'Response to Physical Activity Programs and Their Effects on Health Behavior', *Public Health Reports*, vol. 85, no. 10 (Oct. 1970) pp. 905–11

F. Heinzelmann and D. Durbeck, 'Personal Effects of a Health Evaluation and Enhancement Program', unpublished work presented at the Heart Disease and Stroke Control Programme, Regional Medical Programmes, Health Services and Administration

J. Howard and A. Mikalachki, 'Fitness and Employee Productivity', *Canadian Journal of Applied Sport Sciences*, vol. 4, no. 3 (1979) pp. 191–8

G. Howe, 'Employee Physical Fitness Programmes: Protecting The Company's Investment', unpublished manuscript (1978)

R. Keelor, 'Testimony to the Council on Wage and Price Stability Hearings on Health Care Costs', (Chicago, July 21, 1978)

R. Kreitner, 'Employee Physical Fitness – Protecting an Investment in Human Resources', *Personnel Journal* (1976) p. 340

V. Provosudov, 'The Effects of Physical Exercises on Health and Economic Efficiency', paper presented at the Lesgaft State University of Physical Culture (Leningrad, USSR)

R. Pyle, 'Corporate Fitness: A Business Solution to The Health Cost Crisis', *Business Horizons* (Apr. 1980)

R. Pyle, 'Performance Measures for a Corporate Fitness Program', *Training and Development Journal*, vol. 35, no. 7 (July 1979) p. 32

J. White and G. Steinbach, 'Motivating Executives to Keep Physically Fit', *Harvard Business Review* (Mar.–Apr. 1978)

L. Wonkel, 'Involvement in Vigorous Physical Activity: Consideration for Enhancing Self-Motivation', paper presented at the Fitness Motivation Workshop, Geneva Park, Ontario, (March 26–8, 1980)

L. Zion, 'Body Concept as it Relates to Self-Concept', *Research Quarterly* (1965)

C. Zook, and F. Moore, 'High Cost Users of Medical Care', *The New England Journal of Medicine* (1 May 1980) p. 1001

5 Relaxation in the Management of Stress

Laurence E. Burns
Rochdale Area Health Authority

Stress is universal. It is far more common than the common cold and can be far more dangerous. It can affect our health in dozens of ways, decrease our adaptive functioning in social, occupational, marital and many other spheres of everyday life and even shorten our life span.

Some writers believe that stress has been growing steadily, affecting more and more people. However, there is little doubt that human beings have always been subject to stress. Benson (1975) for example, quotes the writing of a physician in China, 4600 years ago, who wrote that grief, calamity and evil cause inner bitterness, injure the mind, reduce its intelligence and injure the muscles and the flesh. Yet the period from the turn of the century until the 1980s stands apart from all other periods in human history as an era of remarkable change. Galbraith (1977) refers to it as the Age of Uncertainty. During this century each generation has had to cope with additional complexity and stress; in the recent past the pace has accelerated – within the span of a single generation fundamental changes have occurred in life-style and environment.

The behavioural approach to stress

The behavioural approach to stress is based on a model in which anxiety, tension and other effects of stress are viewed as the way in which the individual has *learned* to cope with stress, and the

95

difficulties of living in a changing and increasingly more complex environment. The model is not concerned with obscure constructs such as unconscious conflicts, but concentrates on a detailed description of those behaviours (overt and covert) which cause distress or interfere with the optimal functioning of the individual. As will be seen later, particularly in relation to relaxation training, an important theme underscoring the behavioural orientation is self-management – the extent to which the individual learns to regulate his or her own anxiety or tension or creates changes in his or her own environment. The approach aims to provide the individual with a comprehensive set of coping strategies and skills for dealing with the effects of stress.

From the behavioural point of view it is generally recognised that stressful events lead to three categories of response:

(a) Psychophysiological

Responses at this level include rapid heart rate, increased blood pressure, pallor or flushing, raised muscular tension, headaches, sleep disturbance etc.

(b) Cognitive

These responses usually involve trains of thought which are self-defeating, anxiety generating, unproductive or irrational. Cognitive distortions include:

(i) Magnification – an exaggeration of the meaning of an event.
(ii) Arbitrary Inference – this distortion involves arriving at a conclusion when evidence is lacking or may even support a contrary conclusion.
(iii) Overgeneralisation – a single incident is taken and an unwarranted conclusion is drawn; for example, a single failure is regarded as an indication of total personal incompetence.
(iv) Dichotomous Reasoning – the individual indulges in an overly rigid or simplified perception of events as 'good' or 'bad'.
(v) Cognitive Deficiency – there is a disregard for the importance of the situation.

(c) Behavioural

At this level overt manifestations of stress may be in evidence. For example, occupational performance may be impaired; there may be avoidance of stressful situations, inertia, etc.

Friedman and Rosenman (1974) have described patterns of response which involve cognitive, psychophysiological and behavioural reactions which they refer to as 'Type A Personality', and which they relate to cardiovascular problems. Particular patterns involve an eagerness to compete, self-imposed deadlines, a desire for recognition, an intense drive towards self-selected but poorly-defined goals and quickness of mental functioning. Additionally, there may be impatience at the rate of progress of events, multiple thinking or acting, vague guilt or uneasiness at relaxing, scheduling more things in less time, etc. Some people accept the view that these are personality patterns which are resistant to change. However, as Suinn (1977) points out, such Type A characteristics lend themselves to a different set of premises from the behavioural point of view; Type A patterns are *learned* patterns of behaviour, just as other patterns are learned. Type A patterns may be acquired by individuals over a period of time, as our society places considerable emphasis on achievement, assertiveness, productivity, competitiveness and the work ethic. Thus, the Type A individual has many stresses – work overload, need for promotion and recognition, deadlines, for example. Secondary stress may result when achievement is blocked. Such a client, a candidate for a coronary heart attack according to Friedman and Rosenman, may recognise the need to alter his or her behaviour, but seems unable to do so. As Suinn notes, complex psychological processes are involved; the Type A individual will respond to stress by displaying Type A behaviours, which tend to be valued by our society. A consequence of Type A behaviours is reinforcement, as the individual is likely (a) to achieve his or her goal and (b) to reduce the original stress situation. Type A behaviours, which are strengthened through reinforcement, are themselves stress-producing as such individuals tend to put themselves in situations which involve stress because of a high level of drive. They then react to this increased stress by displaying those very patterns which have been strongly reinforced. Thus, the individual is caught in a vicious circle from which he finds it difficult to extricate himself. He needs to acquire new behaviours incompatible to typical Type A behaviours, while retaining efficiency and competence.

It is clear that responses to stress are complex, manifestations being observed at the psychophysiological, cognitive and behavioural levels. The stressed individual has to contend with many specific problems at the different levels. Accordingly, any programme for the management of stress which would claim to be comprehensive would seek to modify a number of problematic behaviours involving different modalities. The behavioural approach is likely, in a given case, to use a combination of methods to overcome the effects of stress. Emphasis could be placed on cognitive processes, and an endeavour made to ascertain exactly what the client is saying to himself about the stressful situation – whether, for example his cognitions are based on rational or irrational considerations. Having identified cognitive distortions, efforts would be directed at helping the client understand the relationship between the distortions and the effective reaction. Specific techniques, such as accurate feedback, cognitive restructuring and confrontation methods, could be used to help the client think more productively. Strategies to cope with problems at the behavioural level frequently involve *in vivo* training methods; such methods aim to reduce avoidance behaviour, increase performance and generally to resolve the maladaptive patterns of behaviour.

Relaxation is one of a number of methods which could be used in the behavioural approach to the management of some of the psychophysiological reactions. For, if these reactions are made worse through tension, and relaxation is incompatible with tension, relaxation (either on its own or accompanied by other procedures) may be a useful means of decreasing arousal.

The behavioural approach has much to offer in the assessment and amelioration of stress in organisations, a subject of important concern in both academic and organisational circles. Selye (1978) reports that occupational stress forms a major category in the International Institute of Stress library collection of more than 120 000 publications on stress and related subjects. Although occupational stress seems to be a much greater concern to companies in the United States, some progressive companies in Britain (such as ICI) have shown interest in stress management programmes. These programmes have aimed at providing participants with information about sources of stress within organisations, ways of identifying the effects of stress on the individual, and behavioural methods which the individual can apply to coping with the problem. Progressive muscular relaxation training is one procedure which is used quite extensively in stress management programmes.

The history of progressive relaxation training

The history of relaxation training involves two distinct phases. The first phase commenced with the pioneering work of Edmund Jacobson. Jacobson began his investigations in the laboratory at Harvard University in 1908. Later investigations were carried out at Cornell University and at the University of Chicago until 1936. Since then further studies have been conducted in a laboratory to which he devoted his private means, the Laboratory for Clinical Psychology in Chicago.

Jacobson's early investigations led him to conclude that muscle tension results in the shortening of the muscle fibres. Relaxation of the muscle fibres – the complete absence of all contractions – was seen as the direct physiological opposite of tension and was viewed as a logical treatment for the overly-tense person. Jacobson believed that, by systematically tensing and relaxing the tension in various muscle groups, and by learning to discriminate the feelings of tension and relaxation, an individual may almost completely eliminate muscular contractions and experience a feeling of deep relaxation. His theories were published in a book entitled *Progressive Relaxation* (Jacobson, 1938). One drawback to his procedure was that the individual required extensive training over a prolonged period of time.

The second phase in the development of relaxation commenced with the research of Joseph Wolpe (1958) into the counter-conditioning of fear responses. Wolpe demonstrated that fear reactions could be removed by presenting the feared stimulus while evoking an incompatible response (relaxation). However, a serious obstacle to the use of Jacobson's methods was the amount of time required for training. Wolpe used Jacobson's basic techniques of tensing and relaxing muscle groups, but considerably shortened the procedure. Thus, after a few sessions of training in the clinic and at home, clients were able to become deeply relaxed. Further developments and refinements of Jacobson's training procedures have since taken place.

Advantages of deep relaxation

There appear to be numerous advantages in being able to relax deeply. Many of the advantages listed below are based on research evidence; others are based on extensive clinical experience.

Relaxation can enable the individual:

(1) To cope more effectively with the general effects of stress and to avoid over-reacting.

(2) To ameliorate or eliminate specific stress-related disorders such as tension headaches, migraine, sleeplessness and essential hypertension.

(3) To reduce levels of muscular tension, thereby alleviating bodily aches and pains caused by inappropriate tension.

(4) To control anticipatory anxiety before, and maintain feelings of calmness during, anxiety-provoking events such as a significant interview or an important lecture.

(5) To decrease unnecessary fatigue and aid recovery after an exhausting day's work.

(6) To increase overall competence by reducing anxiety levels; the objective is alert relaxation.

(7) To help prevent the onset of stress-related disorders.

(8) To diminish the need to engage in stress-induced behaviours – excessive smoking, consumption of alcohol or compulsive overeating, for example.

(9) To confront anxiety-provoking situations, thereby eliminating maladaptive, defensive mechanisms such as avoidance.

(10) To improve concentration and decision-making, and aid learning.

(11) To enhance personal relationships as there is less likelihood of cognitive distortions arising, and there is increased discriminatory capacity of cues from others.

(12) To help defuse interpersonal conflicts through modelling processes. A relaxed person may have a considerable calming effect on an angry or an anxious person. Relaxation may aid the discussion of difficult problems.

(13) To increase self-awareness of the psychophysiological state; relaxation and coping skills can be brought into play at the onset of psychophysiological arousal.

(14) To improve the level of self-confidence and self-esteem, as a consequence of much improved control of stress reactions.

(15) To raise the threshold of tolerance to pain.

(16) To aid recovery after certain illnesses, surgery, etc.

(17) To help control mood states, (such as depression, anger), more readily, where such states are caused by irrational cognitions.

(18) To reduce the need to depend on tranquillisers, sedatives, etc.

(19) To assist recovery after strenuous physical exercise.

(20) To improve physical skills, for example in golf or music.

(21) To reduce the incidence of accident proneness.

Preparation for relaxation training

Before embarking on the mechanics of relaxation training, a number of points need to be considered:

(1) The physical setting where the relaxation is to be practised is important. Keep the noise-level low. Ensure that the illumination is kept dim. Reclining chairs are ideal for relaxation training but any easy chair will suffice, provided that the individual is sitting or reclining comfortably in such a way as to keep muscular tension to a minimum. During relaxation training the eyes should be kept closed so that visual stimuli from the room can be eliminated.

(2) Bear in mind that learning to relax involves learning a skill, like learning to play a new sport. Individuals *learn* to be tense and anxious and, in an analogous fashion, can be trained to relax, thus reversing the process. Relaxation skills take time to acquire; significant gains can be achieved in a month, with twenty minutes of daily practice.

(3) High levels of tension can lead to rigid control. Some tense individuals have developed a pathological over-awareness to anxiety-producing internal and external cues and, when learning to relax, may have fears of losing control. In our experience such individuals are able to relax to a certain point and find it difficult to proceed beyond this point; this problem can be overcome with reassurance and short training sessions to begin with, gradually increasing the duration of the sessions. The individual, of course, always remains in ultimate control during the relaxation session and should terminate the session if, for any reason, discomfort is experienced.

(4) It is, perhaps, paradoxical that the individual gains control over him or herself by letting go. As mentioned in (3) above, in stressful situations typically, the individual responds by tightening the reins of control rather than by loosening them. As indicated in the section on advantages of relaxation, by letting go of the muscles and conscious control of the body, the individual is able to achieve significant control over a wide range of functions.

(5) During relaxation a number of unusual feelings, such as floating in the air, tingling sensations, etc. may be experienced. These feelings are usually signs that the muscles are beginning to relax. They are not uncommon and are no cause for concern. However, if the sensations become particularly troublesome, they may normally be effectively dealt with by opening the eyes, breathing in and out a little more deeply, and gently tensing the muscles throughout the body, before resuming the relaxation training.

(6) Most people find it difficult to concentrate on the relaxation techniques for a long period of time. It is important that the individual brings his or her mind back to the relaxation process as soon as he or she is aware that it has wandered on to something else.

(7) During the relaxation training various groups of muscles will be tensed; it is important that this tension be released immediately and that the tension does not dissipate gradually.

(8) During training sessions it is necessary to discriminate the feelings of tension and relaxation in the muscles. Thus, during the session, when the muscles are tense, the feelings of tension should be closely monitored; likewise the feelings of relaxation.

(9) Once a group of muscles has been relaxed there is some advantage in not moving that group; thus, do not move in the chair unnecessarily. However, the individual may feel free to move in order to maintain a comfortable position at all times.

(10) The purpose of relaxation training is to relax the mind and body completely. As deeper and deeper levels of relaxation are attained there may be a tendency to drift off to sleep; this tendency must be resisted unless the technique is being specifically used as an aid to overcoming insomnia.

(11) After the relaxation training session, tense up all the groups of muscles and breathe in and out somewhat more deeply *before* arising from the chair.

Relaxation instructions

(a) Introduction

As mentioned previously, during the relaxation training various groups of muscles will be tensed and then relaxed. The reason for this is that all people have some level of tension during waking hours; the amount of tension, of course, varies from one person to another and is referred to as the 'adaptation level'. By first tensing a group of muscles, (for example, the muscles of the right hand), holding the tension and then immediately releasing the tension, a larger and much more noticeable lessening of tension may be achieved than by merely trying to relax the muscles by 'letting them go'. Bernstein *et al.* (1973) believe that the release of tension creates a 'momentum' which allows the muscles to drop far below their adaptation level. By the use of this tensing-relaxing method, most individuals, after sufficient training, can bring about states of relaxation at will.

(b) Contracting the sixteen muscle groups

Sixteen groups of muscles are systematically tensed and relaxed. A particular group is tensed for approximately eight seconds; after the tension has been released the individual's attention is maintained upon the relaxed muscle group for approximately fifteen seconds; the muscle group is then tensed and relaxed a second time. Then the next muscle group is dealt with in a similar manner. Listed below is the order in which the muscle groups are tensed and relaxed, together with the means by which each group of muscles is tensed.

Take a slow, deep breath as each muscle group is tensed. Just prior to releasing the tension and exhaling, say the word 'Relax' or 'Calm' to yourself. After exhaling, and while concentrating on the feelings of relaxation, resume normal breathing. Exercise care when contracting muscles in the neck and legs, particularly in the latter, if there is any tendency to have cramp. If there is any evidence of heart, respiratory or other serious problems, the training procedure should be discussed with your doctor.

(c) Delivery of instructions

The following instructions are of the type given to clients with stress-related problems. By memorising them the reader will learn how to

Muscle Groups	Tensing Procedures
(1) Dominant hand and lower arm.	Tense muscles by making a tight fist.
(2) Dominant biceps.	Press elbow into back of chair, pushing downwards.
(3) Non-dominant hand and lower arm.	Procedure the same as (1).
(4) Non-dominant biceps.	Procedure the same as (2).
(5) Forehead.	Wrinkle up forehead and brow; lift eyebrows.
(6) Nose and upper cheeks.	Squint eyes tightly, wrinkling nose.
(7) Jaws and lower cheeks.	Clench jaws, bite teeth, pull corners of mouth back.
(8) Neck.	Press firmly against back of chair.
(9) Shoulders, upper back and chest.	Take slow deep breath and, while holding it, sit forward slightly, throw chest out, bringing shoulder blades together.
(10) Stomach region.	Pull muscles in.
(11) Dominant thigh.	Press heel into floor.
(12) Dominant calf.	Pull toes upwards.
(13) Dominant foot.	Curl toes downwards.
(14) Non-dominant thigh.	Procedure the same as (11).
(15) Non-dominant calf.	Procedure the same as (12).
(16) Non-dominant foot.	Procedure the same as (13).

administer the procedure. Alternatively a tape recording of relaxation instructions, methods, exercises (basic, intermediate and advanced), may be obtained from the author, (Dr L. E. Burns, Department of Clinical Psychology, Birch Hill Hospital, Rochdale, Lancashire, OL16 9QN).

'Settle back and find a comfortable position in the chair. Ensure that all your clothing is loose. Close your eyes and let your head relax comfortably on the back of the chair. Have your legs in a comfortable position with both feet firmly supported on the floor. Breathe in and out normally. Let the whole of your body become relaxed. Concentrate on the whole of your body, allowing it to become more and more relaxed. Just carry on breathing in and out normally, all the while relaxing, more and more deeply, the whole of your body.

Focus your attention on your dominant hand and lower arm. Tense all the muscles by making a tight fist. Monitor the feelings of tension. Now relax. Let all the tension go, and notice the difference in the feelings. Keep your attention focused on your lower arm and hand, and let all the muscles become more and more relaxed. Good. Now tense the muscles again in your dominant hand and lower arm. Study the tension. Now relax; let all the tension go. Focus on these muscles as they relax completely, noticing what it feels like as the muscles become more and more relaxed. Focus all your attention on the feelings associated with the relaxation.

Now concentrate on the dominant biceps. Tense your biceps – tighter and tighter. Again, just monitor the feelings of tension. Now relax. Let all of the tension go from your dominant biceps. Monitor the very pleasant feelings of relaxation. Fine. Now, once again, tense up all the muscles in your dominant biceps. Hold it and relax. Now, concentrate on the whole of your dominant arm from the shoulder right down to the finger tips and let the whole of your arm become more and more deeply relaxed. Just focus your attention on the very pleasant feelings of relaxation throughout the whole of your arm and hand.

Keep your arm and hand completely relaxed – try not to move it – and concentrate now on your non-dominant hand and lower arm. Tense up this area. Make the muscles tighter and tighter. Again, monitor the feelings of tension. Hold it and relax. Release the tension immediately. Let all the muscles in your non-dominant hand and lower arm become totally relaxed. Good. Once again, tense up the muscles in this area – make them go rigid – hold it – and relax. Monitor the feelings of relaxation – the very pleasant sensations of deep relaxation.

Now focus your attention on the non-dominant biceps. Make this area very tense. Notice the signs of tension. Relax; let all the tension go. Just allow all the muscles in your non-dominant biceps to become more and more relaxed. Study the difference. Monitor the warm, pleasant feelings of relaxation. Now, once again, tense up all the muscles in your non-dominant biceps – tighter and tighter. Now relax. Let the contractions go completely. Let go of all the contractions. Fine. Now concentrate on the whole of your non-dominant arm and hand. Note the sensations of deep relaxation. Allow the muscles to become even more deeply relaxed. Good.

Now keep your non-dominant hand and arm completely relaxed. Concentrate now on the muscles in your forehead. Make them tense. Study the tension and relax. Picture your forehead becoming smoother and more relaxed. Study the growing feelings of relaxation across your forehead. Now tense your forehead again. Monitor the feelings of tension. Relax. Once again, picture your forehead becoming smooth. Allow the feelings of relaxation to flow across your forehead.

Now pay attention to your nose and upper cheeks. Tense up this area; hold the tension and relax. Relax all the groups of muscles in the upper part of your cheeks and nose. Now tense this area again. Study the tension. And, again, relax, noting the difference in your feelings.

Now focus on your jaws and lower cheeks. Tense the muscles in this area. Make them rigid. Hold it – and relax. Let the muscles become more relaxed. Once again, tense the muscles in your jaws and lower cheeks; study the tension. Now relax. Monitor the feelings of relaxation. Now concentrate on the whole of your face – your forehead, eyes, cheeks, mouth and jaw. Let all the muscles in your face become more and more loose; more and more limp; more and more relaxed. There should be no signs of tension. No signs of firmness. Just enjoy the pleasant feelings of relaxation as the muscles go on relaxing, more and more deeply, more and more completely.

Now concentrate on the muscles in your neck. Make them very tense. Hold it – and relax. Let the relaxation grow in the muscles of your neck. Now, tense the muscles again. Study the tension. Relax. Let all the contractions in your neck go and notice the warm, pleasant feelings of deep relaxation. Allow it to continue to develop.

Now focus on your shoulders, upper back and chest. Take a slow, deep breath; sit forward slightly and tense up all the muscles. Tighter and tighter. Monitor the feelings of tension in your shoulders, upper back and chest. Relax. Just slump into the chair. Breathe in and out normally and let all the tension go. There should be no tension in your shoulder, upper back or chest. Good. Now, once again, tense up all the muscles in this area. Hold it. And relax. Notice the difference. Allow the feelings of relaxation to grow.

Now focus on your stomach region. Make the muscles in your stomach very tense. Hold the tension – and relax. Just breathe in and out normally and allow all the muscles in your stomach area to become more and more relaxed. Allow the deep relaxation to develop. Once again, tense up all the muscles in your stomach, and relax. Tell yourself to relax more and more deeply. Continue to breathe easily and regularly.

Concentrate now on the whole of the main part of your body – around your shoulders, chest and stomach region. Let the whole of the main part of your body sink into an even deeper state of relaxation. Allow all of the muscles to become completely relaxed and limp.

Keep the main part of your body very relaxed and still. Concentrate now on your dominant thigh. Tense up this area; make the muscles tight; tighter and tighter. Now relax. Let go of the tension in your thigh. Good. Once again, tense up all the muscles in your thigh. Hold the tension; study the tension – and relax. Allow the relaxation in your thigh to develop. Good.

Focus now on your dominant calf. Make the muscles very tense in this area. Monitor the feelings of tension. Now relax. Study the contrast in your feelings. Once again, tighten up all your calf muscles. Hold it. Tell yourself to relax. Let the tension go completely.

Now concentrate on your dominant foot. Make all the muscles and joints tense; more and more tense. Now relax. Allow the muscles and joints to become very relaxed. Once again, tense up all the muscles and joints in your dominant foot. Hold it. And relax.

Focus your attention on the whole of your dominant leg – from the top of your thigh to your toes. Let your whole leg now become more and more deeply relaxed. There should be no signs of tension – just a very pleasant feeling of deep relaxation.

Keep your dominant leg relaxed. Concentrate now on your non-dominant thigh. Tense the muscles. Tighter and tighter. Relax. Let the tension go. Tense the muscles again in your non-dominant thigh. Allow them to become more and more firm; more and more tight. Monitor the feelings. Relax. Notice the difference.

Focus on the non-dominant calf and tense the muscles. Relax. Let the muscles go completely. There should be no sign of firmness or tension. Again, tense the muscles in the non-dominant calf. Tighter and tighter. And relax.

Now focus on the non-dominant foot and, again, tighten up all the muscles and joints. Monitor the feelings of tension. Hold it – and relax. Study the feelings of relaxation. Again, tense up all the muscles in your non-dominant foot. Monitor the feelings of tension. Relax. Contrast the feelings in your foot. Observe the warm, pleasant feelings of relaxation.

Now concentrate on the whole of your non-dominant leg. Let the relaxation develop. Let the muscles become more and more limp.

Now focus on the whole of your body – from the top of your head to your toes; not on part of it but on the whole of your body – and allow it to sink into an even deeper state of relaxation. Just give in to it – don't resist it. Allow your whole body to become more and more completely relaxed. Just breathe in and out normally.

Concentrate now on your feet and imagine that your feet are becoming heavier and heavier; more and more relaxed. Now your legs are becoming heavier and heavier; heavy as a ton of lead. Imagine that the heaviness is spreading into your stomach region and your chest. The stomach and chest are becoming very heavy. Now your head region; it is becoming more and more heavy and relaxed. Your hands and arms are becoming so heavy; so relaxed. Your whole body is becoming heavier and heavier. Imagine that your body is becoming so heavy that it is beginning to sink down into the chair and, as it sinks down, so it becomes more and more relaxed. Just imagine that you are sinking down – down – down – into the chair; becoming more and more heavy; more and more relaxed. Just monitor the very pleasant feelings of deep relaxation; the warm, glowing, heavy feelings of being completely relaxed and at ease. You feel calm and peaceful. Just keep your thoughts on the very pleasant feelings of deep relaxation. Just continue to relax. Enjoy this period of being completely relaxed.

Relaxation will normally continue for a further ten minutes.'

(d) Abbreviated relaxation

As relaxation skills develop, normally after a week to ten days of daily practice, the number of muscle groups (originally sixteen) which are to be tensed and relaxed are reduced as follows:

Muscle Groups	Tensing Procedure
(1) Dominant arm.	Tense muscles by making a fist while pressing elbow into back of chair.
(2) Non-dominant arm.	Procedure the same as (1).
(3) Face.	Squint eyes, clench jaws, pull corners of mouth back.
(4) Neck.	Press firmly against back of chair.
(5) Shoulders, chest and stomach region.	Take slow deep breath, throw chest out, pulling in the muscles of the stomach.
(6) Dominant leg.	Press heel into floor, curling toes downwards.
(7) Non-dominant leg.	Procedure the same as (6).

Finally, after a further seven to ten days' training with the seven muscle groups, contract all of the seven muscle groups simultaneously; hold the tension for eight seconds as usual, and relax. Repeat three times.

Generalising the relaxation response

After success has been achieved in obtaining deep levels of relaxation during the training sessions, it is important for the individual to generalise the relaxation response to his or her everyday life. The goal is for the relaxation skills to become habitual. There are two basic methods to aid this process:

(a) Self-monitoring

Unfortunately, levels of tension tend to increase gradually over a period of years and become a part of our way of life. Thus, although we may be quite tense generally, we may not recognise it and it is only during acute episodes that we become conscious of our state of very high arousal. The differential monitoring of tension and relaxation during the training sessions should make us more aware of our levels of tension. Self-monitoring involves randomly assessing, on several occasions during the course of a day, our levels of tension. If tension is monitored – for example the tight gripping of the steering wheel of the car while driving, feeling keyed up while doing work at a desk or while in social situations – then general or differential relaxation skills may be brought into play.

(b) Cue-induced relaxation

Certain events in our environment may trigger off stressful situations. Conversely, certain environmental stimuli can also come to evoke the relaxation response. For example, routinely while at important business meetings, working at our desk, etc., we should aim to relax so that these stimuli may, in time, become strongly associated with the relaxation response. With repeated practice, stressful events, (whether external or internal), should provide the cues to bring into operation our relaxation skills.

Although it is acknowledged that other behavioural techniques involving cognitive control, etc., may have a part to play in the management of stress, there are, as already mentioned, many benefits to relaxation, a major one being that it assists the individual in gaining conscious or automatic control over high levels of psycho-physiological arousal.

REFERENCES

H. Benson, *The Relaxation Response* (New York: Morrow, 1975)

D. A. Bernstein and T. D. Borkovec, *Progressive Relaxation Training* (Chicago: Research Press, 1973)

M. Friedman and R. Rosenman, *Type A Behavior and your Heart* (New York: Alfred A. Knopf, 1974)

J. K. Galbraith, *The Age of Uncertainty* (Boston: Houghton Mifflin, 1977)

E. Jacobson, *Progressive Relaxation* (Chicago: University of Chicago Press, 1938)

H. Selye, in P. Goldberg, *Executive Health* (New York: McGraw-Hill, 1978)

R. M. Suinn, 'Type A Behavior Pattern', in R. B. Williams and W. D. Gentry (eds), *Behavioral Approaches to Medical Treatment* (Cambridge, Mass: Ballinger, 1977)

J. Wolpe, *Psychotherapy by Reciprocal Inhibition* (Stanford, Ca.: Stanford University Press, 1958)

PART III

REMEDIAL ACTION

6 An Occupational Health Physician's Experience

Michael McDonald
London, UK

'Was he free? Was he happy? The question is absurd: Had anything been wrong, we should certainly have heard.'

'The Unknown Citizen' (W. H. Auden, March 1939)

Introduction

A recent frank review of some of the books and papers on work stress and mental strain has described them as 'tending to be jargon-ridden expositions of dubious practical utility which tell us little or nothing about the pressures on people in industry and the strains which they produce' (Murrell, 1978). Lloyd Davies (1973) criticised the psychiatric contribution for failing to keep pace with the understanding of the effects of industrialised work. Both authors have pointed out the need for realistic studies which permit the observation and measurement of what is happening to people and their interaction with work and leisure – in essence, studies of the natural history of exposure, which are as relevant to non-physical as to physical stressors at work.

This chapter describes a field investigation into the mental health of employees in a highly specialised section of industry which I undertook as a part-time occupational health physician over the period 1965–73. It also outlines the lessons learned from this investigation, which have subsequently assisted me to cope with the problems of strain in people at work, and which may be of help to others involved in health care in industry.

Personal setting

It may allow greater understanding of the events portrayed if, first, I give a thumb-nail sketch of my professional training and previous experience – if only to show how ill-prepared I was for the tasks that lay ahead. Like many other medical students of 30 years ago, my undergraduate education in the main clinical subjects was thorough, and I felt reasonably well-equipped to cope with the demands of the pre-registration 'house jobs' that followed qualification. However in the lesser known specialities I had not been so well briefed. For example, psychiatry was covered by four lectures, two embarrassing attendances at out-patients and two visits to a forbidding mental hospital on the outskirts of London. Public health was dealt with summarily in two dull lectures given by the local Medical Officer of Health. 'Industrial medicine' were rude words and were not allowed to be mentioned in public – certainly not in front of the Professor of Surgery! In short I received the normal education of a British doctor qualifying in the early 1950s.

It was in a busy casualty department in the Midlands that I had my first encounter with the more gory side of occupational medicine, in the shape of a miner whose pelvis had been crushed in a cutting-machine at one of the local collieries. Within two weeks I went down the pit and saw the machine in which this man had allowed himself to be trapped whilst trying to clear a blockage. Those people with the same degree of curiosity will know what I mean when I say that no-one should pass up a similar 'opportunity'. I emerged not only with a deep feeling of gratitude to those warm and generous men who work underground to give us our daily fuel, but with the seeds of a fascination in people and their work which has never left me. In 1958 I entered general practice in the home counties. To boost our practice's income from the National Health Service, the senior partner and I did sessional work with the local group industrial health service. After eighteen months' apprenticeship, I was appointed visiting medical officer to a modern electronics research laboratory which had just moved to a new location within our practice area. This was to be the start of one of the most interesting and stimulating phases of my life.

The smaller work place

Modern sociology has suggested 500 as the upper order of size of a successful factory, as beyond this many of the employees cannot distinguish their less familiar workmates from complete strangers, or, in Aristotle's words 'know one another's characters'. Above this size the works manager tends to be remote from his work force by the introduction of a level of subordinate management in addition to the foreman. (Revans, 1960).

Revans also suggested that the effect of size may appear in the larger units as heightened absence rates and simple lateness, increased accident rate and greater chance of work loss through industrial action.

The research laboratories to which I was appointed had an initial working population of approximately 500 persons (increasing to 1200 persons after 16 years), and so came within the definition of a 'smaller work place' (Taylor and Wood, 1960). At the time of my entry into occupational medicine in 1958, 60 per cent of the factory population in Great Britain worked in factories of this size. Indeed, industries such as research laboratories were not then required to register under the Factories Acts and so the exact number of smaller work places was not really known. Most of the workers in these factories had no access to medical services at their places of work. In the UK there were only a few restricted areas, such as Slough, Harlow, Park Royal (Central Middlesex), Rochdale, West Bromwich and Dundee, where group services had been set up to meet the needs of occupational health care. Not surprisingly, this lack of health services at work was not confined to the UK, as I confirmed in 1965 when, with the aid of a Council of Europe Medical Fellowship, I was able to study smaller work places in Norway, Sweden and Finland (McDonald, 1966). Many of my impressions were already known to those engaged in small industry health services and had been described by such writers as Taylor (1958), Jeffreys and Wood (1960) and Lee (1962); but it is important to restate some of them here so as to provide a background knowledge of the nature of the worker who opts to work in smaller industry, his work demands and relationships.

In a healthy economy which allows reasonable employment opportunities, most people select the type of work they feel most capable of doing in an environment in which they are happiest, or, as Tredgold (1972) stated: 'Each of us sets a level of need for security and chooses a career or occupation to fit.' Thus a certain type of worker may enter small industry as the work place of choice and this person, by the nature of his or her character and working environment, may present problems and needs which differ from the rest of the working population. I discovered that in the small work place the working-group tends to be self-selected from either friends or relatives. The atmosphere thus created permits better personal relationships both between workmates and with the employer. The individual can work happily despite working conditions which are sometimes poor.

The type of employee is often one who is self-sufficient and independent, and tends not to seek promotion or the comparative security of large industry. He or she is more likely to be able to select their own speed of work and have a variety of tasks to perform. The work tends to be less boring and repetitive and he or she is likely to derive more satisfaction from it than a counterpart on a large assembly line. There is greater opportunity to be a self-managing individual, and to function at an adult level. Small industry generally does not offer as much opportunity to those who are motivated by achievement and who wish to use higher skills.

Group health services offer the greatest opportunity for service to small industry. These may be independent, or based on hospital or larger industry, but whatever form they take they must be flexible to fit in with the constantly changing requirements of this segment of industry. The roles of both doctor and nurse in the service of smaller industry differ from those of their counterparts in large industry. The majority of occupational health nurses in industry work without the constant support and advice of a doctor (Radwanski, 1979) and most of these are employed in smaller industry. The degree of responsibility placed on them is probably greater than in any other branch of their profession. In addition to their occupational health role they may be called upon to act as advisors in safety, and as part-time social workers. This then was my experience and state of knowledge at the start.

The research laboratories

The research laboratories to which I was appointed were established in 1946 to provide research and development facilities for a leading international telecommunications company. In 1959 the laboratories moved to a new purpose-built site in my practice area. By then the activities of the laboratories had been extended to provide research facilities for what had become a multi-industry corporation, whose interests ranged over telecommunications, electronics, engineered products, consumer products and services, natural resources, and insurance and finance. The laboratories comprised two specialist but complementary operating units – one devoted to telecommunications and electronics, and the other to materials and components. In addition, the broad spectrum of expertise and facilities allowed extension of research and development activities into specialist areas directly related to the various needs of the other industries within the corporation.

By 1965, 715 people worked at the laboratories and Figure 6.1 shows their main functional groups. The research scientists were a

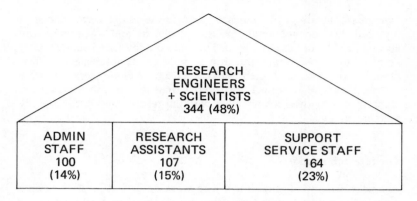

Figure 6.1 Functional groups of laboratories staff

carefully selected group of highly-proficient graduate physicists, chemists, engineers, mathematicians and computer technologists. Together with skilled research assistants they worked in closely-knit project groups comprising as few as three, four or five persons. Because of their potential to the company, expertise, experience, training and costly recruitment, the value of these graduate scientists and engineers was substantial. By tradition, the parent company in the UK had a strong paternalistic attitude towards its employees, and this was particularly apparent at these research laboratories, where no effort or money was spared in order to preserve and promote the health and welfare of its work force. Without this degree of real concern the investigation which is described in the pages which follow would not have been possible.

Medical services

The company had a well-established occupational health service, headed by a medical director located at company headquarters. Medical services were provided at each of the major locations throughout the UK and these were staffed mainly by experienced state-registered nurses backed up by part-time doctors – often local general practitioners. The laboratories employed one full-time nursing sister. I attended initially for four hours, which was later increased to 12 hours per week. An environmental safety committee composed of the site engineer, chief chemist, senior physicist, doctor and nurse visited all parts of the laboratories every month to advise on the proper control of environmental hazards (physical, chemical, biological). This was of immense value to me in the performance of my role as occupational health physician and facilitated my acceptance by the research staff. Not only did my face become better known but, more important, I was seen to be interested in their research projects and their safe working. Welfare services were provided by the Personnel Manager with whom we, in the Medical Department, enjoyed a very close working relationship both formally and informally.

The research scientists

Murrell (1978) wrote that 'most men working in factories are neither acutely discontented with their work nor do they find it stimulating or enjoyable; there is little bitterness but equally little enthusiasm'. This contrasts vividly with the picture of scientific research painted in an interview given by Sir Barnes Wallis (1979) in which he said 'there is no greater joy in life than first proving that a thing is impossible, and then showing how it can be done'. Whilst such stirring statements may serve to illustrate the nature and motivation of research scientists, little hard fact is known about this remarkable section of much-valued individuals, and even less is known about their mental health. MacIver (1969) ventured to suggest that 'the mental health problems of professional and research personnel in industry have an epidemiological flavour of their own' but did not quantify his statement. Perhaps the folk-lore surrounding the eccentricities of wartime 'boffins' provided sufficient barrier to defy penetration.

My own assessment of the research personnel with whom I worked is unashamedly biased in their favour – indeed I found them to be the most colourful and fascinating group that I have ever worked with in industry. They were a group of people who worked happily and derived complete satisfaction from their jobs. Whilst there were project target dates to be met, by and large individuals were free to select their own speed and manner of work – some were even allowed to work at home on certain phases of their research projects and this presented difficulties in the monitoring of sickness absence. By virtue of their training and background they were individualists, and were encouraged to be so by management when bringing their skills and knowledge to bear on problem solving tasks. Each individual was capable of displaying a pattern of behaviour which covered a wider spectrum than is normally found in manufacturing industries. This behaviour could border on the eccentric as far as the 'outside' world was concerned, but was within normal limits for this particular industrial community. Whilst their intelligence quotients were within the top 5 percentile of the general population, many of them were surprisingly naïve and even immature when social and family problems arose. The 'pure' and more dedicated scientists tended not to welcome or perform well in executive roles demanding skills of leadership.

Early days

Before starting employment at the research laboratories, I was interviewed by the managing director, who quickly made me aware of his concern for the mental health of his scientists and engineers. Apparently a number of vital projects had been seriously affected in the previous year by the breakdown of key personnel. He highlighted the thorny problem of a particular lone scientist working on highly specialised research – so specialised, in fact, that he and other senior staff could not discern whether it was bona fide or merely the ramblings of a disturbed mind. He asked that I should make the detection of early signs of mental ill-health amongst his staff one of the first priorities of my job. Whilst I considered that he placed more faith in my clinical ability than it deserved, I did promise to see what could be done. Clearly, if I was to be successful in meeting this request and in carrying out the remainder of my role as the location's medical officer, my main objectives were to gain acceptance by the staff and to obtain detailed knowledge of their work and the related hazards. This was to take longer than I had first appreciated, though to some degree my path was eased by the nearness of my general practice surgery to the laboratories. This allowed me to deal quickly with crises and emergencies arising outside my normal four-hour session, and so provided a much appreciated service for work people who were then strangers to the area. In addition a number of the staff registered as my patients, and I was thus able to gain a knowledge of them (and their families) outside their work environment. Some became my friends and through them I was able to learn something of the intricacies of the company in human terms, and of the rich tradition of service and dedication they had provided in the early days of telecommunications throughout the world. The tradition of pioneering and discovery was part of their make-up, and was one that would always impel them into new areas of greater sophistication and complexity. As their doctor it was hard not to be as enthusiastic as they were.

As I burrowed into the organisation I discovered the few cases that the managing director had been so concerned about. All were known to their managers, who had been prepared to tolerate their odd and, at times, difficult behaviour provided they made adequate contribution to their research projects. What had not been appreciated was the effect these unfortunate people were having on their immediate colleagues. Whilst the presence of the odd personality problem or mentally-disturbed person in a production line of 100–200 persons was unlikely to bring production to a halt, one disturbed man or woman in a project group of three, four or five persons could completely disrupt the whole research project if help was not provided both to the individual and to the group.

One of the first examples of strain presented itself in two or three of the younger graduate engineers. It had been the practice to detach newcomers abroad to assist with the installation of specialised equipment and so provide them with valuable field experience. As this offered young bachelors opportunities of free travel to interesting places 'off the beaten track' these posts were much sought after. Problems tended to arise when they got married whilst on leave at home. As they often lived 'rough', conditions did not allow them to be accompanied by their young brides, and so symptoms of strain were liable to develop because of divided loyalties between the company and the wife. Repatriation was a solution, but contractual obligations and the individual's specialist knowledge of the local technical problems did not always make this easy to effect.

Another type of clinical problem was posed by two young graduate scientists who suffered recurrent schizophrenic breakdowns during their early years of employment. As the laboratories employed a high proportion of young graduates, it was to be expected that this population would contain one or two schizophrenics who would behave in this way. The two that presented subsequently proved to have had previous breakdowns whilst at university. Both were fully supported by the medical department, management and colleagues during their relapses and returned to provide effective work. The two cases provided interesting lessons for the future as to how the employment screening procedure had failed to identify them, and the reasons for their repeated relapses. On the first point, both lacked insight into their clinical condition and did not recognise that they had been 'ill' at university and so, understandably, did not declare a past history of breakdown on employment. On the second point, both suffered relapses because of the instability of their domestic circumstances which did not permit their continuing to take their prescribed maintenance therapy. Both scientists subsequently resigned from the laboratories to pursue normal careers elsewhere. The lone scientist identified by the managing director proved to be an untreatable severe psychotic who was receiving amateur and time-consuming psychotherapy from his senior manager. Whilst I feel that colleagues can help, this case had gone well past the point of benefit. Fortunately the other cases, which I channelled to appropriate agencies, benefited from treatment and so it was accepted that I was a safe person to approach for advice on medical problems.

Elated with this modest 'success' I proceeded to make my first mistake. I had read a paper in a reputable journal of psychology about the possible benefits of personality tests as predictors of mental illness, and I decided to offer one of these tests to all employees who consulted me in the medical department. The test asked people to draw a picture, which would reveal central themes in their personality which were predictive of future mental ill health. As Felton (1969) recorded, 'Organisations with large numbers of research and development personnel are more likely to include psychometric procedures than companies employing hundreds or thousands of new high-school graduates or craftsmen.' The research laboratories were one such organisation, and I had not appreciated the sensitivity of graduates to this type of procedure. At first the test was received with mild amusement, but at the end of six months I was approached by the secretary of one of the unions who asked my reasons for introducing the test and rightly questioned my ability to interpret the results. I saw that the test was not welcomed and withdrew it. It was some time before suspicion of me was dispelled and confidence restored. This was a salutary lesson to me against tinkering with trendy techniques I did not fully understand!

It transpired later that management was divided in its opinion on the desirability of psychometric tests for selection of graduates. One school believed that testing would screen out all unstable recruits and that the survival population would be more efficient. The other lacked conviction in the test anyway, and recognised that genius was not necessarily associated with emotional stability. It was happy to tolerate the 'odd-balls' provided they produced new ideas worthy of development, and provided the company employed an agency capable of dealing competently with any psychological or psychiatric problems. My own view was that the admission of a graduate entrant to a research organisation should depend on his or her technical and specialist skills and ability, and his acceptance by the members of his immediate working group.

I have attempted to set the scene of the concern of management in the laboratories for the preservation of the mental health of employees, and have given examples of cases and problem situations that I encountered in my first five or six years there. In doing so I may have created the impression that there was a higher incidence of mental ill health amongst the company's staff than in other industries. As I pointed out earlier, the spectrum of normal behaviour was different to that in other industrial communities – just as a coal mining community might be different to a hospital community – but the pattern and incidence of mental illness did not lead one to suspect that in extent and nature they were different to those of the general population. However, there was a greater preparedness both to examine this facet of health, and to finance any reasonable investigation of it.

The preventive approach

The notion that 'prevention is better than cure' has always appealed to both the general public and health workers as a desirable approach to the lessening of the incidence and the severity of disease. Lennart Levi (1979) has summarised the three main strategies in the preventive approach in medicine. The first operates by decreasing vulnerability and increasing resistance of populations, for example through immunisation and improved nutrition. The second involves the identification of high risk individuals and the offer of appropriate preventive treatment. The third strategy is the provision of proper control of noxious agents such as radiation. The strategy of the identification of high-risk individuals achieved considerable success in ante-natal care and early childhood, and in the 1960s led to the vogue of pre-symptomatic diagnosis of disease in adults. Unfortunately, because of the limitations of present-day treatment, the expectations of this type of approach have not yet been fulfilled. There is some evidence to suggest that the early detection of symptomless hypertensives in the under 60s, and cancer of the breast in post-menopausal women, may be beneficial, but in no other illness does early detection appear to confer the benefit of restoring normal life-expectancy or quality of life. As far as the early identification of 'at risk' groups to stress is concerned, Cooper and Marshall (1978) stated that some people more than others are 'characterologically' predisposed to stress and that factors such as personality, motivation, fluctuations in ability (as with age), insight into personal motivations and weaknesses may be contributory. In the sphere of stress-related diseases, the stress-seeking coronary-prone Type 'A' behaviour pattern identified by Rosenman, Friedman and Strauss (1964, 1966) is well known. The concept that there may even be a hereditary predisposition to neurosis (in children and young adults) was advanced by Kopelman (1976). In the identification of emotionally-disturbed workers, Felton (1969) placed importance on employment interviews, psychometric testing, supervisors' reports, observations on medical examination, sick absence, labour turnover and excessive medical department visiting. Brook (1976) favoured Holmes' and Rahe's (1967) opinion that people are more prone to emotional difficulties at those times of life when personal, psychological readjustments have to be made. He also considered that, in industry, three periods of life are of particular importance: late adolescence, early middle age and later middle age.

On the basis of these approaches I examined the opportunities which existed at the laboratories for identifying emotionally disturbed workers within its population. I was reasonably happy that late adolescents were already being adequately screened on recruitment by 'in-depth' interviews, psychometric tests and medical examinations. Self-referrals, referrals of employees by management, and persons returning to work after sick leave, were also being accurately recorded in the medical department. However I doubted if these records revealed much more than the 'tip of the iceberg' of the true incidence of emotional problems in the early and late middle-age groups. The significance of labour turn-over was minimal because it was the practice for scientists to move round in various industries to gain specialist experience. Similarly, sick absence records could not be regarded as accurate both because 'study at home' was an accepted practice, and because staff travelled abroad frequently and could be ill there without our knowledge of the diagnosis or the duration of the incapacity. Furthermore I had gained the impression that tense and anxious staff formed part of the conscientious group of employees who tended to remain at work out of loyalty rather than take leave. Depressives or anxiety depressives were more likely to stay at home when incapacitated. I realised that a further strategy needed to be introduced if a realistic assessment of the incidence of impaired mental health was to be attempted. The strategy that I chose was that of a health screening programme for those over 40 years of age.

Presymptomatic health screening

In addition to my study of smaller work places in Scandinavia in 1965, whilst I was there I took the opportunity to examine some of the newer research techniques being employed by several of the institutes of occupational medicine. I was particularly attracted to the work being carried out on the screening of populations for early evidence of disease. This appeared to be particularly effective in Finland, where there is a low-density population, and many areas where people did not have access to medical services. I was able to accompany mobile investigation teams from the Institute of Occupational Medicine in Helsinki on their investigations to industries in country areas. Some of the enthusiasm of the Finns for this type of investigation rubbed off on to me and, on my return to England, I resolved to introduce a similar health-screening programme for the laboratories' population. The proposal was received with enthusiasm by the managing director, who immediately placed the necessary funds at my disposal for equipment etc. On this occasion I took good care to obtain clearance from all interested parties for the scheme before it was launched! In direct contrast to the reaction to my previous investigation the programme was welcomed widely — indeed the problem was to restrict the numbers of participants to the age-groups I considered would be most likely to benefit.

In 1965, voluntary health screening was offered to all laboratory staff of 40 years of age and above. The screening consisted of the administration of a detailed questionnaire to individual volunteers and a full medical examination by myself. In addition they received the following special investigations: electrocardiography, Vitalography, serum cholesterol and uric acid estimations (analysed at the local hospital pathology laboratory), blood sugar estimations by Dextrostix (proceeding to a glucose tolerance test if abnormal) and screening for proteinuria by Albustix. One-and-a-quarter hours were allotted to each individual for the completion of the total screening process. By the end of the first year I had screened 83 of the 232 employees (206 males and 26 females) who were eligible, and had taken stock of my findings. As it was possible that most of those who had sought examination first were employees who were most anxious about their personal health, I considered that I had been looking at a biased sample of the population and so the results could not be considered to be statistically significant. My overall impression was that they were a group of individuals who displayed a normal pattern of existence, both at home and at work. Most appeared to be happily married with children and enjoyed normal domestic lives. They seemed to derive great satisfaction from their work and enjoyed good interpersonal work relationships at all levels. By and large they displayed the same tendencies as most Western Europeans to over-eat and under-exercise but, surprisingly, showed no evidence of harmful drinking. Those who smoked cigarettes tended to have twice as many symptoms and signs of respiratory and cardio-vascular disease as non-smokers. As far as physical illness was concerned, I detected a few cases of piles, hernias and varicose veins of which the volunteers were mostly already aware. Of greater interest was the fact that 85 per cent of volunteers examined complained of one or more symptoms of ill health. Some of these I considered were symptoms of mental ill-health masquerading as physical illness. As only 12 per cent of those examined were subsequently referred to their family doctors for further advice, it can be seen that the majority of symptoms uncovered were of a minor nature. Nonetheless it was my impression that some employees had been nursing anxieties about these and other health matters which had tended to act as stressors to them in their everyday lives. Most recognised the true significance of their symptoms and that they did not warrant the seeking of medical advice but, in others, they created doubts and uncertainties which could develop out of proportion, and affect both the quality of their lives and their effectiveness at work. Thirty per cent of those examined admitted to symptoms of strain related to either home or work, and the vast majority of these were in positions of responsibility, with some managerial or supervisory role.

I concluded from this review of my findings that, whilst I had carried out an investigation which had been greatly appreciated by the laboratories' staff (and had thereby risen in their esteem), I had not been able to confer any benefit on their existing or future physical health status by discovering any significant treatable disease early. However, it appeared that health screening could provide a means for both the early detection of those suffering from impaired mental health, and an additional opportunity for the assessment of its incidence in the population. It was this strategy, then, that I added to the existing procedures of screening after sick leave and medical department referrals, in order to assess the incidence of employees suffering from impaired mental health.

The investigation

The primary objective of my investigation was to estimate the annual incidence of employees who developed symptoms and signs of impaired mental health during the period 1965–73. Data was collected from three sources – self-referred and management-referred employees to the medical department, employees reporting to the medical department on return from sick leave and employees identified as a result of the 'over-40s' health screening programme. By the end of nine years, 80 per cent of the population of 232 over 40 years of age had been screened. Thus it could be said that all employees had had equal opportunity of access to the three screening processes available, and that the results obtained were likely to be statistically significant. Data from recruitment medical examinations were not used, as it was presumed that these persons had developed symptoms before joining the company. Each case was identified by me during the course of personal consultation, and the diagnoses were made as at a general practitioner's surgery. Additional objectives were to identify the age group(s) of greatest incidence in both sexes, and to assess the relative importance of work and domestic factors in the causation of impaired mental health.

The results

1 The denominator population (total work force)

Information on the exact size of this population was not easily available and was eventually obtained by the nursing sister, my wife and I

searching amongst piles of dust-covered accounts department records
to find what we wanted. I was surprised to find that as many as 1878
people had been employed at the laboratories during the nine years
1965–73, as I had not previously appreciated the high labour-turnover
associated with the needs of particular projects. Many of the short-
stay staff were transfers from associated companies within the
corporation. The distribution by age and sex of the total work-force
taken at the mid-point (1969) in the investigation appears in Table 6.1.

TABLE 6.1   Distribution of total work force by age and sex

	Total	<30 years	31–49 years	50+ years
Male	1207	557	444	206
	(64%)	(30%)	(24%)	(11%)
Female	671	439	190	42
	(36%)	(24%)	(10%)	(2%)

Equally surprising was that as few as 251 (216 males and 35 females)
remained in employment throughout the nine years. The total annual
staffing-levels and man-years worked appear in Table 6.2. The latter
has been included because the labour-turnover was so high that
'numbers employed' does not give a sufficiently accurate indication of
the risk population.

TABLE 6.2   Annual staffing levels and man years worked 1965–73

	1965	1966	1967	1968	1969	1970	1971	1972	1973
Total numbers of staff	715	750	785	825	860	896	935	971	1011
Man years	605	664	682	686	726	787	787	804	848

The distribution of total annual years worked by age and sex
appear in Table 6.3. It shows a remarkable consistency throughout
the nine years for, whilst the population appears to the practitioner to
change, he or she is dealing with a very usual consistency because of
the types of job and the people available.

TABLE 6.3 Distribution of total annual man years worked by age and sex of employees

Man years	1965 M	1965 F	1966 M	1966 F	1967 M	1967 F	1968 M	1968 F	1969 M	1969 F	1970 M	1970 F	1971 M	1971 F	1972 M	1972 F	1973 M	1973 F
<30 years	139	75	153	80	151	68	157	62	160	68	173	79	172	80	177	88	186	95
%	23%	12%	23%	12%	22%	10%	23%	9%	22%	9%	22%	10%	22%	10%	22%	11%	22%	11%
31–49 years	211	49	232	53	239	68	240	69	257	75	275	79	276	78	281	80	297	80
%	35%	8%	35%	8%	35%	10%	35%	10%	35%	10%	35%	10%	35%	10%	35%	10%	35%	9%
50+ years	120	11	133	13	136	20	137	21	146	20	157	24	158	23	154	24	160	30
%	20%	2%	20%	2%	20%	3%	20%	3%	20%	3%	20%	3%	20%	3%	19%	3%	19%	4%
Total	470	135	518	146	526	156	534	152	563	163	605	182	606	181	612	192	643	205
%	78%	22%	78%	22%	77%	23%	78%	22%	78%	22%	77%	23%	77%	23%	76%	24%	76%	24%
Total man years	605		664		682		686		726		787		787		804		848	

TABLE 6.4 Numbers per year of employees who developed symptoms 1965–73 (excluding the diagnosis of 'personality disorder')

	1965	1966	1967	1968	1969	1970	1971	1972	1973
Male	6	11	8	8	6	5	8	13	7
Female	2	1	1	0	3	3	1	0	4
Total	8	12	9	8	9	8	9	13	11

2 The numerator population – employees who developed symptoms or signs of impaired mental health during 1965–73

Eighty-seven employees (72 males and 15 females) developed symptoms or signs of mental ill-health during the nine years of the investigations (see Table 6.4).

3 Means of detection

Thirty-nine (45 per cent) were either self-referrals or were referred to the medical department by management. Sixteen (18 per cent) were detected on return from sick leave and 32 (37 per cent) were discovered as a result of the 'over-40s' health screening programme. This last finding clearly demonstrates the advantage of the newly-introduced technique in uncovering what would otherwise have remained a hidden population.

4 Functional groupings

Forty-six (53 per cent) were research scientists or engineers, 10 (11 per cent) were research assistants, 12 (14 per cent) were in the administration group and 19 (22 per cent) were members of the support staff. Twenty-nine (33 per cent) of the 87 were in positions of responsibility with some management or executive role. Many other studies of this kind have been preoccupied with the effects of stress on executives. Whilst executives are undoubtedly subject to strain, the results of this investigation show that stressors can affect persons of any job status. What may be a stressor to a person of one job status may not be so to a person of another job status, and each of them will react to differing levels of stress in their own way. An individual's reaction depends on his or her experience, skills and attributes. The way in which a person reacts is determined largely by his or her upbringing.

5 Diagnosis

I found there was a normal range of diagnosis such as a GP would expect to find in his or her practice. Thirty-four (39 per cent) had symptoms or signs of anxiety states, 23 (26 per cent) of depressive states, 25 (29 per cent) of anxiety depression and 5 (6 per cent) had symptoms suggestive of schizophrenia or schizoid states. It was difficult to differentiate between states ('I am') and traits ('I generally feel') of anxiety and depression, but those persons with traits of anxiety and depression − the anxious or depressive personalities − were excluded from the numerator population.

6 Precipitating factors

It was interesting that only 15 (17 per cent) considered that their symptoms were associated with their work. Of the remainder, 40 (46 per cent) had domestic precipitating factors and 32 (37 per cent) were of mixed work and domestic origin − mostly domestic.

Age and sex

Table 6.5 shows that the rates of occurrence per cent man-years are fairly even, and approximate to a little over 1 per cent per year. The highest rates of occurrence for both sexes were in the 31−49 years age-group, which supports Brook's findings.

8 Incidence of illness

Totalling the annual rates of occurrence for each of the 9 years shows that the rate of risk of impaired mental health for this population was approximately 12 per cent from 1965 to 1973. I considered it significant that nearly half (41) of these employees remained in employment with the laboratories throughout the nine years 1965−73. This could be interpreted in a number of different ways. It may be that this sort of person is better tolerated by this type of working population, or simply that most of them seek to avoid the stress of change more than does the rest of the laboratories' population. I noted with interest that the 87 employees who developed symptoms between 1965 and 1973 worked a total of 605 man years in the nine years, which equalled the total man years worked by all staff employed during 1965. This gives some indication of the potential loss to the company in the unlikely event of all these breaking down at the same time.

Discussion of results

Varying estimates have been made of the proportion of the general population suffering from mental ill health. In one study carried out between 1968 and 1974 on a random sample of the Swedish population aged 15−75, one Swede out of three reported experiencing

TABLE 6.5   Rates of illness occurrence per cent man years

		1965	1966	1967	1968	1969	1970	1971	1972	1973	*Mean*
Overall rates per 100 man years		1.32	1.80	1.32	1.17	1.23	1.02	1.14	1.62	1.30	1.32
Male	<30 years	0.72	0.65	0.66	1.27	nil	nil	nil	1.69	nil	0.55
	31–49 years	0.95	2.58	1.67	2.08	1.55	0.73	2.17	2.14	1.68	1.73
	50+ years	0.64	0.77	0.57	0.19	0.36	0.49	0.33	0.65	0.31	0.48
Female	<30 years	nil	1.25	nil	nil	1.47	nil	nil	nil	1.05	0.41
	31–49 years	4.08	nil	nil	nil	2.66	2.53	1.28	nil	2.50	1.45
	50+ years	nil	nil	0.64	nil	nil	0.55	nil	nil	0.31	0.17

impaired mental well-being during the previous year (Levi, 1979). MacIver (1969) estimates that 25 per cent of the industrial population have significant emotional problems. Viewed against this background, my own estimate of the rate of risk of mental ill health of 12 per cent in 1965–73 would not appear to be high.

Because of the adverse effects that mental strain and ill health at work can have on absenteeism, productivity, time keeping, accident rates and quality of work, managements seek that these are quantified and costed, and in doing so tend to assume that the causative factors are confined largely to the work situation. Tredgold (1972) suspected that the onset of neurosis in industry is often the result of a combination of many factors, of which insecurity at work is only one and is often less important than domestic stress. As Murrell (1978) states 'pressures which have produced strains which are reasonably tolerable may suddenly be exacerbated by something which has gone on outside the factory'. My own findings suggest that domestic and social stressors outweigh those at work in giving rise to symptoms of disease.

Because of cost factors, some managements may either seek to limit the employment of persons with symptoms of impaired mental health, or to identify early others in a declining mental-health state. I was able to show that most of these people (excluding psychotics) can be safely employed and can go on to provide a normal input, providing there is access to adequate medical advice at work. I was also able to show that health screening provides a valuable means of detecting a not inconsiderable 'hidden' fraction (37 per cent) of employees with symptoms of strain or mental ill-health who would otherwise have been missed. The health screening process also serves to establish sound lines of communication between employees and caring agencies, and tends to lessen the severity and duration of the more acute mental crises. The procedure provides prior knowledge of individual normal behaviour patterns and allows earlier detection of variation from these. Thus assistance can be provided for minor or potential problems before they have had a chance to escalate.

Lessons in coping

Mental health forms only a part of the spectrum of normal day-to-day responsibility of the physician and nurse in industry.

The means of control of physical, chemical and biological hazards in the work place are now well-known, and their effectiveness is largely related to the amount of expenditure that management is prepared to make. The means of controlling, or of limiting, psychological hazards at work are less certain, and the desirability of attaining these goals is even debatable. Certainly more is needed to be known of the likely causes of strain and impaired mental health, their effects on work populations and methods of coping.

In the preceding pages I have described my own attempts, albeit in an atypical work community, to quantify some of the related factors. Now it might be useful to outline a few of the lessons I learned, which helped me to cope with effects of stress in that population. These can be divided into community or organisational, and individual coping measures.

1 Community or organisational measures

As I pointed out earlier, I was blessed with an interested and reactive management. Thus it was easier for me than it might be for others to cross the first and all important hurdle – that of creating an understanding in management and unions of the importance of stress and its possible effects on the work community. Once this has been achieved, then the doors are opened for the introduction of acceptable executive policies, and the provision of adequate investigation and caring agencies. Whilst harmful drinking was an insignificant problem for my industry, it is that sort of problem that requires appropriate policy introduction. In addition, this helpful atmosphere facilitates the rationalisation of the conflicting interests of management, unions, medical and other agencies in this problem area.

As far as the provision of material help is concerned, this boiled down to ensuring that there was adequate availability of consultation and ease of access (formal or informal) to the doctor and the nurse. Regrettably, both the nursing sister and I lacked previous specialist training in counselling, and so we had to learn in the school of experience.

2 Individual measures

Access to trained caring-agencies within the work location is essential. These may be found within the occupational health service, welfare or personnel departments. Whoever undertakes the task should be capable of assisting the affected employee to recognise his or her own problem(s), the various options for their solution and the consequences of adopting the options selected. This is always a difficult matter for doctors and nurses who are used to telling people what to do! Where a possible option involves executive action by management, then the caring agent should only intercede if specifically requested to do so by the employee. Last, but not least, the caring agent should be aware of his or her own limitations, and should know when to stop or to hand over to a more experienced colleague or specialist agency.

Conclusion

Perhaps the reader was hoping that I would have commented on the rates of incidence and level of risk that I discovered in the laboratories population. Since I have been unable to discover similar studies on other industrial populations it has not been possible to make comparisons. I hope that the data that I have elicited from this investigation will stimulate others to do the same, so that a store of information can be built on this important subject.

REFERENCES

W. H. Auden, *Selected Poems*, E. Mendelson (ed.) (Faber & Faber, 1938) p. 86

A. Brook, 'Psychiatric disorders in industry', *British Journal of Hospital Medicine* (May 1976) pp. 484 and 485

C. L. Cooper and J. Marshall, *Understanding Executive Stress* (Macmillan, 1968) pp. 26–7

J. S. Felton, 'Psychiatric orientation in the education of occupational physicians', *Occupational Psychiatry* (Collins, 1969) pp. 127–8

J. Holmes and R. H. Rahe, *Journal of Psychosomatic Research* (1967) pp. 11, 213

M. Jeffreys and C. H. Wood, *British Journal of Industrial Medicine*, vol. 17 (1960) p. 10

L. Kennart, 'Psychosocial Factors in Preventive Medicine', *The Surgeon General's Report on Health Promotion and Disease Prevention* (1979), *Healthy People*, US Department of Health Education and Welfare DHEW (PHS) Publication no. 79-55071A (1979)

M. D. Kopelman, 'Discuss the evidence as to the relative importance of parental genotype and parental attitudes in the genesis of neurotic reaction in children and young adults', Mental Health Foundation Prize Essay (1976)

W. R. Lee, *British Journal of Industrial Medicine*, vol. 19 (1962) p. 3

J. M. MacIver, *The Epidemiology of Mental Illness of Industry – Occupational Psychiatry* (Collins, 1969) p. 273

M. A. McDonald, 'The provision of occupational health services for the smaller work place in Norway, Sweden and Finland', *Transactions of Society of Occupational Medicine*, vol. 16 (1966) pp. 78–82

H. Murrell, 'Work Stress and Mental Strain – A review of some of the literature', *Work Research Unit Occasional Paper*, no. 6, Department of Employment, (Jan. 1978) pp. 2, 30 and 75

T. A. Lloyd Davies, *Proceedings of the Royal Society of Medicine*, vol. 66 (Aug. 1973) pp. 818–22

D. Radwanski, *Current Approaches to Occupational Medicine*, A. Ward Gardner Wright (ed.), vol. 13 (1979) p. 219

R. W. Revans, 'Morale and the size of the working group', *Modern Trends in Occupational Health*, R. S. F. Schilling (ed.) (Butterworth) pp. 196–208

R. H. Rosenman, M. Friedman and R. Strauss, 'A Predictive Study of CHD', *Journal of the American Medical Association*, vol. 189 (1964) pp. 15–22

R. H. Rosenman, M. Friedman and R. Strauss, 'CHD in the Western Collaborative Group Study', *Journal of the American Medical Association*, vol. 195 (1966) pp. 86–92

Lord Taylor, and C. H. Wood, 'Occupational Health Services in Smaller Work Places in Britain', *Modern Trends in Occupational Health*, ch. 19, (Butterworth, 1960)

S. Taylor, *The Practitioner*, vol. 181, (1958) p. 133

R. F. Tredgold, 'Insecurity in Industry'. *Proceedings of Royal Society of Medicine*, vol. 65, no. 12, pp. 1087 and 1091

Sir Barnes Wallis, 'Personal Comment from "The Great Inventor"', BBC 1, 20 November 1979

7 Counselling in Organisations

John Lightbody
Shell Chemicals UK Ltd

Introduction

'I weep every time I see a removal van,' said Carol. Everybody looked at me. I gazed as the wide expanse of green baize table-top which separated us, feeling like a man who had forgotten what trumps were at a critical stage in the game. 'You weep every time you see a removal van?' I queried. 'Yes,' said Carol, helpfully. She leaned slightly to her right to see me better round the intervening bulk of the heavy bronze microphone, *circa* 1931, which occupied the centre of the table. She seemed composed and confident, clearly expecting me to finesse her lead. I moved my plastic chair a little to my left and the red recording light winked out at the noise.

'That's fine for sound,' said the producer, emerging from behind plate glass. 'But try not to move about so much'.

Carol and I were recording a counselling session for a well-known radio programme. She was a genuine client who had written to the BBC about the problem of being married to an itinerant executive. An employee counsellor with a large organisation, I had been invited into the studio to act as counsellor for the afternoon.

Driving down to Manchester to make the broadcast, I found myself going through in my mind a check-list of issues around making counselling happen – confidentiality and respect for the client, for instance. How could the session be confidential with four million listeners? Did Carol's husband know she was going to confide in me?

How long did we have? If the BBC was paying for the time of everybody involved, whose property was the interview?

Over lunch I found that the producer of the programme had in fact thought through the issues more thoroughly than I. He said that the client was happy about there being an audience; she even had a very clear idea of using the audience as an agent of change. 'My concern, you see, is not just for me but for others like me,' she had said. Under the heading of respect for the client, the producer was quite clear that it would be my task as counsellor to reach a statement of the client's situation which she could not only cope with at the time of the interview but live with afterwards. He would edit the tape with issues like privacy, confidentiality and integrity well in mind.

So we began. As Carol explained the problem and I listened, the strange studio with its green baize table, ancient microphone and listening audience slowly transmuted into a counselling agency. The little red light blinked on, and counselling happened.

Employee counselling

I tell this story quite deliberately at the beginning of this chapter on counselling in an organisation because it lets me raise quite quickly some key things about counselling in unfamiliar settings. The first point is how easy and 'natural' counselling can be. The second point is that making counselling happen in a situation where it would not occur naturally is actually quite difficult. The story is therefore a paradigm for employee counselling.

Counselling often does feel a bit as if it occurs quite naturally. There is nothing stilted or artificial about good counselling. The rules of the game are fairly simple, even proverbially simple. One of the most widely accepted proverbs for example is that 'a trouble shared is a trouble halved'. If the listener reacts with a reasonable degree of attentiveness and displays an attitude of acceptance, the proverb comes true and the alleviation of distress is a virtually inevitable outcome. Despite this apparent simplicity however there are issues and practicalities which must be considered.

Things can go wrong. On the one hand, therefore, counselling is an easy, enjoyable process. Most people with the time, the right circumstances and an interest in the other person, display a great deal of natural counselling skill. On the other hand, where conditions are extreme, time is short and clients many, someone needs to know what they are doing. That skill must be explicit and thus becomes professional. In my view, a counsellor who is ambiguous about contracts, confidentiality or client autonomy, for example, transfers that feeling of ambiguity to the client and may create, rather than alleviate, anxiety. Counselling in an unfavourable climate is difficult, and if ineptly done may make matters worse. This latter observation in my view is not an argument for hesitation but for competence. It is an argument for the development in the work-place of explicit professional skills applied to human situations. I call it employee counselling.

How does counselling work?

Counselling takes place in an interview or series of interviews, and usually arises when one individual has in some way sought the help of another, because he or she perceives a need to change in some way. There are of course different kinds of processes by which one person can help another to change. Persuasion, information-giving and simple instruction are, for example, among them. When the helper chooses counselling as a method, he or she is deciding upon the development of a relationship with the other individual, with a view to resolving the difficulty which initiated the contact. I have recently come across a useful little book by John Shaw of the University of Manchester called *'Basic Counselling'* (Shaw, 1973) which deals simply, but in adequate detail, with the process. It is beyond the scope of this chapter to go into such detail but I should perhaps give a definition.

Counselling, as I see it, is a way of responding to another person, by relating with them, so that the other is helped to explore their thoughts, feelings, behaviour and situation; in order to reach a clearer understanding of their self and of their situation; so that they can use their strengths to cope more effectively, to make appropriate decisions and to take action to change. For counselling is about change. Change is a matter of an individual producing adjustment, either in themselves or in their environment, or in their perception of the fit or misfit between themselves and that environment. To a large extent counselling is a typical problem-solving activity. It is a coping method based on data-gathering, followed by understanding, which leads to action for change. Richard Lazarus, quoted in the *Journal of Occupational Medicine* (Lazarus, 1980), reminds us, however, that 'an enormous amount of coping is emotion-focused . . . For many serious sources of stress in life, there is little or nothing that can be done to change things. If so, you're better off if you do nothing except take care of your feelings.' Counselling is a way of switching from one coping method to another, (from cognitive to emotional, for example) and sometimes back again, as suits the strengths of a particular client in a particular situation. The interview structure in which either mode operates is the same – listening, forming hypotheses, taking action, making decisions and receiving feedback.

A further introductory point is that this easy, humane activity alleviates stress. This alleviation has been recorded not only in cases of simple distress but even in cases of extreme anxiety. A counselling attitude is always appropriate, even where it is not of itself sufficient. Isaac Marks, in summarising his excellent paper on 'Modern Trends in the Management of Morbid Anxiety' (Marks, 1975) reminds us that 'a multivariate model is required to account for the various ways in which morbid anxiety can be managed'. He deals with drugs, of course, which play a 'palliative role'. He closely examines the various procedures which can be regarded as methods of anxiety extinction – flooding, cognitive rehearsal and the rest. He then speaks of coping mechanisms, stress-immunisation and abreaction (which latter we 'ill understand today'), and then the penultimate sentence of his paper is as follows: 'Subjects often experience great relief simply by talking about their problem, a confessional effect that so far has not been subjected to scientific study and which must be brought under experimental control if we are to understand it further.' Experience teaches most counsellors the wisdom of these closing remarks. I would suggest that the experience of great relief, which clients fairly consistently report back to the counsellor, is to be attributed to a lowering of anxiety levels; my hypothesis being that this can be attributed to the nature of the counselling process.

The counsellor as behavioural scientist

The introduction of a counselling service into industry with which I have been associated was not 'experimental', in the sense that it was not in any way tentative. But it was nevertheless quite explicitly an attempt to bring the study of stress under some form of experimental control. One felt that the introduction of a well-designed and fully-understood service would produce a reaction in terms of client use which would tell one much about stress, particularly if carefully measured over time. I should emphasise here that I introduced my service into a perfectly normal, efficient organisation, average in representing a diverse community. We were specifically *not* in any way trying to combat any particular pathology. The new counselling service had no hidden agenda. I was not trying to 'reduce absence rates', 'increase morale' or 'increase productivity'. We were not planning any major redundancy or other change which could have been seen as a reason for introducing a counselling capacity. The counselling service was a deliberate, limited, understood, controlled intervention into a social system, which was itself reasonably aware and relaxed about it. It was anticipated that the results would be at least interesting, at most a contribution to the problem of understanding and coping with organisational stress.

The counselling contract: confidentiality and risk-taking

The working hypothesis of counselling is that the client has experienced anxiety resulting from a loss of perceived control over his or her own situation. The counsellor knows that the clients will experience a drop in anxiety which is little-researched and not widely understood. Typically, this restores to the client his or her perception of control. They regain composure. In this operating mode they can usually see their own way out of the impasse, and will be able to drop the relationship. Sometimes there appears to be no way out, but then at least two risk-takers are better than one. Becoming a client is in itself an exercise in risk-taking. The clients risk being rejected, in order to experience acceptance. In communicating their feelings they risk having their feelings hurt. In order to make their own decisions, they risk being exploited. They are usually intensely aware of some danger threatening their ability to exercise control over their own life space, have discovered their inability to regain control, but preserve belief in the possibility of doing so. These needs are so strong they give the client the drive to seek out the counsellor.

Like the client, the counsellor is a risk-taker. Like the client, he needs competence, confidence and the willingness to present himself as an individual ready to share with another individual aspects of his inner self. By listening, the counsellor risks one day finding that he cannot accept, that he will not respond appropriately to feelings, that he will impose a stereotyped solution, make a judgement or betray a confidence.

Confidentiality is not primarily about secrecy, although secrecy is the client's right. Confidentiality means that the client is in control of the information and decides with whom to share it. This gives a new meaning to the term confidentiality. There are two points I wish to make in consequence of this definition of confidentiality. The first is that clients are always interested in change. Mere secrecy may, in fact, have a low priority in relation to other needs. In the introductory case study, Carol's choice of agency and process was dictated by a desire to share a problem, and thus not only to be helped personally but also to help others by producing a wider change in attitude. She felt that this would not merely alleviate her own distress but also in some way channel the distress already suffered and somehow change the situation for others. Counselling, as I practice it, is not narcissistic but is a robust outward-looking activity. It may begin with two people looking at each other, but it ends with the two participants looking outwards in the same direction, if I may be allowed to adapt an old French proverb.

The second point I wish to make about confidentiality is that the client is not the only one in control of the situation. The BBC producer and I also exercised control, each one of us acting within our own roles, neither of us making a profit at the client's expense, which seems to me to be the principal definition of professionalism. Another important aspect of professionalism can be seen in the fact that the producer had done his homework, and that the counsellor did his by checking out the setting, the issues and the contract before the event. (A further indication of professionalism, of course, is that counselling happened at all in the extreme conditions of that broadcasting studio.)

Agencies and referral

Sometimes the need of the client is met adequately in the one-to-one relationship, and in that case the agency setting of the Counsellor is almost irrelevant. More often, however, the meeting of the need only buys temporary space or time to use for the construction of social support systems designed to meet the need more permanently. The need to construct support systems, for both client and counsellor, gives rise to the idea of 'agency' in counselling. I have elsewhere defined agencies by their activity of referral (Lightbody, 1979): 'I think of agencies as points in the social structure towards whom the counsellor feels able to make referrals and from whom he accepts referrals. This activity of agency creates the varying structures which are social support systems.' The company doctor, the personnel department and local social services are some of the more obvious agencies. I give a complete list below. Agencies provide expertise and resources. In addition, they often legitimate the counsellor's work and allow him to operate as a 'socially-sanctioned healer', to use Garfield's felicitous phrase.

An agency may well have functions other than counselling, some subordinate to counselling, others taking precedence. Agencies also have characteristics which largely determine the profile of the typical client population. It seems to me that some of these agency functions and characteristics either promote or impede counselling, either at the input, process or output stage. For example, in the story with which I began, the green baize table, the lack of contact with Carol's husband, my total unfamiliarity with my surroundings, are all examples of negative characteristics of the agency we were using that day. The major function of the agency was broadcasting. Broadcasting, while it is of course a positive and admirable function viewed in itself, is negative with respect to the counselling process in that it forces the latter to take place in a physically uncomfortable environment and effectively 'in public'. So the conspicuous bronze microphone represented a prevailing, if not countervailing, function of that day's counselling agency!

Conceptually, agencies are created by referral. In this context, 'referral' has its own precise rules. Referral happens when, with the client's consent, a counsellor creates a link with another person who, through expertise or availability, is able to assist in the solution of the problem, or provide appropriate support. Occasionally such referral means the end of a case as far as that particular counsellor is concerned. Always, however, there is the possibility presented to the client, of going out and testing the suggested resource, and then coming back to share the experience with the counsellor. Referrals are characterised by client autonomy and confidentiality. Referral does not take place without informed consent, and is always seen in the context of concern for the well-being of the autonomous individual in his or her occupational and community setting.

The varying characteristics of agencies mean that there are, of course, a wide variety of possible models for the development of a counselling capacity in an occupational setting. A useful review of the options is contained in Watts (1977). Some of these models have been realised in practice. Perhaps the most obvious model is for the organisation to employ the services of a professional counsellor. I shall describe in this chapter such a counselling service. An account of the only service of a similar nature that I have encountered in an extensive search is to be found in Kelsey (1975). By way of preamble, however, first I should like briefly to outline some other options and second to look at two reasonably accessible enquiries into the advisability of setting up counselling schemes in occupational settings.

One model for a counselling service would be to set up networks within the organisation of employees who have been given some training in counselling skills, but who are still primarily employed to do other jobs of work. This method can employ different types of network giving rise to different forms of peer-counselling. The Natural Environment Research Council's is a good example and is described in Watts (1977). This scheme shares with that of Imperial Chemical Industries Ltd the distinction of being first off the mark – as early as 1971. A description of the latter scheme is to be found in the *British Journal of Guidance and Counselling* (Hopson, 1973). A third method is to focus on, and strengthen, the counselling which is already carried out by employees working in roles which bring them into face-to-face contact with troubled individuals – notably the fast-expanding occupational health teams, personnel and welfare officers, and, of course, shop stewards and other employee representatives. Organisation development practitioners share many of the techniques and values of the working counsellor. The 1970s have seen a growing interest in development and training in counselling skills as an integral part of management and supervisory roles.

Two published enquiries throw some light on the planning required if one is to weigh the options fully. The first concerns the army, and the second the health service. Early in 1976 the *Report* of the Army Welfare Inquiry Committee was published (Army Welfare Inquiry Committee, 1976). It seems to be a document well worth reading in the context of counselling within an organisation, despite the fact that its main recommendations were not accepted by Parliament, for reasons which were principally economic. The report's excellent surveys reveal the type of personal difficulties encountered by a body of highly-organised and efficient men, their wives and families. The mean age and sex distribution of this population is not too far away from that of an industrial organisation. The report highlights the effects of 'turbulence', for example, by which they mean frequent changes of posting at home and overseas. Again this is not too far removed from the mobility expected of, at least senior, management in a typical large commercial firm. My main interest, however, lies in the responses of those who felt that there should be a particular person on the camp to whom one could go with a personal problem. What type of person should this be? The answer reveals a strong preference for a professionally-qualified person, 'in civilian dress', available at regimental, that is local, level. On balance there was a wish that he or she should be 'a military person', this preference was associated with being married (rather than single), and it increased with age.

A second organisational setting in which counselling has been much talked about in recent years is the National Health Service. The Report of the Parliamentary Committee on Nursing now known as the *Briggs Report* (1972) led, by way of two conferences organised by The Royal College of Nursing (June and October 1975), to a nurses' working party being set up in October 1975. This working party published a report – *Counselling in Nursing* – early in 1978. It is not, as one might expect, a study on how the nurse might seek ways of counselling patients. It is in fact a study of how the nurse can herself receive counselling, within a rapidly-changing organisational setting. The report indicates the great need for this. In relation to who should supply this need, it states that student nurses would prefer being counselled by someone who 'knows what it is all about, is experienced, approachable and often around'. Table 10 of the report shows that all nurses surveyed would clearly prefer being counselled (should the need arise) by a nurse trained in counselling. If I read the figures rightly, nurses are a little more suspicious of 'trained civilians' than soldiers are. An article in the nursing press by Jef Smith, a Director of Social Services, calls attention to this fact (Smith, 1978). It also widens the discussion to social services, identifying similarly high needs for counselling there: 'The case seems inescapable for organisations like social services departments and hospitals to provide expert counselling for both staff and students, placing the job away from the hierarchical functions of line management and giving the job facilities and resources which allow workers to admit their need and seek help without stigma.'

My own organisation early in 1974 had reached the same, rather obvious conclusion, that counselling was an apparently efficient and humane response to distress. It further concluded that, this being the case, perhaps the simplest thing to do was to hire someone who is quite good at it, and give him a reasonably free hand to ensure that counselling would happen inside the organisation.

Setting up the service

The setting of this, the first, professional counselling service in British industry is a petrochemical plant situated in flat Cheshire countryside. The plant is kept going twenty-four hours every day of the year. There are 3000 employees of whom about 1000 are shift-work operators. The rest are engineers, craftsmen, technicians, scientists and managers.

The service began on 1 August 1974, and has continued without a break ever since. The beginning of the service was announced in a brief management circular, and a short article appeared in the house magazine. It is important, I think, to bear in mind that while the introduction of the service was a considered decision at senior level, it was deliberately 'low-profile', and that no attempt was made to publicise or encourage its use. One started with a basic company commitment to the concept in general. Decisions about the design of the service were based upon realising in practice a model of a counselling agency which can be chiefly characterised by the fact that I am a company employee who is an experienced post-graduate practitioner of counselling, and that my sole function within the organisation is that of counselling fellow employees. The only function of the agency would be counselling. This made it unique at that time. It is still unique.

I was allocated a secluded but central office with reception facilities, a name in the telephone book and the facility to keep confidential records. It seemed to us self-evident that the counsellor should be located on site, and not be initially a member either of the medical department or of the personnel department. In this way the client could be helped to see that each of these agencies had specifically distinct functions. At the very least it would mean that the counsellor might pick up problems which had not yet been defined as medical, personnel, management or union matters. At best the service could provide a method by which presented problems were sorted out, and suitable resources contacted. The counsellor was therefore established as a services manager, one of six reporting to the overall service manager, who himself reported to the manager of the site.

In the first month I introduced myself around, explaining what it was hoped to achieve. I had meetings with medical and personnel departments, and got out to social services offices in the immediate area. The chief officer of local social services made me welcome, as did all social-work staffs. Links with hospitals and voluntary organisations were forged.

Counselling can be, and is often thought to be, an isolated activity. In reality, of course, great weight is given to the advantages of team work, particularly with medical and social services. I brought with me into the work setting a highly-developed notion of referral. The activity of referral creates the support structures used not only by the clients but also, of course, by the counsellor. Conceptually, referrals create agencies. As stated above, counselling referral must be congruent with confidentiality and client autonomy. For example, if a manager or someone from the personnel or medical functions rings up about someone who has a problem, I will accept the case as long as the person ringing clears it with the employee he or she thinks has a problem. If the employee freely consents to becoming a client, I can take it from there, but I don't go back to the referral source unless I have, once again, the consent of the client. Outward referral happens when, again with the client's consent, the counsellor creates a link with another person who, through expertise or availability, is able to assist in the solution of the problem, or provide appropriate support.

My list of agencies is as follows:

Senior management
Direct-in-line supervision
Union representatives
Personnel department
Internal medical department
Family and friends
Social services
Family doctors
Community psychiatric nursing service

Department of clinical psychology
Medical specialists
Voluntary organisations devoted to specific problems
Other external agencies (solicitors, etc.)

Clearly many of the agencies I have listed have functions other than counselling. Some of these functions might even be thought at first glance to be negative with respect to counselling. I like negative characteristics and functions, not least because they concentrate the mind. When negatives are present they throw into relief elements of the counselling process which are essential, elements without which counselling cannot be said to be taking place. The first essential characteristic to surface under the etching process of contrary winds is confidentiality. Confidentiality, as we have said, is controlled by the client. With his or her informed consent it can be extended to include other people. Without that consent it cannot. The counsellor respects that confidentiality in the context of the support of his agency, and that agency's support systems. This is implicit in every contract and should normally, in my view, be made explicit, especially in the presence of countervailing agency functions. All of these agencies I have listed, however, have shown themselves perfectly capable of co-operating correctly in the counselling process. Some have since been encouraged to play an active role themselves as counsellors, helped, perhaps, by knowing that back-up in the process is only a phone call away.

The above sections have concentrated on the counsellor's role in relation to clients and to the wider community of caring agencies. A further important consideration is the position he or she adopts (or is assigned!) in relation to the official 'host' organisation. Just as the client's ultimate aim is survival, the counsellor is interested in survival too − the survival of himself, his clients and his agency. The organisational counsellor who is not a change agent risks indulging in manipulating well-being. Integrity demands that he or she be a change agent at an organisational, as well as an individual, level. It is in this aspect that the organisation-based counsellor departs most significantly from the role adopted by social case-worker colleagues. I have discussed this subject in depth elsewhere, (Lightbody, 1979).

Reactions to the service

The most striking thing, in that first wet month of August 1974, was the number of clients. It was like being sole 'duty officer' in a busy county town, day in, day out. It was as if I had never been away. By the month's end I had conducted 110 interviews with 70 people. Of these, 40 became longer-term clients. Of the 40, 14 were simple advice cases, clients seeking and receiving advice on a wide range of personal problems; 26 were clients who accepted a genuine on-going counselling contract. Of the latter, 14 had been referred in by the personnel department; others came at their own initiative or were referred by line management. By the end of the third month, I had conducted 300 interviews and acquired 93 clients, of whom 60 were 'simple advice' on a wide range of family and interpersonal matters. The other 33 were evaluated as being able to benefit from counselling, and had accepted accordingly.

Nine months into the job, I was able to report the same high use of the service, with 97 advice cases and 92 of counselling 'proper'. Of these latter, 51 were closed and 41 remained current. Of the closed cases, a very high proportion had been settled satisfactorily, there had been no missed appointments and I had a general feeling in every case of 'having got somewhere'. Many of the cases were among the most complex and worthwhile that I had ever been associated with.

The above pattern has continued. At the time of writing, six years into the job, I have been in personal contact with some 8 per cent per annum of all employees. I have accepted as clients for the service, a figure equal to 5 per cent per annum of all employees, of whom half have been simple advice cases and half have been true counselling. Simple advice has ranged across a wide variety of subjects, including education, family matters, housing, divorce, separation, children, aged parents and consumer affairs. The advice service has thus been deeply involved in keeping up-to-date with the bewildering changes in legislation which affect most of these matters. Counselling clients have generally exhibited signs of having difficulty in the management of anxiety.

The response to the counselling service in terms of client use is strikingly representative of the overall employee population. There is above all, an even distribution in terms of age, sex and organisational level of clients. The average age of simple advice cases is nine months younger than the population average, that of counselling cases three months older. The standard deviation of age around the mean is within 3 per cent of that of the employee population. Absence rates (of clients) are no higher than the general population of the plant, which is itself considerably better than the national average.

The agency has survived in this form until now. On its fourth anniversary, as it became obvious that much of the work was in the area of health, we decided to locate the service in the medical department. It is perhaps too soon to evaluate the effect of this change but early results show 'business as usual'. I have recently seen a follow-up article by Dr Kelsey and his associates (Kelsey, 1980), describing his service referred to earlier which began in the USA in 1975. His results in terms of client reaction are very close to those described above, despite the apparently different nature of the organisation.

Discussion

And so counselling actually happens. The clients are generally perfectly competent people, with the confidence to present themselves in person, as it were, in order to take the risk of examining their own situation which is generally one of some anxiety. The immediate and classic effect of the decision on the part of the client to undertake a counselling interview is a lowering of his or her anxiety level. This sets them free to re-examine the situation in which they find themselves. Normally they can then take action to deal with the root of the problem. The counsellor produces the micro-climate in which this can happen. He or she guarantees confidentiality. (S)he is reasonably resourceful. If more resources than (s)he or the client possess are needed to solve the problem these can be mobilised by the provision of referral. The activity of referral creates for the client and the counsellor a network of social support which can be built up and serviced to suit individual needs. It is the business of the counsellor to make sure that such networks do not create unnecessary dependency. On the contrary, the object of the exercise is to increase self-confidence through greater self-awareness on the part of the client. When counselling is properly done, the client will feel valued, get appropriate help and experience reduced alienation. Technically, he or she acquires an increased perception of self-control.

Modern organisations allied to complex industrial processes can easily produce in the employees the perception that they have little or no control over their own life-space. Such a shift in perception produces abnormal, anxious, stereotyped behaviour. And yet modern organisations, moving towards open systems, demand from the individual relaxed, aware, responsible behaviour. A counselling capacity seems to me to provide the ideal type of neutral bypass switch which, used or not, puts into the system a mechanism capable of producing the heightened perception of self-control necessary for mental well-being.

REFERENCES

Army Welfare Enquiry Committee Report (HMSO, 1976)
A. Briggs, (Chairman), *Committee on Nursing Report* (1972)

B. Hopson, 'Career Development in Industry and the Diary of an Experiment', *British Journal of Guidance and Counselling*, Vol. 1 (Jan. 1973)

J. Kelsey, 'Professional Counselling in a Company with a Broad Dispersal of Work Locations', *Journal of Occupational Medicine*, vol. 17, no. 11 (1975)

J. Kelsey, *Journal of Occupational Medicine*, vol. 22, no. 2 (1980)

R. S. Lazarus, 'Coping by Thought and Feeling', *Journal of Occupational Medicine*, vol. 22, no. 2 (1980) p. 113

J. Lightbody, 'Employee Counselling, What Kind of Change Agent?' in *Change Agents at Work* R. Ottoway (ed.) (London: Associated Business Press, 1979)

I. Marks, 'Modern Trends in the Management of Morbid Anxiety' in *Stress and Anxiety*, Spielberger and Sarason (eds) (New York: John Wiley, 1975)

Royal College of Nursing, *'Counselling in Nursing'* report (1978)

J. Shaw, *Basic Counselling* (Vernon Scott Assoc., 1973)

J. Smith, 'How Nurses can Help Themselves', *Nursing Mirror* (9 Nov. 1978)

A. G. Watts (ed.), *Counselling at Work* (London: National Council of Social Services, 1977)

8 The Plessey Experiment

Peggie Kellam,
MIND, Northamptonshire, UK

Starting out

In 1975, the Northamptonshire branch of the National Association for Mental Health (MIND) Executive decided to ask its members, of whom I was one, to look at different aspects of their work that needed developing – for example, group homes, education, stress at work – and to take on responsibility for these developments. Later, in 1976, when the Executive asked me to lead a group, in conjunction with the director of a large business organisation, to look at stress among people at work, I readily agreed. Of the aspects to be covered, this was the one which most appealed to me. I had previously been involved as an observer in such a project during the war years, when I worked in a military psychiatric hospital quite near to what was then known as the 'Austin Motor Works'. At this hospital there were several very eminent psychiatrists involved with 'The Austin', and their work was more meaningful to me later on reflection than at the time, due to my then limited experience. This was, however, a new direction for me personally, as my background in various forms of hospital and community social work had seldom brought me into direct contact with the world of industry.

Starting out on the project, both the director and I had ideas which we wanted to pursue to achieve our aim, which was 'To look at the stress at work which comes from outside, and inside, the gates.' But how to get inside those gates? I felt at times that I was being asked to

147

accept too much responsibility by my partner, given that my knowledge of industrial workshops was practically nil. Already a previous attempt made by Northamptonshire MIND to involve industry in this subject had failed through lack of support. I wanted to make sure that this project was going to be successful. As a social worker I am interested in working in depth and for long, rather than short, periods, and I applied the same principles to my approach to this problem. I adopted a way of working with which I feel most comfortable. During this time my partner moved on, or maybe I was a disappointment to him – I was too slow.

Much discussion took place at the very beginning as to how we could get this project off the ground. I talked with all sorts of people – in hospitals, in industry, in social services departments, to company doctors and trade unionists – trying to find a starting point. All were helpful – but some were just as confused as I was at times, and would say, 'But how will you do it? What do you really want to achieve?' Gradually, month by month, a plan was crystallising in my own mind, and I was beginning to capitalise on all the comments and advice obtained during the year in my many conversations.

Then my thoughts went back to Northfield Military Hospital in 1944, and the professionals with whom I had worked, including Harold Bridger, now at the Tavistock Institute of Human Relations, London. I hadn't lost touch with him, and so I discussed my project and the information I had gleaned from my year of part-time voluntary work in the field with him. As usual, he was caring and helped me gain the confidence that was necessary at this point to launch the project. He allowed me to use him as a sounding board, and also introduced me to Dr Joseph L. Kearns (then Group Medical Advisor, J. Lyons Company) and to Dr Alexis Brooke. At that time, I also spoke with professionals with whom I work on a regular basis. With guidance from all these sources, I looked for the necessary people to form a 'team'. I sought out people who were interested, who would give me support and who could provide expertise from their own fields, so that together we could achieve a more comprehensive view.

At this point Mike Herbert, an industrial chaplain sharing my interest, agreed to assist me. Later in the year, at Dr Kearns' suggestion, we called together the nucleus of a group of people with concern for the subject. This group felt that perhaps the best and quickest way to raise local interest in stress at work would be to have a seminar inviting well-known people to speak on the subject, a Northampton 'mini-Windsor' (see Kearns' book, *Stress at Work*, 1973). This idea was at first accepted, but then doubts developed as to whether it would succeed. Dr Roy Payne (of Sheffield University) pointed out that this had been tried in Sheffield and failed. I reminded the group that a similar approach had already been tried by MIND in Northampton before I became involved, and had failed. Also, Dr Kearns did not want to play a prominent role in such a seminar, as he was a newcomer to Northampton and might be seen as an 'outsider' trying to impose his views on the area.

When it was decided that a seminar would not be the right approach, Dr Kearns suggested that we arrange for him to meet a small group of 'unconverted' senior industrialists from the town, and seek their reactions to the subject. The Chairman of MIND made this approach for me in July 1976, and the companies invited were British Timken, Express Lifts Ltd and Plessey Connectors Ltd. They were invited to meet Dr Kearns, a few professionals and myself. British Timken did not send a representative at that point, but later became temporarily involved with our group. We discussed their views openly with the two representatives of senior management who did attend, and the outcome was that Plessey's Director agreed to help us with our project, and to come back for further discussion with us.

The 'stress at work' group

Meanwhile, the initial group of interested people continued to grow. Stated in broad terms, its main objective has been to provide external assistance to local businesses where needed, using myself as a professional psychiatric counsellor. Why counselling? As a volunteer with only a limited amount of time, I felt that counselling, which is an area of work in which I have a wide experience, would be something I could offer and the most profitable use of my time. It was likely to be acceptable to interested companies, and would enable me to remain in the background rather than appear to be pushing forward and become known as an individual. Dr Roy Payne had impressed on me that there is suspicion amongst both management and employees towards outsiders looking at stress within an organisation, as they seldom wish to admit that it exists. He felt the most important tool I had to offer was counselling, and in practice this proved to be of value. I use the group, then, as a support mechanism. It serves, however, many other important purposes, particularly those of helping individual members who bring their problems to it and of promoting education about stress at work, initially locally but increasingly on a national scale.

The group is multi-disciplinary, as can be seen from the list of members given at the end of the chapter. It has attracted, for example, people from industry, the church, trade unions, social services and the medical profession. Its members are busy people who give their spare time voluntarily. To avoid evening meetings, we meet regularly every month for two hours over a working lunch. We sift and discuss local workforce problems that have been submitted for consideration and solution, plan future developments, and sometimes entertain interested guests. It is very rewarding to note that many of the original group are still members, and our attendance seldom falls below two-thirds. Having worked together for so long now and 'jelled' as a group there is a great deal of 'give-and-take' between us, and this has reinforced the common interest which initially brought us together. I feel now that the group is at its maximum size, and should not get bigger, otherwise it might become unmanageable. This is something to watch, as quite a number of people are currently interested and want to join, and it is difficult to turn people away.

The Plessey experiment

Plessey, then, become the partner in our group's first 'experiment' in employee counselling. They were 'chosen' because they agreed to cooperate, and, as stated earlier, it is extremely difficult to get into a company, or even past the gates. On behalf of the Director and General Manager of Plessey (Mr J. G. Edwards), Don Smith, the then General Manufacturing Manager, accepted the group's invitation to further discussions. At that meeting, Dr Kearns and Dr Payne expressed views that although there is a vast area to be studied under the heading of 'stress within an industrial society', few people in industry wish to know anything about it. Don Smith's feeling at that time was that their views probably represented an 'outside looking in' perspective. As a result, he and Cecil Pettit (at that time Apex Union representative with the business) decided to set up an experiment within their company to establish any trends in data about illness or psychological factors within the workforce. The work we did at that point was mainly to look at the statistics already compiled by the company to see how many people regularly attended the nursing sister at the surgery with minor, potentially stress-related, ailments, and from which departments they came. After a very short time, it became obvious that stress problems did exist, and also that the business was fairly well-equipped to deal with them, albeit in a fairly basic manner. The nursing sister and a long-serving member of the personnel department had, in fact, been dealing in their own way with such problems for a very long time. They usually referred employees back to their own doctors. This meant, however, that unless a problem was a very obvious one, only the presenting problem was being dealt with, and the situation was not investigated beyond that.

As a result of these findings it was decided to improve existing facilities, but that this should be done in a very 'low-key' way. Management also felt that this could be done with very little extra cost. One member of the personnel department was set aside as a counsellor. Her room was made more comfortable and sound-proofed for the purpose (at that time only partitions existed between her office and the one next-door). I was asked to provide a professional back-up counselling facility on a voluntary basis, as and when required – the 'mechanics' to be worked out between the personnel department, the nursing sister and myself. No attempt was made to publicise or encourage use of these services – here again, a 'low profile' was thought to be most appropriate.

It is very important in setting up such a service that the chief executive of the company is seen to be in full agreement. Mr Edwards, Managing Director of Plessey, reinforced his approval by inviting me to lunch after two Board meetings. I thus had an opportunity to meet with senior management, the doctor, the nursing sister, and members of the personnel department, and explain the objectives of the exercise in an informal setting. At all times I have, if necessary, access to Mr Edwards. My 'contract' with other members of the workforce is equally important, and I was very aware that I must earn the trust of the company's staff generally. Trade unionists, at times, could misunderstand the reasons behind such a service, and, if suspicious, could interpret the help offered as a manipulative tool of management rather than as a benefit to employees.

It was agreed that I should meet with the personnel department and the nursing sister jointly once a month to discuss individual cases and any problems that had arisen. A key task at this stage was to establish credibility. The nurse and a member of personnel had been dealing with problems as far as they could without extra help, and I was very careful not to be seen as taking over from them. I listened and tried to make only comments which I felt might be useful (and which later did prove to be so). I was careful to remain in the background, lest I should be thought to be seeking to become the leader.

The source of clients through the system is varied. Some are referred by senior management, and a number of immediate in-line supervisors. Some come via the personnel or medical departments or via union representatives. A few are referred by family or friends or by external social service agencies. Some people contact me directly, and all my senior management clients have used this method. (The latter feel particularly unable to approach people within the company, even those in 'welfare' functions, because of the admission of weakness involved. The service has therefore been especially valuable to this group.)

I am now receiving growing numbers of referrals from companies other than Plessey, either directly or via the group. Some hear of our work through Don Smith's talks to other business organisations (see below), others through satisfied clients. Despite our lack of official 'publicity', demand has increased and I can no longer cope with the workload, working as I do voluntarily. The group is therefore applying for funds to employ a full-time counsellor to take on much of the work and to extend the group's activities. My only reservation about this is that the service might grow too large and lose its personal approach and involvement.

I do not become involved in a particular case unless the nurse and personnel department feel the help needed is beyond their capabilities. Arrangements are then made for me to see the individual and he/she knows that none of the information disclosed is reported back to management unless he/she has agreed and it is in his/her interests. These interviews are sometimes carried out at the Leicester University Annexe, in a room paid for by MIND to provide a 'neutral' territory outside the factory premises. (This happens especially with longer term cases.) In emergencies I sometimes see people at my home. Discussion with senior management has only been necessary in a few cases. This was, however, helpful when action or understanding became necessary from some one in a position of authority.

It was firmly established early in the operation of the service that although there is a phenomenon that can be called 'industrial stress', it cannot be taken as something separate from other causes of strèss. It is related to a person's *whole* experience of pressure and stress – at home, in personal relationships, in their career, dealing with financial problems etc. Some people can cope easily with some or several potential causes of stress, others succumb easily, and in many cases people are stimulated by, and enjoy, pressure that they are quite capable of handling.

After a four-year operating period, a number of case histories from within and outside Plessey have been prepared. These have been selected to give a fairly representative coverage of the spectrum of stress problems likely to be found in an industrial community. A selection is included at the end of this chapter. For reasons of confidentiality, I have disguised the identities of those involved. (Confidentiality, and the integrity of the staff, is an essential key to the scheme's success.) During these four years, approximately 300 people have been seen, and I have been involved in about a quarter of these cases. It is interesting to note that approximately 85 per cent have been the result of 'external' problems manifesting themselves in the work place. Of these 300 many have been helped through discussion with the staff involved in the service and with the sympathetic management team in the company.

My role during the first year was played at a very low key and, as already explained, I was trying to establish credibility. Even when I reached the gates of Plessey and was invited in, I still continued to work slowly. I saw my role as assisting the nursing sister and personnel department to become sensitive to signs of stress, and to look beyond the presenting problem. Now this has been accomplished and these staff have in turn educated the work-force within the factory to be sensitive to the needs of their colleagues. The work-force is a very caring one, and is helping the Managing Director to reach his goal that his factory will be known as the best in Europe, and not only the best in Northampton. The absentee rate is low, for example, at 4 per cent.

This experiment has shown that:

(a) Similar projects could be started in many other companies where personnel and/or welfare functions already exist, merely by extending the terms of reference of these functions. Whatever advice is needed for starting the project can be provided by the local multi-disciplinary team.

(b) It is necessary for some advisory group, of a similar make-up to the Northampton one, to be available to industry as and when needed. There is almost certain to be a point at which the company concerned feels that a particular case has reached the limit of their financial and functional capability, and that external guidance is needed.

(c) Concentrated efforts to analyse and help an individual can result in a total failure to detect stress developing amongst his or her colleagues.

Despite this initial success and our apparent acceptance, credibility and confidentiality are still important issues today. If what we are doing becomes too well publicised and it can be seen that we are analysing our activities this could be eyed with suspicion as a 'management tool'. Individuals working at management or shop-floor levels could be afraid to voice their problems in case they are seen as part of a research project, or earmarked as people suffering from stress, which could later block promotion.

The pay-offs

In the current industrial climate, there are needs for greater flexibility and stability in the work force. Legislation centred around protection of employment, health and safety at work etc. provides a keystone for stability, but also makes necessary increased management efforts to maintain and support an existing labour force, rather than create or allow constant labour turnover. Absenteeism too is, without doubt, a vital factor in any business control set-up. It is also a factor which, in the present social climate, can very quickly escalate for a wide variety of reasons, many of which would not have been acceptable in industry a few years ago – such as domestic troubles, boredom, frustration, lack of incentive and demotivation. Although the Plessey experiment has not completely eliminated absenteeism, and will not necessarily do so, the results are already showing that potential long-term absenteeism has been brought completely under control by virtue of early intervention and action. The ultimate goal is to maintain an activity which will minimise absenteeism, but will, in addition, develop an industrial climate within the business, which is harmonious and at the same time efficient.

Activities such as this would seem to have an ever greater role to play in the future. The next five years will almost certainly produce major changes in the fundamental approach to the employment of people in industry. Shorter working weeks and longer holidays will bring a need for people to learn how to manage their lives outside work. New technology and increasing automation will mean fewer jobs, and a need for all levels of workers to undergo more frequent training and retraining. Formal 'management development' programmes have been considered a necessity for a number of years, but development programmes will now need to cover personnel at all levels, in order to maintain continuity of interest and skills, and ultimate efficiency from the total work force. Industry will need to adapt and organise the management of people to enable the needs, problems and aspirations of individuals to be understood and catered for. Development of the organisation's ability to deal effectively with its employees' stress problems will become a major factor in the management of people. The experiments carried out in Plessey, Northampton over the last four years have shown that the analysis of work-environment stress, followed by a logical approach to the elimination of problems, has significant benefits to both business and personnel.

The Tavistock visit and expansion of our work

At the end of 1977 the group was looking for future direction. We realised that a great deal of experience was available in our interdisciplinary team, and that what it had learned should not be kept to itself. It was therefore agreed that four members of the group – Don

Smith, Cecil Pettit, Mike Herbert and myself – should visit the Tavistock Institute for Human Relations and consult Dr Alexis Brooke, who has considerable experience in the area of industrial stress.

Dr Brooke agreed with the aims of the group, and commended its interdisciplinary nature. He was interested to learn of the project at Plessey and recommended that the group undertake a three-year research programme, with similar experiments in other local companies. At the end of this three-year period, the group might consider organising a seminar for leading industrialists, to appraise them of the work and to discuss its merits and benefits to industry. He suggested we try to continue the work at Plessey, and to formalise what we were doing on an ad hoc basis with other companies from whom we were receiving referrals. He pointed out that each scheme has to be tailor-made to each individual company; the scheme at Plessey could not just be transferred as it was. Each company has to be looked at as a separate entity: each director has to be consulted, and with his/her consent and that of the personnel department, the medical officer and trade union, a separate scheme has to be devised.

At that time the group made one or two approaches to companies to begin other projects, but no great enthusiasm was shown by them. Instead, the group's activities have developed in less formal ways and have consisted mainly of developing a reputation and credibility, and furthering 'education' about stress at work in a wide range of contexts. For the time being we are leaving research to those who are more academically qualified, and we are concentrating on action. The group is now becoming known and members are often approached with invitations to take part in seminars and talk to interested managements. For example, Don Smith, now Personnel Executive of Plessey, takes every opportunity to talk to industrialists about what is happening in his company, and he is often asked to speak on this matter. The opportunity came for him and me to speak to the Northamptonshire and Leicestershire branch of the Institute of Personnel Management in April 1978. Considerable interest was shown by its members who came from a cross section of industry – for example, banking, food manufacturing, county council and the Co-operative Society. We have also presented a paper at the 1980 Annual Seminar of ACAS (Advisory Conciliation and Arbitration Service) held in Northampton. The latter gave an opportunity for discussion amongst participants, and it was interesting to listen to the difference in views expressed by those employing technical staff and those employing purely manual workers. The latter were not very impressed. They felt that if someone had problems at work that was not the responsibility of management, and that workers could easily be replaced by going to the employment exchange. But people employing technical staff viewed this quite differently, and were interested.

One large company in the area has now expressed a wish to join the supportive group and become involved in the scheme to a somewhat lesser degree than Plessey, and this is happening. Referrals are currently made on an ad hoc basis and I have access to the company personnel department and nurse, but I feel that until I have more time to spend working out the details this service will probably not develop further. We have also been contacted by members of a nearby branch of MIND (Corby) who are interested in setting up a group similar to our own, and would like to use the Northampton team as advisors and supporters in doing so. As a final illustration of how the network is growing, only this week (May, 1980) I have been asked to talk to chief officers in the local county council, at a workshop. They are being prepared to help employees who could be affected by cuts in personnel. The workshop is intended to help them become sensitive to the needs of staff involved in redundancy, early retirement or redeployment. I am using the group from Plessey to show how this can be done.

In conclusion, we are greatly pleased with the success we have achieved so far, and feel that our way of working has much potential for the future. We have particularly learnt that it is essential for each new development to be approached carefully, and for time to be allowed for it to progress at the speed of the particular organisation. We are only speaking so far of one fully-developed 'experiment', but there are now many openings through which our work can expand in the future. We expect each of these to present different problems and new challenges.

Case histories

The final section of this chapter is taken up with disguised case histories of people referred for counselling. These have been selected to give a fairly representative coverage of the spectrum of stress problems likely to be found in an industrial population.

Mr M: Senior engineer in a key position (aged 57 years)

The presenting problems were that he looked physically ill and was acting out of character, upsetting other people in the department and holding up work. Also he would not stay away from work although colleagues thought he should. He had discussed his anxieties with the Personnel Department in vague terms, but at first refused to see me.

One day I received a phone call at 4.30 p.m. – could I see him that day as he really couldn't cope at work. He had agreed to this. I visited him at 8 p.m. I found that he had a problem wife who was suffering from a neurological illness; his father had died six months previously of cancer; and his mother had died two years ago having been an in-patient at a local psychiatric hospital for 20 years. Mr M was depressed and thought he had cancer. He said 'I wish the doctor had given me sick leave; he didn't suggest it.' Mr M agreed that I could speak with his doctor. Initially I acted as co-ordinator between his doctor, a consultant and social services. Throughout, I have seen this man on a weekly basis. He should soon be returning to work. Social services are now very much involved with his wife, the hospital and the home situation. I am now only involved with Mr M.

Mr C: Tool maker (aged 51 years)

Mr Edwards, Managing Director of Plessey, walks around the factory and talks with the employees. This particular day he spoke with a key man, who immediately broke down and cried, saying his wife had left him. He expressed suicidal ideas. His marriage had been a very good one, but one year ago his son's name hit the headlines in the local paper and as a result he had been sent to prison – something unheard of for this family who led very 'respectable' lives. Plessey had already helped considerably by supporting this couple in different ways, but the stress was still there. Now the marriage appeared to be breaking up and Mr C was behaving in a very unpredictable way and out of character. I was able to meet this urgent request for a meeting that lunch time and, with a doctor's help, to support the man until he felt he could cope. The couple are now together again.

Mr W: Key man in sales dept (aged 55 years)

This man had been having time off each morning for almost 12 months, to enable him to see his wife onto the bus for the day hospital, and allow him time to do the shopping. His colleagues were now 'getting tired of this policy and voicing their displeasure and wondering how much longer this would continue.' It was reported that this man was depressed. He agreed to see me. The situation was more involved than I had expected. His wife was attending a psychiatric day centre, and being seen by a consultant. One daughter, a university student, had broken down and had been treated as an in-patient at a private mental hospital. His other daughter had been placed with foster parents through borough social services, and it seemed that she was having a disturbing effect upon the marital situation of the foster-parents. In this case I acted purely as co-ordinator and arranged a meeting of the consultants, social workers and the general practitioner at Leicester University Annex – neutral ground – and then withdrew from the whole case.

Mrs B: Canteen worker (aged 34 years)

Mrs B worked in a department where there were two managers of the same status – one man and one woman – and it was thought that some of the difficulties in the day-to-day working of this department were due to the fact that Mrs B was having an affair with the man – her senior. On examination this was found to be untrue and the difficulties were mainly external to the workplace. Discussion and advice helped her to resolve these problems.

Mrs L: Sales dept (aged 36 years)

This woman presented herself at the works surgery with headaches, upset stomach etc. at regular intervals. After some time she confided in the Nursing Sister, who suggested that she should see me. I saw her at first weekly, then fortnightly, now monthly. Her visits to the surgery have ceased. She has insight into her problem and she herself has to decide what she wants to do.

Miss B (aged 26 years)

This was an intelligent blind worker who presented the works with many problems. She went through a period when a lot of time was spent in adjusting the bench at which she worked. Then the seat was wrong – 'It doesn't support my back', and so on. I suggested that we look beyond the problems at work, and we found that this young woman was pregnant. Support is being given by the personnel department and her doctor.

Mrs M (aged 40 years)

This Italian lady has worked for Plessey for 9 years and has been in this country for 18 years. Although she seems reasonably intelligent, she cannot read or write English. She has worked in the same group for 6 years and just recently was moved to another through lack of work. She misses the original group because she had a particular friend – an Irish woman – who was sensitive to her. She is having difficulty in breaking into this new group. She is also depressed due to her mother's death. In cases such as this, counselling and personal insight on the part of the client seem able to do little to solve the problem, which seems more one caused by work structure and organisation. Could management not have transferred someone else with her when this move occurred?

Through satisfied Plessey clients, and the talks Don Smith has given to other companies, the following people from outside the company have also asked for help:

Mr P: An accountant from County Council (aged 28 years)

Mr P was depressed and very anxious; he felt he couldn't cope. Both parents had been in-patients at a local psychiatric hospital and he felt he was going mad. However, in discussion it became evident that the problem lay with his immediate superior, whom he was carrying and trying to protect. His superior had a marital and drinking problem, and was seldom at his post. Support given to Mr P helped him to gain insight, and he now copes quite well, even though he is still carrying his superior.

Mr R: Forklift truck driver (aged 53 years)

This man had been given three verbal warnings because of drinking on duty. Then he was found drunk again. He drove a little forklift truck between the aisles where women worked in the factory. Management was afraid that whilst under the influence of drink he might not react quickly enough, and might injure one of the women as she stepped out from her machine. This man was given another chance on the understanding that he would work with me. He was an ex-Royal Marine, he did like a drink, but his need was greater than normal for other reasons. His wife was a patient at a psychiatric day centre, and his mother, who lived with them, was a very difficult woman. Mr R drank rather than go home. Again my role was one of co-ordinator. I contacted his doctor who became involved, and we involved the day centre with Mr R's wife and the health visitor with his mother. I continued to see Mr R every two weeks for three months.

Mr L (aged 52 years)

Polish. He had been educated to grammar school level. He had been a head waiter in a hotel, but due to his mental state had come down in the world, and he was now a cleaner. He would have found it difficult to work in this situation if he had been well, as he had particularly high moral standards and was not interested in the chit-chat amongst the men. Unfortunately his paranoia increased. His doctor was anxious that we should try to keep him at Avon because he realised Mr L would find it difficult to get another job. I continued to support Mr L but unfortunately he died suddenly.

Mrs T (aged 35 years)

(This lady has agreed that I do not need to disguise the information about her case.) One day during normal working hours in social services at the county council, the telephone rang and Mrs T spoke to me. At first I thought it was a client from the community and when I began to make enquiries she asked 'Are you the same Mrs Kellam mentioned by MIND who works on the Stress project at Plessey and helps people with stress?' When I replied 'Yes' she then introduced herself as a member of our own switchboard, and explained that her husband had been treated at a psychiatric hospital. He was now working in a non-union setting and she felt the firm was using his illness to get rid of him and he was being victimised. I listened at length and then suggested that I put her in touch with Mr Cecil Pettit – a member of our group – who has a vast Union experience. When approached he very kindly agreed to see Mrs T and her husband, and did so on two occasions initially for two hours each time. There were other interviews, and they all helped very considerably. The man lost his job, but, with this support not his confidence, and he is now employed by another firm. Mrs T talked to me from time to time about this and I was able to support her in other areas of stress. I was also able to interpret this stress to my colleagues who had been voicing the difficulty that they had recently been experiencing from our switchboard. I was able to give them an explanation, and asked them to be more caring.

REFERENCE

J. L. Kearns, *Stress in Industry* (London: Priory Press, 1973)

APPENDIX

MEMBERS OF THE 'STRESS AT WORK' GROUP

Mr K. Briers	Personnel Dept, Thames Case Ltd
Dr J. M. St V Dawkins	Community Physician – Social Services, Northamptonshire Area Health Authority
Mr I. Gawn	Hon. Secretary NALGO (National and Local Government Officers Union), Northamptonshire County Council (recently resigned and awaiting replacement)
The Revd. M. Herbert	Industrial Chaplain
Mr B. Hopewell	Personnel Dept, Thames Case Ltd

Mrs P. Kellam	MIND Executive
Miss P. Kingerlee	Principal Clinical Psychologist
The Revd. R. Jones	Deputy Director, Council for Voluntary Service
Dr D. McGrath	Consultant Psychiatrist
Mrs N. Muttock	Personnel Dept, Avon Cosmetics
Mr C. Pettit	Training Officer, Plessey Business Systems
Mr D. Smith	Personnel Executive, Plessey Connectors
The Revd. I. Prentis	
Dr I. Robertson	General Practitioner and Medical Adviser to Anglia & Thanet Building Society
Miss P. Swinburn	Psychologist
Mr H. Wreschner	Managing Director, Deanshanger Oxide Works

CONSULTANTS

Dr Alexis Brooke	Consultant Psychiatrist, Tavistock Clinic
Mr H. Bridger	Tavistock Clinic, London
Dr J. Kearns	Private Consultant

9 Alcohol and Drug Misuse

Charles Vetter
ACCEPT, London

As Director of ACCEPT (Alcoholism Community Centres for Education, Prevention and Treatment), the largest alcoholism treatment centre in the United Kingdom, I have a special interest in promoting concern about the escalating national problem of alcohol and drug misuse, and in encouraging individuals and policy-makers to take appropriate preventive and remedial action. In this chapter, I shall first set the scene by explaining some of the important facts about alcohol and drug misuse. Certain stress-prone, and therefore highly vulnerable, life-styles will then be described. The second half of the chapter covers available treatment facilities, with particular emphasis on new developments and how the growing number of concerned companies can offer assistance to employees.

Current trends

Alcoholism has been described by the Royal College of Psychiatrists (1979) as 'an endemic disorder of frightening magnitude'. It is now twenty times more common than all other drug addictions combined, and after heart diseases and cancer is the third major health hazard in developed countries.

Researcher Jan De Lint, of the Toronto Addiction Centre, Canada, revealed in a recent survey that drinking is rising steadily in twenty-four of the twenty-five countries studied, and more people are being hospitalised for alcoholism and are dying of cirrhosis of the liver than ten years ago (De Lint, 1978). In Britain, compared with twenty years ago, we are drinking: three times more spirits, five times more wine and much, much more beer. During 1979, over 25 million prescriptions were issued for 'soft' drugs such as tranquillisers, antidepressants and sleeping pills. The government's Committee on the Safety of Medicines has expressed concern over the high numbers of patients who receive repeated prescriptions from their doctors. They are equally concerned over the question of withdrawal symptoms and 'hangover states' which may include anxiety, apprehension, tremor, insomnia, nausea and vomiting.

While statistics are not available as to the numbers of people suffering from drug dependencies or drug-related road, home and work accidents, there is ample evidence to indicate that misuse of 'soft' drugs now constitutes a severe national problem. Very often people who misuse alcohol also misuse drugs, thereby creating cross-dependencies not infrequently leading to overdosing, brain damage and death.

Typical cases

How this overall, escalating consumption and misuse affects individuals can best be demonstrated by studying some cases referred during a typical day at the ACCEPT main treatment centre in London. A few examples:

1. 'I never thought it could happen to me ... I had a good job, a wonderful family and I thought I had a bright future in my company. But one morning, I woke up and realised that I had become hooked on drink ... on my way to work my first thoughts were how soon I'd be able to get out of the office and into a pub to calm my nerves.'

2. The medical officer of a large company refers a young man of 24, an administrative trainee, who has been showing up tipsy at company meetings.

3. A hospital phones and asks if we can send a counsellor to visit a 23-year-old nurse, now a patient in the psychiatric ward. She had taken an overdose – trying to kill herself in shame and despair over the mess she has made of her life through addiction to alcohol and tranquillisers.

4. The personnel officer of a company brings along a 'successful' man, aged 55, who is at the end of his tether. He had been a social drinker until five years ago when he was put in charge of

an important new venture. The extra socialising, the pressures and worries of his new job had slowly led to continual, excessive drinking, to the point where he made a series of business mistakes and the new venture failed. He then tried to drown his sorrows in still more alcohol but that only made his predicament worse. He was on the verge of being made redundant and his wife was thinking of leaving him.

5. A train driver shows up, shaking like a leaf. He is worried that drinking while driving his train will eventually result in a fatal accident, but he is afraid to tell anyone for fear of being disciplined. We explain that we have a working arrangement with his organisation; if he sees the transport medical officer he will be given generous sick leave, and his job will not be at risk. Three months later he is back driving trains, fit and healthy.

Stress is a factor

In each of the above cases, stress played an important part in the development of alcohol/drug dependence. To understand this fully, perhaps it is best first to review some questions and answers that will provide a straightforward background to the complex problems of alcoholism.

Questions and answers

Q. *What is alcoholism?*

A. Dependence upon the drug alcohol, involving a complex group of physical, psychological, behavioural, cultural and environmental factors.

Q. *How does one know when a person has become alcohol dependent?*

A. When excessive drinking of beer, wine or spirits, on a regular or intermittent basis, continues to harm or interfere with bodily or mental health, family well-being, social interactions, or job effectiveness. When attempts to return to normal drinking, or to achieve complete abstinence, continue to fail, one may be entering the area of chronic alcoholism.

Q. *How much drinking is too much?*

A. The amount may vary with each individual. Any amount, no matter how little, that leads to problems puts you in the area of problem drinking and at risk of becoming alcohol dependent, *particularly when mixed with tranquillisers, sleeping pills, anti-*

depressants and other drugs. The effect of alcohol on one person may be quite different from that on another. Recent studies have demonstrated that too much social drinking can cause serious damage to the liver, even though the drinker may feel fine, act normally and not be alcohol dependent (Leiber and Rubin, 1977). In addition to liver problems, persistent drinking may also lead to other toxic conditions in the body, including damage to mental faculties (Shaw, 1978).

Q. *Is alcoholism really an illness?*

A. Yes. It is recognised as such by the British Medical Association, the American Medical Association and the World Health Organization. However, important behavioural factors may be involved as well. The depth of illness may be determined by the extent of alcohol-related problems and alcohol-related disabilities which develop during the course of a person's drinking career.

Q. *How widespread is the illness of alcoholism?*

A. In Britain, it is estimated that there are 600 000 dependent drinkers, with perhaps another 600 000 to 1 200 000 with serious drink problems. Add to these figures the families, the children, the friends and workmates who may be seriously affected by a person's alcoholism and you can readily see the grave extent of the problem.

In Britain in 1978, the amount spent on alcohol was £7500 million. As a nation we spent more on alcohol than on fuel and light; much more than on newspapers, cigarettes, books or other forms of entertainment, and nearly as much as on clothing and footwear. We have as a nation been spending a steadily-increasing proportion of our expenditure on alcohol since the early 1960s. We are not alone in spending more of our incomes on alcohol. Most of Europe, the USA and Japan are also spending increasing proportions of their incomes on beer, wines and spirits.

The Royal College of Psychiatrists (1979) in their Report *Alcohol and Alcoholism* state that it is 'time to respond to a large and threatening problem ... an endemic disorder of frightening magnitude.'

Excessive drinking is as lethal a danger in the home as on the roads. Of the estimated 800 000 accidents that occur in the home each year, a sample study revealed that 65 per cent were caused by alcohol or had alcohol as the major contributing factor. Convictions for drinking and driving in England and Wales increased by 50 per cent between 1971 and 1976. Surveys show a clear link between road accidents and social activities, particularly after 10 p.m. Accidents reported on both Friday and Saturday nights show a sharp increase, and alcohol is much more likely to be a factor during the weekend. Of all male deaths between the ages of 15 and 24, 50 per cent are caused by road accidents, and the largest factor in these casualities is alcohol.

Offences involving drunkenness have increased steadily for both men and women during the past five years. During the last ten years, the rate for males in the age group 18–21 has almost doubled. For females, 18–21, the rate is more than four times what it was ten years ago.

Whilst drunkenness is not alcoholism, it is evidence of alcohol misuse (particularly amongst many more young men and women) which may lead to alcoholism. Trends towards younger persons presenting themselves for treatment indicate support for this view. In the USA, 10 million of the 100 million people who use alcohol are believed to be either alcohol-dependent or problem drinkers. An American yardstick is that in every group of ten/twelve so-called 'normal drinkers', one person has or will develop a serious alcohol problem. In France it is estimated that 43 per cent of all hospital expenditure is alcoholism-related.

Q. *How does alcohol dependence affect the individual?*
A. Alcoholism is a progressive illness, developing over a period of from one to twenty-five years.

Some direct effects may be: uncontrolled drinking; forgetfulness and alcohol amnesia (blackouts); social delinquency; irrational behaviour; chronic anxiety and depression; accidents and frequent minor illnesses; loss of job, home, family and friends; harm to children and relatives; psychiatric problems; gastric disorders; chronic alcoholism; liver damage; cirrhosis; facial deterioration (particularly among women); serious loss of memory; nervous system damage; brain damage and dementia.

Alcohol related illnesses may include chest and other infections; pneumonia; anaemia; heart illnesses; hepatitis; pancreatitis; ulcers; malnutrition; certain types of cancer.

Continued alcohol misuse may lead to a ten to fifteen years shortened lifespan, parasuicides and suicide.

Some warning signs and symptoms: (courtesy of the Medical Council on Alcoholism): Can't eat breakfast; gastritis/diarrhoea; heart irregularities; flushed face; nocturnal sweating; bruises on body or limbs; cigarette burns; impotence; tingling fingers or toes; frequent minor illness; anaemia; bleary eyes; inability to sleep; nervousness; missing work – especially on Mondays – and frequent sick leaves; family and job problems; frequent accidents: job/home/car; resentments and jealousies; unknown fears and anxieties; depression and isolation; sudden mood changes; misuse of tranquillisers etc.; missing appointments.

It is not unusual to find some of these warning signs in teenagers, and young men and women in their 20s.

An 'Alcohol Questionnaire' which can be used to help in the identification of problem drinking forms an appendix to this chapter.

Q. *What about families?*

A. Alcoholism is often called the 'family illness', because other members of the family (as well as friends, firms and the general public) may be harmed by a person's excessive drinking. Wives, husbands, children and grandchildren are highly vulnerable to both emotional and physical battering. Children growing up within a family troubled by alcoholism are far more likely to develop alcohol problems or other emotional or behavioural disturbances. Family and friends are often drawn into the dependent drinker's 'neurotic games' and, unless wisely counselled, are likely to become unwitting accomplices in the escalation of the illness.

Q. *What kind of people become dependent drinkers?*

A. Almost anyone may be affected. Some, because of personality problems, job pressures or 'hard-drinking' social or work environments, are more vulnerable than others.

Q. *What about people with good jobs and homes?*

A. This may well be the area of greatest danger. A recent survey suggests that the cost to Britain of lost industrial production due to alcohol abuse was around £350 million last year, with the total cost to the nation in the area of £1000 million per year. Another study states that most problem drinkers, in their most productive years, are employed most of the time and sick leave due to alcohol misuse amounts to more time lost than through all strikes and stoppages in any given year. Furthermore, problem drinkers have three times more accidents at work than other workers.

At ACCEPT, we find that 80 per cent of our referrals are employed people or housewives with good, stable homes. Ages continue to drop, with one quarter of our clients under 30 and one half under the age of 40 (ACCEPT, 1979).

Q. *You mention housewives. What about women in general?*

A. Ten years ago, the ratio of referrals for treatment was one woman to every eight men. Today, it is two women to every three men (ACCEPT, 1979). We soon expect referrals of women, probably young women, to equal or exceed men.

Q. *Can beer or wine drinkers become addicted?*
A. Yes. It is useful to know that one pint of beer, or two glasses of wine, contain the same amount of alcohol as a double whisky.

Q. *How does alcohol work as a stimulant?*
A. It does not, although it may seem to. It actually depresses the central nervous system, first lowering the sensitivity of critical faculties and thereby relieving layers of anxiety and restraint. Continued drinking may remove additional restraints, resulting in quite foreign or anti-social behaviour. You will be able to think of countless examples. It is claimed that one-half of all murderers are drunk at the time of the crime, and alcohol is an important factor in half of the assault and violence crimes within the family.

Q. *Does alcohol increase sexual abilities?*
A. It may increase inclinations through lessening tensions and inhibitions, but it doesn't increase ability. As a matter of fact, excessive drinking may be a frequent cause of impotence.

Q. *Can drinking affect pregnancy?*
A. Recent studies in the USA suggest that heavy drinking during pregnancy may lead to deformed and mentally-retarded babies.

Q. *What about drinking and driving?*
A. Drinking affects driving from the first drink onwards. Over half the drivers involved in fatal accidents have alcohol in their bloodstream. The more a driver drinks, the less able he or she is to detect the fact that judgement is impaired. In an experiment with professional drivers, the more they drank the more certain they were that they could drive expertly. A simple driving test revealed how wrong they were – they made potentially dangerous mistakes.

Stress inducing life-styles

Perhaps few people realise that basic psychological and environmental factors leading to stress (which may lead to alcohol/drug misuse) are directly related to the type of life-style each person chooses to follow. The choice of life-style depends upon many factors, but the importance of childhood conditioning in determining life-style choices is often seriously under-estimated. Listed below, with brief descriptions, are popular examples of life-styles which may lead to stress within individuals, as well as having the potential to create stressful interactions with their families, friends and workmates. (This classification is by courtesy of Dr Nyana Rowley, ACCEPT, St Georges Hospital, London.)

1   The getter

Actively or passively manipulates life and people by employing charm, shyness, temper or intimidation to put others into his/her service.

2   The driver

Perpetually in motion, the over-conscientious, over-ambitious person constantly striving to achieve a goal. Each day is viewed in terms of how best to get the 'most mileage', with as few 'pit-stops' as possible. Life is a perpetual race for such persons, although the goal or finish-line is seldom attained. As one individual said, 'I don't know where I'm going, but I've got my foot to the floorboard.'

3   The controller

Either wants to control life, or is afraid that it will dominate him or her. Surprises are disliked, spontaneity controlled, and feelings largely masked or hidden from others. Intellectualism, rightness, orderliness and neatness are favoured actions. Such a person is always concerned about 'saying the right thing at the right time'.

4   Need to be right

Persons who need to be right scrupulously avoid making errors. Should they be caught in an error, they will more often rationalise that others are wrong than that they are. 'Being right' becomes their obsession.

5   Need to be superior

People who need to be superior may refuse to enter life-tasks in which they cannot be the 'centre' or the 'best'. Such people may engage in socially non-constructive activities, such as seeing how many consecutive times they can jump on a pogo stick, for the purpose of breaking the world record. 'If I can't be first or best, then I'll settle for last or worst' often characterises such individuals.

6   Need to be liked

People who need to be liked, to 'please everybody all the time', are sensitive to criticism, lack self-assertion and feel crushed when not enjoying universal and constant approval. They are adept at discovering how to be accepted by others, and feel that such opinions are the only measure of their personal worth.

7   Need to be good

People who need to be good prefer living by higher moral standards than their peers. Such extreme goodness may serve as an instrument for moral superiority, so that such persons not only elevate themselves over others, but may actually discourage the 'inferior' person. As Mosak notes, this is a frequent device of the 'model child' or the alcohol dependent's wife or husband.

8   The opposers

People who oppose everything can rarely be found to be for something. They are quick to identify faults, constantly finding themselves opposed to the programmes or desires of others.

9   The victim

Innocently or actively becomes a 'disaster chaser', characterised by feelings of nobility, self-pity, resignations or proneness to accident. Is constantly seeking the sympathy or pity of others. Is also commonly employed by such people.

10   The martyr

Is similar to the victim, except that his or her 'death' is for a noble or righteous cause. Moral indignation or silent suffering at the hands of 'unjust' others are common characteristics.

11   The baby

Finds a place through the use of charm, cuteness and the exploitation of others. Often (but not always) the youngest in the family constellation, such persons may have high-pitched voices and childlike mannerisms employed to put others into their service.

12   The inadequate

A person who can do nothing right, being thoroughly awkward or clumsy. Often activities are limited to those in which some success is guaranteed, and assuming responsibility generally results in failure. Such a person loudly proclaims his/her own inadequacies, a living symbol of an 'inferiority complex'.

13   Avoiding feelings

People who avoid feelings believe that logical thinking and rational living can solve all life's problems. Their most prized characteristics consist of their logic, rationalisation, intellectualisation, and 'talking a good game'.

14   Excitement seekers

Despise dull, routine activities, preferring constant thrill and motion. In searching for excitement, others are often employed in providing new exhilaration. 'Let's party tonight' is a frequent theme. Self-excitement of fears or masturbation may also be employed. May be bored in recovery from alcoholism or other illnesses, and so may relapse to create excitement and involve others such as doctors, nurses and counsellors.

15   The escapist

Escapes from life by not getting involved. Refuses to take even small risks to accomplish anything. Hides away inside him/herself and makes excuses, rationalises, dreams, but never acts.

In addition, there are a number of special factors which may make a person more vulnerable to stress and subsequent alcohol and drug misuse. These include:

a. Ignorance about alcohol as a depressant, anxiety-producing, potentially addictive drug.
b. Inability to understand and cope with own emotions.
c. Personality vulnerabilities such as shyness, anxieties, emotional insecurities and low self-esteem.
d. Impatience: desires for immediate gratifications.
e. Inability to endure frustration and tolerate adversity.
f. Poor problem-solving and coping skills.
g. Lack of social and self-assertion skills.
h. Inability to entertain oneself, to be alone without being lonely, narrow leisure-horizons.
i. Vulnerability to peer-group pressures (herd syndrome).
j. Lack of self- and social-responsibility or of an effective life-style.

Treatment responses: 'picking up the pieces'

Until fairly recently, and with few exceptions, the general response to the problems of alcohol and drug misuse by both government and voluntary organisations was to create a patchwork of services, without due regard to overall direction or effective co-ordination. Most services tended to be passive, 'sitting back' and waiting for alcohol-problem people – usually males in their 40s and 50s – to present themselves for help or treatment. Typically they would do so after they had suffered from mental and physical damage – as well as social deprivations such as loss of jobs, homes and so forth – and, in many cases, become deeply entrenched in long-term maladaptive behaviour patterns that were extremely difficult to treat.

Amongst the early responses was the decision of the Department of Health and Social Security (DHSS) to establish Alcohol Dependence Inpatient Units throughout the country. Today, there are twenty-six such units, at least one in each regional health authority. Treatment programmes, including various forms of group therapy, usually extend over a period of six weeks to three months. However, the total number of beds provided by all the units is less than 700, which is an extremely meagre response when considered against the national need. Most units lack sufficient resources for local community outpatient aftercare, and there is often a long list of desperate people awaiting admission.

Various voluntary organisations, sometimes in partnership with local authorities, have gradually opened a number of hostels or 'half-way' houses where persons can live in a supportive environment for varying periods of time, while preparing to return to their community to work and live. The therapeutic input within these residential facilities varies from non-existent to intensive. At the end of 1978, there were approximately 60 hostels in service providing some 800 beds, mostly for the chronic homeless. However, some hostels may now be closed due to government funding cutbacks. A government-sponsored agency, FARE (the Federation of Alcohol Residential Establishments), based in London, is now providing support for, and development of, the national residential establishment network.

Perhaps the most widespread service over recent years has been provided by the voluntary self-help fellowship, Alcoholics Anonymous. They have established a national network of group meetings, and support themselves by their own contributions. The general opinion of many professional observers was that – with the exception of those people who 'caught on' to the AA spiritual philosophy and who attended AA meetings regularly – most of the services tended to have rather indifferent results in the long term.

It is arguable then that previous responses have, with a few exceptions, tended to be 'too little and too late'. Furthermore, it was found that many persons suffering from severe alcohol or drug misuse were unable to gain immediate admission to the National Health Service Treatment Units because of the long waiting lists and other factors.

They were usually admitted to outlying psychiatric hospitals where they were heavily sedated or tranquillised, then 'dried out' and discharged a week or two later, without any real therapeutic or even educational input being provided. This pattern of response is known in the trade as 'drug 'em and jug 'em', and while the general situation is improving today, this procedure continues to be the only option in many localities.

For hard drug users (heroin, LSD etc.), there now exist some twenty drug rehabilitation projects in England and Wales, mostly residential. There are also a scattering of drug dependency clinics attached to hospitals throughout Britain. At the last count, thirteen such dependency clinics were based within Greater London, where it is thought a high proportion of the 4100 registered hard-drug dependent persons reside. It is generally accepted that there are many more unregistered hard-drug users, but accurate statistics are simply not available.

Today's trends in new services

There appears to be a definite trend towards providing primary care services within local communities with the emphasis on much earlier recognition, thereby reducing the need for long stays in hospitals and hostels. Of course, no matter how successful primary and secondary treatment methods become, there will always be a need for long-stay services for a small percentage of the alcohol/drug misuse population. However, in the case of alcohol misuse, the vast majority of people can be reached earlier while their physical and mental resources are still intact, and *before* jobs have been lost and homes broken up. This has been demonstrated quite clearly by the work of ACCEPT in the Greater London area, where, last year, as noted earlier, some 80 per cent of the referrals dealt with were still in employment, and where some 97 per cent had stable home environments ranging from bed-sits to palatial homes. Based upon the work of ACCEPT, which is itself setting up additional centres, voluntary and statutory bodies in other areas are establishing education, prevention and treatment centres. For instance, Birmingham now has the Aquarius project functioning effectively while, in Liverpool, a co-ordinating body supported by local council and health authority is initiating a similar project. It is hoped that many more communities will be following these pioneering efforts, but government funding cutbacks may delay and discourage numerous projects.

Another encouraging sign has been the steady progress of the National Council on Alcoholism (NCA). Over the past twenty years, they have been successful in establishing twenty-seven local and regional councils which provide advice, information and counselling services in key cities such as Bristol, Coventry, Manchester, Newcastle and so forth. Many more general hospitals are now taking an active interest in alcoholism and are providing short-stay detoxification facilities in general wards. They are also increasing interactions with non-medical community resources such as AA, ACCEPT, NCA and others. The Medical Council on Alcoholism, based in London, has increased its efforts to provide more education and a better understanding of the problems which, in the past, have tended to be ignored by many doctors, psychiatrists and hospital consultants.

The Alcohol Education Centre (AEC) at the Maudsley Hospital, London was formed in 1973. Funded by the DHSS, it has maintained a rapid rate of expansion in providing education and training for those involved in working with alcohol-problem people. Each year, the AEC organises Summer Schools, Advanced Schools, special courses, seminars and workshops. More recently, they have appointed a Development Officer to encourage and assist major business firms and government agencies to establish employee-assistance programmes, which are described more fully in the next section. Professor Griffith Edwards and the team at the Addiction Research Unit, The Institute of Psychiatry in London, have diligently widened their research activities and have published many papers and reports which are of inestimable value to planners and those working in the field.

For those who wish to study present and future trends in more detail, the following publications are recommended:

Alcohol & Alcoholism, a report by the Royal College of Psychiatrists (Tavistock Publications, 1979).

ACCEPT 3rd Annual Report, 1979 (Accept Publications, Western Hospital, Seagrave Road, London SW6).

The Pattern and Range of Services for Problem Drinkers, (Department of Health and Social Security, Alexander Fleming House, Elephant and Castle, London SE1, 1979).

Business, industry and government – new approaches

Most encouraging of all the current developments is the fact that organisations such as ACCEPT, AEC, MCA and NCA are making important progress not only in educating the general public and the medical profession, but in stimulating and helping major firms and government agencies employing large numbers of people to establish employee assistance programmes especially geared to alcohol and drug misuse. Key elements of these programmes include education in sensible drinking habits; information about the dangers of alcohol and drugs, such as tranquillisers, pain killers, anti-depressants and sleeping pills; and the training of supervisors, health, welfare and personnel staff in early recognition and treatment management procedures. Employees are encouraged to seek help voluntarily through multiple-referral channels before their problems become obvious to staff or workmates.

Basic guidelines for an employee assistance programme usually contain the following points:

An employee's choice to drink alcoholic beverages is a personal matter which does not concern the employer.

However, when the use of alcohol (at times extremely well hidden) affects job performance or attendance, or affects other workers, the matter becomes of justifiable concern to the employer.

Employers will develop a comprehensive alcohol education and alcoholism/drug misuse awareness programme, training staff and using appropriate literature, and display posters to alert all employees including executives.

Employees can, in confidence, discuss their problems with the medical, nursing, welfare or personnel staff who will maintain complete confidentiality. Neither jobs nor promotion prospects will be affected, providing positive action is taken.

However, if no action is taken by the problem drinking employee and there is a decline in job performance including absenteeism, and/or chronic lateness, the supervisor will discuss the matter with the employee and refer him or her to the medical, nursing, welfare or personnel staff, or to a special employee-assistance counsellor. Supervisors do not attempt to act as drinking problem counsellors.

Problem drinking and alcoholism are dealt with as bona fide illnesses. However, if the employee refuses to follow the employer's treatment recommendations and job performance does not improve, then normal disciplinary procedures are followed. In certain cases, the employee may be retired on grounds of chronic illness.

A good example of this type of information disseminated on a company-wide basis to all employees is the following extract from Imperial Chemical Company Limited's *Plastic News* (1980):

Tips for sensible drinking

When you choose to drink, sip your drink slowly instead of gulping. Pace yourself. Avoid drinking another drink quickly on top of your last drink. If you're always the first to finish and ready for another before your friends are, it's time to start worrying.

It is helpful to eat something, even a snack, during any drinking occasion. Try not to drink on an empty stomach. Try to avoid drinking too much except on very special infrequent occasions. Avoid drinking more than you plan or intend to drink.

Avoid frequent business, expense account or pub lunches where the focus is on heavy drinking. Effective sales persons, administrators and plant-workers don't have to misuse alcohol to do business or relax.

If you can handle large quantities of alcohol without getting drunk or without suffering hangovers, be particularly wary. Over the years, it may catch up with you and you may wake up one morning and find you can't do without it. Beer and wine drinkers are just as vulnerable.

To sum up: drinking in moderation can be enjoyable, drinking to excess can sneak up on you over a period of time and become a serious health, social and financial hazard. There is no substitute for your own common sense, bearing in mind that each one of us is responsible for our own behaviour and our own well-being.

If you think you're developing a problem, nip it in the bud. Take immediate action by making an appointment to see your firm's medical officer, nursing officer or your welfare officer. Keep the appointment. You can discuss your problems freely as the medical and welfare staff will maintain complete confidentiality – it won't go on your record and will not affect your job or promotion prospects.

Alternatively, see your doctor, or telephone ACCEPT on 01 381 3155 for information, advice or an appointment. In areas outside London, most cities have councils on alcoholism where you may receive information and counselling.

Family, friends and workmates

If someone in your family, a friend or a workmate is developing a problem, there are ways you can help.

It is not unusual for dependent drinkers to go through what is known as a 'denial phase' wherein, despite all evidence, they deny any problem exists.

A careful, calm approach is necessary. Explain quietly that you believe a drinking problem exists. Give specific examples, if possible, indicating where harm or dependence is taking place. Give the person some literature to read such as the very popular ACCEPT leaflet,

'Now is the Time', which contains a list of warning signs and symptoms.

If you are rebuffed, don't despair. Try again in a month or so, preferably the morning after some unpleasant drinking episode. Avoid recriminations or lecturing, bearing in mind that alcoholism is a bona fide illness often complicated by fear, shame and mental confusion.

I might add that if you cover up for a workmate, you might eventually be helping to kill him or her. You may become what is known as an accomplice in the illness and this usually leads to more serious troubles for all concerned, sometimes accidents and deaths.

Self and social responsibility factors

The Royal College of Psychiatrists has pointed out in clear, unmistakable language that:

> ... it is a fundamental misunderstanding to suppose it (alcoholism) can simply be handed over to doctors and social workers. The people who must share this concern are the mass of ordinary citizens, as well as a wide range of professionals, and those whose work calls on them to implement local and national government policy.

It would appear to be a matter of personal concern for each and every one of us to develop stress avoidance skills and sensible drinking habits. There is wide scope for the use of sports for relaxation, as well as special relaxation techniques, including relaxation cassettes, yoga, bio-energetics, meditation, encounter and psychodrama groups. We can examine and adjust our life-styles to ensure we are not trapped in continuing stress-inducing, emotional habit patterns. Many more counselling and psychotherapy resources are becoming available to assist individuals in improving their inner resources and living more comfortably and effectively.

REFERENCES

ACCEPT, Third Annual Report 1979 (Accept Publications, Western Hospital, London, SW6)

J. De Lint, 'Research Report', *British Journal on Alcohol & Alcoholism*, 13, 2 (1978)

C. S. Leiber and E. Rubin, Joint Study, Mount Sinai School of Medicine (New York, 1977)

Royal College of Psychiatrists, *Alcohol and Alcoholism* (London: Tavistock
   Publications, 1979)
S. J. Shaw, 'Detoxification Evaluation Project', Addiction Research Unit,
   Institute of Psychiatry, London (1978)
'Tips for Sensible Drinking', *Plastics News*, (Imperial Chemical Industries
   Ltd, Welwyn Garden City, Jan. 1980)

OTHER SOURCES AND USEFUL ADDRESSES

British Journal on Alcohol & Alcoholism, 1978/79 issues, B. Edsall & Co.
   Ltd, 36, Eccleston Square, London, SW1
Comments of Sir George Young, M.P., *Hansard* (March 1979), Health
   Education Council, London
Federation of Alcohol Residential Establishments (FARE), 3, Grosvenor
   Crescent, London, SW1
Medical Council on Alcoholism, 3, Grosvenor Crescent, London, SW1
National Council on Alcoholism, *Alcohol and Work*, NCA report (London,
   1978)
Social Trends (HMSO, 1979)
Standing Conference on Drug Addiction (SCODA), 3, Blackburn Road,
   London NW6 (1980)
World Health Organisation, Geneva

APPENDIX: ALCOHOL QUESTIONNAIRE

1. Do you occasionally drink heavily after a disappointment, a quarrel or
    when the boss gives you a hard time?
2. When you have trouble or feel under pressure, do you always drink
    more heavily than usual?
3. Have you noticed that you are able to handle more liquor than you did
    when you were first drinking?
4. Did you ever wake up on the morning after and discover that you could
    not remember part of the evening before, even though your friends tell
    you that you did not 'pass out'?
5. When drinking with other people, do you try to have a few extra drinks
    when others will not know it?
6. Are there certain occasions when you feel uncomfortable if alcohol is
    not available?
7. Have you recently noticed that when you begin drinking you are in
    more of a hurry to get the first drink than you used to be?
8. Do you sometimes feel a little guilty about your drinking?
9. Are you secretly irritated when your family or friends discuss your
    drinking?
10. Have you recently noticed an increase in the frequency of your memory
    blackouts?
11. Do you often find that you wish to continue drinking after your friends
    say they have had enough?

12. Do you usually have a reason for the occasions when you drink heavily?
13. When you are sober, do you often regret things you have done or said while drinking?
14. Have you tried switching brands or following different plans for controlling your drinking?
15. Have you often failed to keep the promises you have made to yourself about controlling or cutting down on your drinking?
16. Have you ever tried to control your drinking by making a change in jobs, or moving to a new location?
17. Do you try to avoid family or close friends while you are drinking?
18. Are you having an increasing number of financial and work problems?
19. Do more people seem to be treating you unfairly without good reason?
20. Do you eat very little or irregularly when you are drinking?
21. Do you sometimes have the shakes in the morning and find that it helps to have a little drink?
22. Have you recently noticed that you cannot drink as much as you once did?
23. Do you sometimes stay drunk for several days at a time?
24. Do you sometimes feel very depressed and wonder whether life is worth living?
25. Sometimes after periods of drinking do you see or hear things that aren't there?
26. Do you get terribly frightened after you have been drinking heavily?

If you have answered 'yes' to any of the questions, you have some of the symptoms that may indicate alcoholism. 'Yes' answers to several of the questions indicate the following stages of alcoholism:

Questions 1–8   – entering the risk area;
Questions 9–21 – middle stage;
Questions 22–26 – beginning of final stage.

Reproduced by kind permission of National Council on Alcoholism, New York, USA.

PART IV

CHANGING THE ENVIRONMENT

10 Changing Structural Conditions of the Work Environment: Stress Reduction through Legislation and Worker Participation

Thoralf Ulrik Qvale
Work Research Institute, Norway

Introduction

In this introduction we first give a brief historical presentation of the socio-political development in Norway leading to a new way of considering work environment problems, and including psycho-social ones. New legislation was passed by the Parliament in 1976 reflecting this reconsideration both in form and content. The central parts of the new legal rules are presented with particular emphasis on those covering psycho-social aspects.

1 Background to the new legislation

When the new legislation replaced the old Norwegian Workers' Protection and Safety Acts, effective from July 1977, the old legislation had been under pressure for a number of years, criticised by the labour movement for being too weak in traditional areas, partly irrelevant in relation to new problems emerging and generally leaving too much to company management's discretion. A wave of wildcat strikes in 1971 in chemical and other process industries in Norway, following a strike in the Swedish iron mines at Kiruna, was the first large-scale indication of unrest. Here the quality of the working environment was a major issue, combined with reactions against low pay and centralisation in the bargaining and union structure (Qvale and Karlsen, 1971). During the Trades Union Congress in 1973, the results of a survey of working environment problems within union constituency (Karlsen, 1972) were discussed and led to decisions about pressing for reforms. At this stage psycho-social problems were not seen as particularly central. Karlsen (1972) mainly reported large-scale conventional work environment problems (noise, dirt, toxic materials, gas, heavy work loads and similar) across all industries. His study covered working schedules, however, and demonstrated strong connections between shiftwork and psycho-social-somatic problems such as stomach problems, little contact with family and little community life.

In line with Norwegian traditions, a committee composed of the interested parties (politicians, union leaders, employers' representatives, civil servants) and specialists (researchers) worked on the reform which eventually was made effective from mid-1977, against little resistance. The emphasis on the solution of psycho-social problems through workers' participation in the work environment improvements developed during the period this committee was drafting the rules.

2   General principles of the new law

Some of the *new* principles built into the Work Environment Act should be mentioned:

The old act required a satisfactory level of security against accidents and health hazards when considering *each factor separately*. The new act requires an adequate (in relation to the economic, technological and social development of society) standard of the *entire work environment* (all factors seen as a whole) and for each factor separately. Thus the concept of 'total load' is introduced. Although each single environmental factor (noise, heat, gas, shiftwork, monotony, pace etc.) may be better than the required level, they may together add up to an unacceptable load for the employees.

The old act stated *minimum* requirements. The new act requires continuous improvements (as well as minimum standards). The responsibility for this lies primarily with the employer and the employees together. There is a legal basis for the employees to raise demands for improvements beyond minimum standards, (Gustavsen *et al.*, 1978).

The old act left it to the factory inspector to decide whether standards were kept. Until the inspector had decided, the employer had the right to use his sole judgement. The new act intends to promote the following changes:

a.   To make development of the work environment an integral part of the general developmental work of the enterprise. In practice this means that work environment factors shall be considered at the design stage and checked by the factory inspector before planning permission is given. Further technical changes shall be submitted to the Work Environment Committee.

b. To bring the employees into this work through their unions and the plant level Work Environment Committees. Here 50 per cent of the seats are allocated to the employees who also elect the chairman (with double-vote) every second year.

c. To establish the employees' right to take part in the decisions relating to the work environment – as a veto right if a dangerous situation arises; as the right of initiative; and as a partner with extended rights in the development of an environment above the minimum levels.

d. To enforce *planned development* of the work environment. Administratively this is achieved through the legal requirement that all changes in the work environment should be according to a *plan* made by the Work Environment Committee. Unilateral action, for example by management, is in principle no longer permitted.

e. To bring the factory inspector into the supervision of the implementation of these plans. This creates a new role for the factory inspector. In addition to being able to forbid substandard solutions, this institution is now to sanction the planning of systematic, positive development, and to monitor its implementation.

This law represents new principles of legislation and of reform in working life which were quite unique at this time. Gustavsen (1977, 1980) has given descriptions and very thorough analyses of these aspects. It is still early to decide whether the new principles really mark a breakthrough in practice. We cannot, however, discuss such questions referring to the *national* level in any detail here, but some comments are given in the concluding section.

3 The section of the law which deals specifically with psycho-social factors

The central text of this section (Section 12) runs as follows:

a. *General requirements* Production methods, work organisation, working hours, (e.g. shift work schedules), and payment systems shall be so designed as to avoid harmful physiological or psychological effects on employees, including any negative influence on the alertness necessary for safety reasons.

Employees shall be afforded opportunities for personal development and the maintenance and development of their skills.

b. *Job design*   Full account shall be taken of the need for employee self-determination and maintenance of skills in planning of work and design of jobs.

Monotonous, repetitive work and machine or assembly-line work that does not permit alteration of pace shall be avoided.

Jobs shall be so designed as to allow some possibility for variation, for contact with other workers, for interdependence between their constituent elements, and for information and feedback to the employees concerning production requirements and performance.

c. *Planning and control systems*   Employees or their representatives shall be kept informed about planning and control systems, including any changes in such systems. They shall be given the necessary training to understand the systems adopted, and shall have the right to influence their design.

d. *Dangerous work*   Piece-rate and similar payment systems shall not be used where they may lead to non-observance of safety standards.

4 Participation

For our purposes, the most central innovations are the Law's emphasis on *employee participation* in evaluating and improving the work environment, the *inclusion of social and psychological variables* as relevant aspects of the work environment, and the general *'total-load' perspective*. This combination of what are usually seen as different issues, i.e. political, psychological, social and physical, reflects the basic thinking behind the Law: those who are exposed to the work environment must be involved in evaluating and improving it. Thus a key concern must be to create conditions for active employee involvement. Practical considerations certainly speak for the same kind of strategy. The task of measuring and combining the multiple work environment factors, if this is to be done by 'specialists' (e.g. factory inspectors), is immense and will give dubious results for many reasons including theoretical ones. Some of these will be dealt with later in this chapter.

The foundations for this theoretical and practical approach are found in a research programme that started at the Tavistock Institute of Human Relations in the 1950s and was continued in Norway through the 1960s. We shall concentrate here on the relevance of this research for the emergence and handling of stress problems in working life.

Conceptual background: The role of structural conditions in causing and coping with stress

Definitions and operationalisations of 'stress' vary widely once we go outside the field of mechanics where it originated, and we will not attempt to review the current theories here. We use the term 'stress' as synonymous with 'total work environment load' and will assume that only stress above a certain (although difficult to define) limit is assumed to give irreversible negative human and/or social consequences and hence should be avoided. Consequently we will not discuss strategies or tactics at the level of the individual to cope with a given (stressful) situation, but will instead concentrate on strategies at several levels in order to keep the load within acceptable limits. Thus, we are introducing technological, organisational, social and administrative factors. Our theoretical approach is therefore close to that of Frankenhaeuser and Gardell (1976), but the main emphasis is on strategic (change-oriented) aspects, building on experience from action research (Thorsrud, 1975; Susman and Evered, 1978).

1 Coal mine studies

The classic coal mine studies performed by Tavistock researchers in the 1950s (Trist and Bamforth, 1961; Trist et al., 1963; Herbst, 1962) opened up a new road to the study of production systems. Departing from what was a psychoanalytical tradition, they moved toward the understanding that 'socio-psychological factors are in-built characteristics of work systems rather than additional,' (Trist et al., 1963, p. xii).

In coal mining, where working conditions are difficult and continually changing, and a number of dangers are always present, the situation would be potentially very stressful. The Tavistock studies contributed the understanding that the traditional, democratic *work group* arrangement at the coal face provided social support, and also made it possible for the workers to cope with the potentially dangerous work situation. This was not only because they were not working *alone*, but also because they trusted and helped each other in a flexible network of mutually-supporting work roles. Each group member knew the others would behave responsibly and be conscious of the safety of the whole group. This had some very practical implications. Those who worked at the coal-face knew the others would be listening for signs of movements in the rocks and warn if there were any danger. Job-rotation meant they shared the good and bad jobs. They also shared equally the outcome of the work and controlled their own work pace and working hours. The surrounding local community and family life reflected the work schedule, values, and norms of the basic job design and work organisation.

New technology (conveyor belts and other machines) broke up this structure, specialised the workers and spread them geographically in the mine. Negative psychological and social consequences followed. Productivity dropped seriously. But with modification of the technology, some of the main features of the early work organisation could be reinstated, and the total system was then stabilised again. The idea of *organisational choice* was developed. In a potentially dangerous and stressful work situation, like the one in the Durham coal mines, autonomous work-groups seemed to provide better safety, social and psychological conditions, and productivity. The negative psycho-social effects of the combination of conveyor-belt technology and a specialised work organisation were clearly demonstrated.

2   Industrial democracy

The Norwegian Industrial Democracy Programme (Emery and Thorsrud, 1969, 1976) was aimed at utilising Tavistock's socio–technical concepts in a national action research strategy for democratisation (Qvale, 1976). The point of departure was not specific work-environment problems, but a broadly defined objective of improving employees' conditions for participation in their own work situations. Job redesign and the introduction of autonomous work groups; training of workers and managers; and changes in technology to allow for this, were central measures. The basic idea was to create a more stimulating work-situation for workers. Without more discretion, and hence learning opportunities in the job, workers would generally remain passive and lacking basic abilities to utilise formal arrangements for participation in decision-making.

A set of psychological criteria for job design were developed. A job should offer the job-holder possibilities for variation, learning and decision-making; should give social support and recognition; appear as meaningful (contribute towards something useful for society) and lead towards a desirable future (Emery and Thorsrud, 1976). At this stage (the mid-1960s) new technology (automation, computers) was seen as opening new opportunities for *technological choice*. The researchers and industrial and union leaders involved in the project thought we should be able to design the technology to give room for a better work organisation, and then also open up new career opportunities and ways of integrating work, education, and private life.

The relevance of this approach for work environment problems including stress should theoretically be two-fold: a better basic socio–technical design should in itself give a better working environment, and the resulting more democratic company structure should also create worker-involvement beyond the production tasks of the individual. We expected a spill-over effect both at plant level (and hence on work environment issues too), and local community level (higher involvement outside the work situation, better adaptation of work to private life).

3 Experiments

Plant-level experiments with new socio-technical solutions and forms of worker participation progressed through quite heavy researcher involvement, but the expected diffusion through union, management and educational networks did not take place to any appreciable extent within the country. The 'scientific management' principles (high specialisation in jobs; piece rates; close supervision; standardisation in job requirements and working hours, etc.) had been replaced with success only in a limited number of enterprises, while they were living on in most others.

Continuing causes of stress

1 Interaction between technological and organisational variables

New syndromes of psycho–social and physiological problems seemed to be appearing and accounting for an increasing part of the sum of occupational diseases. The reasons for this are numerous: growth in company size and hence in large-scale production; application of 'scientific management' techniques in new sectors (offices, hospitals, retailing etc.); automation reducing variety in the job and also increasing the load on a limited number of muscles. These can be summed up as increasing centralisation in decision-making and monotony in work in many industries. Growth in the application of computer control in the process industry, for example, created work situations where the operators merely monitored the equipment, and were expected to remain passive until the appearance of problems the automatic equipment could not control. Increasing absenteeism, labour turnover, sickness and the rapidly growing reporting of 'nervousness', 'stress', 'headache', cardio-vascular diseases, stiff necks, shoulders, pain in the back and legs and similar, indicated the negative effects of this kind of automation.

Although the symptoms were stemming from the *interaction of several* factors (organisational, technological), a common effect was a *reduction in the individual's control over his own work situation.* Karasek's (1979) re-analysis of US and Swedish survey data on work and health confirms the connection between job demands, control ('job decision latitude') and mental strain, using 'exhaustion' and 'depression' as indicators of the latter. He finds that mental strain, and hence psycho–social problems, appear at all organisational levels as the effect of a combination of high job demands and low decision latitude. He concludes that constraints on decision-making, not decision-making per se, are the main problem, and this problem affects not only executives but workers in low-status jobs with little freedom to make decisions. These findings also confirm the emerging recognition within the Norwegian Industrial Democracy Programme in the early 1970s, that we were not merely trying to change the production engineering techniques on the shop floor, plus some closely related work-roles (for example foremen and maintenance), but were actually attacking the basis of the bureaucratic organisational structure. While centralising processes were going on in the companies' organisation, new production technologies requiring in principle fast reaction (decision-making) at the lower levels were introduced and created increasing stress for the employees.

Some of the clearest examples of this combined effect of organisational structure and technology may be seen in recent studies from nuclear power plants (Khemeny, 1979), and oil-production platforms (Scandpower/WRI/IFA, 1980) where heavy governmental control (and centralisation) is combined with company bureaucracy and semi-automatic, potentially dangerous, production processes. It is not by chance that the operating companies claim that 65–90 per cent of all accidents are caused by human error (Blomsnes, 1980; Wright, 1979), and that a basic 'safety philosophy' in nuclear plants is 'general distrust in the human operator to take appropriate safety actions under time pressure in an emergency situation' (Blomsnes, 1980). A vicious circle where 'human error' leads to more automation and even stricter administrative control tends to appear. Selection of workers, exclusion of those who do not cope, and intensified training of workers outside the work situation are the main conventional measures applied to keep the system running in spite of deteriorating working environments (and increasing stress).

2 Strategy

The convergence of the experiences from the Industrial Democracy Programme and the growing concern over psycho–social working environment factors, both emphasising increased control over one's own work situation as a basic key to improvements, led to an attempt to develop a new strategy. The use of legislation; the factory inspectorate; training courses; building up company, union and researcher networks; and public grants for technological improvements were parts of this strategy. The obvious dilemma arising when *central* initiatives are supposed to create *local* activity, and the manner in which this is to be resolved, can probably better be discussed after presentation of two cases.

Work redesign in action: two case studies

1 A case from the industrial democracy programme (Qvale, 1969)

(The socio-technical analysis inherent in this description is parallel to that found in other studies arising from the Tavistock tradition (e.g. Engelstad, 1972; Hill, 1972).)

The project started in 1968, in a light metal smelter company employing about 800 workers in all. The concrete changes started in the most problematic department where labour turnover was around 60 per cent per annum; production yield very low; work very heavy; the chemical working environment extremely bad (very hot, smoky with fumes and toxic gases like chlorine, etc.); and the danger of being burnt by molten metal constantly present. The production process required continuous shift work. The workers on each shift were organised in specialised groups, each led by a chargehand. Maintenance was going on continuously during the day, performed by specialised groups representing the various crafts (electricians, bricklayers, mechanics) and led by their own set of foremen. The production process was very complex, production control extremely difficult, and very large unexplained dips in the yield occurred frequently. Workers were paid at flat, but different rates according to the skill-level of the job to which they were permanently allocated. Thus the heaviest, most taxing jobs were lowest paid.

A local action committee with local union leaders and managers held meetings with all employees, presented experience from earlier projects in the corporation, and also held a 3-day seminar for key workers and managers to plan the project. Workers complained about bad working conditions, authoritarian managers, extremely hot and heavy work, and high labour turnover giving the stable people extra work load and safety problems. Management was very concerned over 'negative', 'uninterested' workers, low productivity, low performance levels, very high maintenance costs and a very uncertain future for the plant.

Characteristics of the production process should in principle make it possible to improve production yield and, at the same time, reduce the work-load on the workers and improve the chemical working environment. (When the process is under control, many heavy tasks do not appear (cleaning, maintenance etc.), and less toxic gas and fumes are released.) The general plan made was to reorganise shift workers so that they formed small groups sharing all production tasks in one part of the department, and to create a new payment system, graded according to the skill of the *worker* and to give feedback about performance. Before this could be done, the workers had to be better trained, 'multi-skilled', and also to be taught process technology and theory. A system of short and longer courses plus on-the-job-training was designed, but persistent labour turnover made it impossible to use. Eventually the company employed 16 extra workers to replace people attending courses. Then the new group system was tried out, after considerable internal discussion and shifting of personnel.

The changes led to the gradual disappearance of the very strong conflicts between groups of specialised workers, who earlier competed for equipment and space between the ovens for moving their vehicles, and in order to finish their particular jobs fast and get away from the heat and fumes. On the other hand the process was still out of control, so the bonus did not pay off. This created pressure on management to intensify development work to stabilise feedstock and establish process parameters to use. After about 6 months, production stabilised, the yield increased and the bonus started paying off. Labour turnover dropped. Parallel projects started in the adjoining department, where workers were pressing for training courses. At this stage the company could offer a combination of courses and on-the-job training to give a career for shift operators leading to a status equal to skilled craftsmen.

This kind of development continued, although there were numerous setbacks. The shift-holiday plan was changed so that the workers could have their 3 weeks' summer holiday during the school summer holiday, in part at least every year and completely every 2nd or 3rd. In addition, they had one week 'daywork' off every 8th week so that they could attend courses, cover for absence of work group members or take part in development work. (Weekly working hours on shifts were reduced by two hours. Later, the Work Environment Act plus further internal development had led to other improvements in the shift/holiday schedules.) A new computer system for processing production data and giving guidance in the control of the ovens was developed locally and acted to stabilise practices within the work groups on each of 5 shift crews in the original department. Recruiting of new workers was transferred from a central office to the particular plant where a new personnel secretary was employed. Better equipment was slowly developed and hundreds of practical, smaller changes were made following suggestions from workers and supervisors. The maintenance crew was reorganised about 2 years later into teams containing all the necessary crafts and doing complete overhaul jobs, with less need for management planning and coordination. Productivity in maintenance then increased immensely. In the following years, labour turnover remained stable in the area of about 5–10 per cent, which is better than in most of the corporation's other plants in this district.

The strategy of this particular project was one of worker/management joint participation in a step-wise analysis of problems, experimenting with solutions and evaluation. This was a kind of learning spiral where new factors and problems appeared when old problems had been solved. The reduction in labour turnover and increase in production were probably the best indicators of some level of success. The change process brought the work organisation gradually closer to the pattern and level of autonomy of the work groups in the coal mines (Gulowsen, 1972). A basic condition for the relative success of the development was the creation of the integrated 'process worker teams'. This ruled out the in-built conflicts that earlier existed between specialised groups, which competed for resources and prevented learning about cause–effect relationships across the specialities. The new teams, however, did not function until the level of training was improved, better tools developed and the crews somewhat stabilised. Then the physical working environment also started improving. Through this period of trials, frustration and struggle, the joint leadership of local union representatives and managers was vital for maintaining some level of workers' commitment to the 'project'.

2 Strategy implicit in the work environment legislation: A case history

The new Law intends to create local activity. The plant level work environment and safety committee (50 per cent worker representatives, 50 per cent company (management) representatives) is obliged to study work environment problems, make a plan for improving the environment, and to implement this plan. A comprehensive course on the new Law, work environment factors, hazards, etc., and how to work with the Law has been distributed to all companies. About 90 000 workers and managers in a national working population of 1.3 million had completed the course approximately 2 years after the Law went into effect. The course includes examples and exercises whereby workers and managers together make analyses of the working environment of several jobs they select for this purpose within their own plant.

Ødegaard (1977) made a follow-up study of one particularly successful case in one company where the participants tried two different approaches in the implementation of the training course. In the particular plant, (a medium size shipyard specialising in repair work and building complicated ships), management had been working for years to decentralise the organisation to increase autonomy and learning possibilities at the shop-floor level, and reduce administrative problems at higher levels. Here the course was tried as a means to start a shop-floor development process. The local union was strongly involved in this, and had earlier made a survey of the work environment problems in the yard.

The first attempt involved a group composed of managers, technicians, foremen, shop stewards and a nurse. They worked together for 8 weeks (about 35 hours) following the course's text books and exercises. In addition they made, in smaller groups, analyses of job situations in the shops and offices. The conclusions were compiled and handed over to the work environment and safety committee. But all participants agreed the exercise was unsuccessful. In the next attempt they formed the course into three groups (one from each of three production departments), each nominated by the Department Council members (one foreman, the local shop steward, who doubles as safety representative, and a worker). In addition, the two managers leading each department were in their group. The groups worked quite similarly to those in the first attempt, but confined the analysis to their own departments. The reports were given to the safety committees, but in addition the group was to try to make plans for improvements in the environment.

The second approach was evaluated as highly successful by the participants, management, and the local union. Ødegaard explains this by pointing to the difference in formal set-up:

In the first attempt single persons from different departments analysed the job situation of other people through inspection.

In the second attempt, groups of participants from the same department work together on analysing problems in their own departments, and they have a formal link to the department through the department council.

Then, turning to the outcomes of the analysis made, the training course on 'Improved Work Environment' which was followed uses the following classification:

Physical factors (noise, ergonomics, chemicals etc.),
Risks of accident,
Social and psychological factors.

Content analysis of the reports from the work groups (17 jobs were analysed through the 'inspection of others' model, and 15 through the 'analysis of our own situation' model) gives the following classification of the causes and remedies to problems suggested:

Technical: the problem is caused by the technical system, or can be solved through technical change,
Human default: the problem is seen as stemming from lack of attention, care, observance of the safety rules etc.,
Organisational causes and means: work organisation, planning, working-hours, stress, social conditions etc., are identified as the key factors.

Table 10.1 below gives the results of the analysis. The main differences in the results of the two ways of analysing are that:

(a) Inspection of others' jobs only leads to the tracing of technical and human factors, while analysis of own situation can also conclude that the way in which work is organised can be the cause of problems.
(b) Inspections of others allocate accident hazards to the traditional human error, while the alternative model brings structural factors into the picture.

It is interesting to note that the workers who analyse their own situation to a very large extent suggest different planning/scheduling as a means to reduce negative physical environment loads. For example, having a job done in the shop rather than on board the ship under repair, thus avoiding welding in places where many workers are present. Thus the welding fumes, flashes, noise, etc. from the work of

TABLE 10.1 Causes of work environment problems according to type and model of analysis (from Ødegaard, 1977)

Type of factors	Model of analysis	Causes as % of total			Total	
		Technical	Human	Organisational	%	(N)
Physical	inspection of others'	75	25	0	100	(36)
	own situation	65	13	22	100	(23)
Accident hazards	inspection of others'	8	92	0	100	(13)
	own situation	39	44	17	100	(23)
Psychological/social	inspection of others'	100	0	0	100	(5)
	own situation	45	0	55	100	(11)

some, will not affect others. The parallel 'analysis of others' solution is to take the way the work is organised for given, and to suggest technical improvements like fans, air ducts etc., plus better personal protection measures (which are frequently cumbersome). This means that the problems are left to be solved either by management or by the individual workers.

3   The need for a multilevel strategy

Both the described cases are exceptional when compared with most other Norwegian industries, and both progressed partly due to common interests shared by management and workers in improving productivity through improved working environments. In both plants these two objectives or steps in a means–ends chain seemed to be compatible, but only in the former (the metal smelter) was this empirically tested. Both cases should illustrate that workers' direct involvement aided in the identification of complex problems, and in the generation of new combinations of technical and organisational factors to solve these. In the first case solutions were also implemented, and so tested in reality.

In most other single plants/enterprises, the need for improving the work environment is usually less strongly felt on the part of management, or management will more usually tend to solve problems they have defined in a unilateral manner, working through experts. As a reaction against this, there have been serious attempts to improve working environments, and increase workers' control generally through joint researcher/local union projects (e.g. Nygaard and Bergo, 1974). These have contributed towards raising consciousness about problems among workers, but seem to have limited impact. The national unions on their side seem as strongly tied up in the same organisational model and managerial practices as the industry itself. Hence they are not able to contribute to the solution of complex environmental/psycho–social problems at plant level either. The factory inspectorate, which has a statutory right to interfere, is similarly caught up in its traditional role of measuring identified, single environmental factors against scientifically/legally established threshold values, and then issuing orders on this basis. The combination of, for example, irregular working hours, variations in work load in periods of understaffing, speed requirements, heat, heavy lifting and little control, which Karlsen and Næss (1978) demonstrated, lead to psychological and physiological wear and tear and psychosomatic illnesses in hotel and restaurant workers, cannot be controlled through such practices.

Obviously a multilevel strategy is needed to create sustained development of the work environment in industry in general. The new legislation and the programme of which it is a part intends, as we briefly have described, to give such a strategy. A major dilemma then is that several parts of this programme (unions, factory inspector, research, financing, the educational system) are based on the same principles of specialisation (in departments, professions, disciplines) and operate according to similar conventional bureaucratic, and frequently authoritarian procedures as the industrial companies whom they are seeking to change.

Summing up – some conclusions

Because of the way we use the concept of total work environment load (and hence stress) the interaction between a number of factors (psychological, social, technological and organisational) has to be considered. We see systematic changes in such factors as a central strategy for reducing organisational stress. Participation by those exposed to the work environment is seen both as an environmental factor in itself, as well as a necessary condition for adequate definition of problems and achievement of successful changes. A sufficient degree of control over resources in order to manage one's job demands is a key factor behind absence of psycho–social problems in relation to work situation. As argued, much more technological and organisational choice is available to create conditions for autonomy than is usually exploited. When, for example, plant-level change programmes within the Industrial Democracy Project were stopped and/or reversed by management, these moves were rooted in social values rather than technical/economic ones. There is, then, a basic problem that the workers who have the lowest degree of control over their work situations (for example, assembly-line workers who are completely machine-paced with short work cycles and no possibility of leaving the work station) will also be those in the weakest position for participation in the improvement process. As demonstrated by Frankenhaeuser and Gardell (1976) the combination of machine-pacing, repetitive work and quick decision-making under strict restrictions is not uncommon, and gives high levels of stress as measured by psycho–physiological methods. The same research also demonstrates implicitly that expert judgement and measurements gave a diagnosis compatible with the workers' own. One conclusion is therefore that to avoid *some* serious negative effects of combinations of socio–technical factors, expert judgement and the application of specific workers' protection rules can work. This is expected to be the case in Norway where the factory inspector should be able to forbid machine pacing, extremely short work-cycles and piece-rates under certain conditions.

To realise the more optimistic part of the Law's intentions, that is creating positive, sustained improvement towards better quality of working life, a much more sophisticated strategy has to be applied. At the level of the single plant, there are numerous demonstrations of solutions and strategies achieving sometimes remarkable improvements in the working environment with similarities to the two cases referred to here. In some of these social scientists have played constructive and active roles, but they have frequently found that the development has become too strongly contingent upon their initiative. The alternative, now under trial within the Industrial Democracy Programme, is to work with groups of people from several enterprises at the same time, to allow direct learning and mutual support through a network, and to avoid creating dependency. A combination of this approach and the use of the resources made available through the legislation is probably the most feasible solution.

A strategy of direct worker participation in the work environment improvement process tends to bring up organisational variables and solutions. Frequently these are alternatives to much more expensive and complex technical solutions. But they may require very determined (multi-level) organisational development work, and they tend to run contrary to basic company and union organisational principles. The fairly simple industrial relations systems in Scandinavia have made projects in this area comparatively easy to carry out. Still, a time perspective of 3–5 years is not very long in this connection.

The use of legislation to improve the quality of working life is becoming increasingly central in Europe (IDE 1980a, 1980b). The main thrust of the rules has so far been, however, to protect workers against well-defined hazards and management's arbitrary use of power. Thus the rules may contribute to improved working conditions in specialised areas and create defence against certain types of changes in negative directions. On the other hand this specialisation in the rules and regulations creates very strong barriers at all levels against working with complex problems and against redefining problems as experience accumulates. The provisions of the Norwegian Work Environment Act for employee participation in the definition, planning and execution of improvements have not yet fully been used. Although there exist a number of interesting cases, even the central bodies which are supposed to assist in the process generally tend to continue working as before with single factors, branch level prescriptions and control measures. In terms of implications for research and development work it seems that levels above the single enterprise now are strategic targets.

REFERENCES

B. Blomsnes, 'Nuclear Power Plant Control: State of the Art Study', in *Platform Control Technology and Organization*, Scandpower, Work Research Institutes (Halden, Oslo, Kjeller: Institute for Atomic Energy, 1980)

F. E. Emery and E. Thorsrud, *Democracy at work* (Leiden, The Netherlands: Nijhoff, 1976)

F. E. Emery and E. Thorsrud, *Form and Content in Industrial Democracy* (London: Tavistock Publications, 1969)

P. H. Engelstad, 'Socio–technical Approach to Problems of Process Control', in L. E. Davis and J. C. Taylor (eds), *Design of Jobs* (Harmondsworth: Penguin, 1972)

M. Frankenhaeuser and B. Gardell, 'Underload and Overload in Working Life: Outline of a Multidisciplinary Approach', *Journal of Human Stress* (Sept. 1976) pp. 35–46

J. Gulowsen, 'A Measure of Work Group Autonomy', in L. E. Davis and J. C. Taylor (eds), *Design of Jobs* (Harmondsworth: Penguin, 1972)

B. Gustavsen, 'A Legislative Approach to Job Reform in Norway', *International Labour Review*, vol. 115, no. 3 (May–June 1977)

B. Gustavsen, *Strategies for Reform of Working Life* (forthcoming)

B. Gustavsen, A. Seierstad and A. Ebeltoft, *Hvordan skal vi gjennomföre arbeidsmiljöloven?* (Oslo, Norway: Tiden, 1978)

P. G. Herbst, *Autonomous Group Functioning* (London: Tavistock, 1962)

P. Hill, *Towards a New Philosophy of Management* (London: Gower, 1972)

Industrial Democracy in Europe, IDE – International Research Group (London: OUP, 1980a)

Industrial Relations in Europe, IDE – International Research Group (London: OUP, 1980b)

J. J. Karlsen, *Arbeidsmiljö og Arbeidsskader. En undersökelse blandt LO's medlemmer om helserisikoene på arbeidsplassen* (Oslo, Norway: LO, 1972)

J. J. Karlsen and R. Næss, *Arbeidsmiljö i hotell- og restaurantnaeringen* (Oslo, Norway: Work Research Institutes, 1978)

J. G. Khemeny, *Report of the President's Commission on the Accident at Three Mile Island* (Washington, 1979)

K. Nygaard and T. Bergo, *Planlegging, styring og databehandling* (Oslo, Norway: Tiden, 1974)

L. A. Odegaard, *Arbeidsplass-undersøkelsene i miljøarbeidet* (Oslo: Work Research Institutes, 1977)

Platform Control Technology and Organization, Scandpower, Work Research Institutes (Halden, Oslo, Kjeller: Institute for Atomic Energy, 1980)

T. U. Qvale, 'A Norwegian Strategy for the Democratization of Industry', *Human Relations*, vol. 29, no. 5 (1976) pp. 453–69

T. U. Qvale, 'Samarbeidsprosjektet i Magnesiumfabrikken', *Work Research Institutes* AI/Doc. 23/71 (Oslo, Norway, 1971)

T. U. Qvale and J. E. Karlsen, 'Tariffstridige Aksjoner', *Work Research Institutes* Doc. 5/71 (Oslo, Norway, 1971)

B. I. Susman and R. E. Evered, 'An Assessment of the Scientific Merits of Action Research', *Administrative Science Quarterly*, vol. 23 (Dec. 1978) pp. 582–603

E. Thorsrud, 'Collaborative Action Research to Enhance the Quality of Working Life', in L. E. Davis and A. B. Cherns (eds) *The Quality of Working Life* (London: Collier-Macmillan, 1975) pp. 193–204

E. L. Trist and K. W. Bamforth, 'Some Social and Psychological Consequences of the Longwall Method of Coal Getting', *Human Relations*, vol. 4 (1951) pp. 3–38

E. L. Trist, W. Higgin, H. Murray and A. B. Pollock, *Organizational Choice: Capabilities of groups at the coal face under changing technologies: The loss, rediscovery, and transformation of a work tradition* (London: Tavistock Publications, 1963)

W. Wright, interview in *Mobile Explorer* (Stavanger, Norway: MENI, 1979)

11 Towards Organisational Coping with Stress

Nico van Dijkhuizen
Royal Netherlands Navy

In this chapter I will not provide you with a detailed programme of how to deal with your own stress, nor with the stress in your company. In the first place because I think I know by now rather well how to measure an individual's or a company's stress, but have little or no practice in dealing with it, although I feel rather well myself. But, in the second place, because I don't know you or your company, and thus giving you detailed advice on how to deal with your stress would be rather tricky. However, what I will try to do is to tell you about recommendations I and my colleagues wrote at the end of a research-report on stress in middle management, and to give a broad outline of a procedure of how to tackle the problems at a company-level. It is up to you to decide whether this chapter is of any use to you; you know yourself and your company much better than I ever will.

The study

In the middle of 1978 a study into the problems of middle management in production departments in industry in the Netherlands was concluded with the report *Middenkader en stress* (*Middle Management and Stress*; Van Vucht Tijssen, Van den Broecke, Van Dijkhuizen, Reiche and De Wolff, 1978). The stress part of that study (the other part being the charting of the middle manager's job) was done with the *Vragenlijst Organisatiestress* (*VOS, a questionnaire for*

organizational stress; Van Dijkhuizen and Reiche, 1976), a transla-
tion and elaboration of the questionnaire used by Caplan *et al.*
(Caplan, Cobb, French, Van Harrison and Pinneau, 1975) in their
study *Job Demands and Worker Health*. The study was organised in
line with the stress model of French and Caplan (1972) and the role
set model of Kahn *et al.* (Kahn, Wolfe, Quinn, Snoek and Rosenthal,
1964).

In the context of this chapter stress comprises all those
characteristics of stimuli in the work environment which, in relation
with his personality, are threatening to the person. By being threatening they may generate harmful consequences, not only for the person
himself, but also for his environment (his family, his organisation).

A model of stress

Not all people will experience a given job situation as stressful, nor will
a given individual experience all job situations as equally stressful.
Rather, stress occurs when the abilities of a person are not congruent
with the demands of the job environment, or where clear obstacles
exist to fulfilling strong needs or values. In such situations there is a
bad fit between the individual and his environments. A good fit exists
to the extent to which the person's motives for working are matched
by supplies for these motives in the job environment, and/or to the
extent to which job demands (or job requirements) are met by relevant
abilities in the person.

This idea may be represented by the model in Figure 11.1. It can be
seen that, on the one hand, the organisation makes demands on the
person, i.e., by giving him a high workload and demanding a high
degree of creativity, but, at the same time, offers reinforcement in the
form of an autonomous job and recognition.

The person, on the other hand, has got certain abilities that may (or
may not) meet the demands of the organisation. But, at the same time,
the person brings with him certain needs the organisation may or may
not meet. If the organisation meets the needs of the person (by giving
him career possibilities, a salary, recognition) and the person's abilities
are useful for the organisation, no stress occurs and the person
experiences satisfaction. If the person meets the organisation's
demands, and the offered possibilities are able to get the person into
the organisation and to keep him inside, the organisation may be said
to experience 'satisfactoriness'.

Should, however, the organisation's demands and/or possibilities
deviate to an important degree from the person's abilities and needs,
the person may experience this as threatening and find himself in a

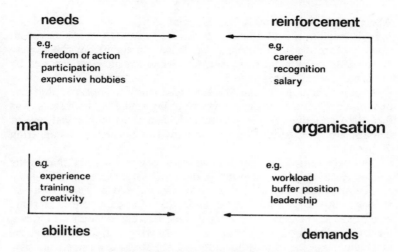

Figure 11.1   A model of fit and misfits between man and organisation
Source: Lofquist and Dawis, 1969.

stressful situation. The greater the discrepancy, the more the stress. This kind of discrepancy may come into being in various ways. Having insufficient skills and abilities may be threatening, because it may lead, for instance, to qualitative work overload: the work is beyond one's abilities, knowledge and experience. Having too many abilities may come to the surface as under-utilisation of skills and abilities: there is no way in which they may be used fully in practice. This may give rise to the 'big fish in a small pond' syndrome. Moreover, one's needs may exceed the organisation's possibilities, like wanting the responsibility of a more senior job when one has reached one's personal ceiling.

However, the situations as described above are part of a photograph instead of a film. In reality the situation is, almost inevitably, much more complicated. It is very likely that, over a period of time, changes occur both in the demands and the supplies of the job, and in the values and the abilities of the employee. We must remember this, but shall repeat the simpler, essential, point before progressing: the greater the discrepancy between the organisation's demands and the person's abilities, and between the organisation's possibilities or reinforcements and the person's needs, the more stress will result from the job.

I will not go into detail about the negative consequences of stress; the fact that this book is on coping with the phenomenon implies that such negative consequences are well-known and worth dealing with.

Allow me to give you just a few examples.

In a medium-sized company in the Netherlands (Metals Division) that was forced to fire a quarter of its staff, a significant rise in psychosomatic complaints was observed, while absenteeism reached 25 per cent.

Another example. In the *Middenkader* study it appeared that one out of every three predecessors of today's middle managers was forced to abandon his job prematurely due to psychological and/or somatic ailments. In one (large) company this figure was a staggering 70 per cent.

And very recently a Dutch newspaper covered a story that in the city of Rotterdam absenteeism among civil servants was to be given special attention. It costs the city, it was calculated, a yearly 100–180 million guilders, the equivalent of about 25–45 million pounds sterling. The costs to industry may thus include decreased quality of work, increased absenteeism, increased staff turnover, and, for example, the increasing expense of health insurance. Job stress can impair the psychological and physical well-being of the individual, and thereby affect the well-being of the worker's family. On the societal level, these effects can be manifest in increased welfare costs, increased socially-disruptive behaviour, such as alcoholism and drug abuse, and less involvement in the community.

How to recognise stress

To recognise stress in our organisation it might be useful to pay attention to the following 'signals':

Lower productivity by decreased work performance

Production stays below planning, or below what might be expected, if expectations are based on technical possibilities; rejects at quality control point to decreasing care in production; faulty and uncaring handling of machinery brings more breakdown than necessary from a technical point of view.

High absenteeism

Absenteeism may result from illnesses with a clear medical diagnosis, such as breaking a leg when skiing, but it is increasingly ascribed to less clearcut, often psychological, illness. It is widely believed that this leads to a need to flee from stressful situations or circumstances. If flight does not result in 'full' absenteeism, it may show itself at work in the avoidance of problems or persons with whom poor relations exist.

This may lead to less efficient problem solving, or even to no pro
solving behaviour at all.

High staff turnover

If the stressful circumstances stay in action long enough, and flight
into absenteeism no longer alleviates the problems, the tendency to
leave the situation and to look for other, less stressful jobs, gets
stronger. High turnover and high absenteeism lead to manpower
problems which again negatively influence productivity and overload
those who stay.

At the interpersonal level we may run into the following
phenomena:

Irritability and much interpersonal conflict

'Stress' tends to make people irritated and annoyed in their reactions
to demands and communications from others. This disturbs
relationships, giving rise to more frequent conflicts. About 50 per cent
of middle managers indicate that they are frequently irritated or
annoyed.

Less support giving

Being interested in others' problems, giving mental and actual support
is inhibited when under tension. This means that, in moments of stress,
less than 'normal' support may be given, while the person demanding
support needs above 'normal' amounts.

Family problems

Usually one can't 'wash oneself clean' from job stress when leaving
the factory gates; very often the family gets its share as well and this
may result in a tense atmosphere at home. Inevitably this atmosphere
will feedback into the organisation again, thus closing the circle, or,
more likely contributing to the upward spiral of stress. One third of
the middle managers in the *Middenkader* study reported that they
were unable to give sufficient attention to their families due to work-
problems.

At the level of the individual the following may be observed:

Increased smoking

It is a well known fact that smokers under stress usually smoke more
than their ordinary average (considering smoking to be a stress-
reducing habit). The addictive effects cause the raised dosage to be
continued longer than strictly necessary.

Sleeplessness

Endless thinking about work problems makes it difficult to fall asleep. About 35 per cent of the middle managers in the *Middenkader* study report regular sleeplessness.

Clothing habits

Clothing habits may be observed to change under stress. People we do not expect to may suddenly appear in an extravagant version of the latest fashion (like the ones of the 1960s 'Carnabition Army'), or appear in very casual or even neglected clothing.

Eating and drinking habits

Either one forgets to eat, because one lacks time to do so; one eats very fast, usually on the work-spot, because one does not allow oneself to take proper time to eat; or one eats excessively, in order to forget one's problems. Moreover, excessive drinking may take place. Stress appears, be it only temporarily, to be soluble in alcohol. To continue in chemical terms: the temporary solution appears from the gradually developing noxious 'precipitation' on the liver.

High blood pressure

Blood pressure, especially the systolic pressure, reacts very quickly to tensions. Prolonged tension may raise the normal or base level, giving rise to hypertension.

High cholesterol level

The same story applies as with blood pressure. An elevated or too high cholesterol level, as shown by 25 per cent of our middle managers, enhances the chances of coronary and cerebrovascular diseases.

Fight-flight reactions

As we have seen above with absenteeism and high staff-turnover, stress often causes flight reactions. However, fight reactions occur too. Examples are making others look ridiculous; not listening to others; starting sentences with: 'I thought I could expect from you . . .' or 'We can discuss this at great length, but . . .'. Examples of flight reactions in this context are: talking round a subject, poor visual contact with the environment, waiting till others make the decisions and the frequent use of phrases like 'Sorry, no time' and 'Upstairs decided . . .'.

When these phenomena are recognised in our organisation, in our co-workers or in ourselves, it is time to tackle the stress problems. One could say that we are already too late. These symptoms mean that we have exposed the organisation and its employees to a, possibly unnecessary, amount of stress. In many cases it might have been avoided; in any case it has already cost us a lot, both materially and psychologically. In these circumstances, we shall have to cure first, but eventually we ought to aim at prevention.

Organisational coping

The aim of organisational coping is to reduce stress in work situations, more specifically to attune the organisation's demands to the individual's skills and abilities, and the organisation's possibilities or reinforcements to the individual's needs. We must not aim at total elimination of stress in organisation; it simply is not possible, nor even desirable. A certain, however limited, amount of stress is necessary to stay alive and perform well. What we must aim at is to diminish the amount of stress to a level equal to the tolerances and needs of the exposed individuals. Organisational coping with stress may consist of three phases: research, classification and attack.

Stress research

In order to be able to attack stress in the right way and in the right places it is important to look for 'stress-centres' in our particular organisation. It is useless to recommend any one 'prefabricated' coping programme, just as it is useless to administer medicine to a patient without first diagnosing the disease. Stress may be diagnosed with an abridged version of the VOS, our organisation stress questionnaire: translated, elaborated and validated by my colleague Martin Reiche and myself, and used in the *Middenkader* study (Van Dijkhuizen and Reiche, 1976; Reiche and Van Dijkhuizen, 1980). This questionnaire measures stressors, strains and personality characteristics present in the particular situation. The questionnaire-data are given form and specific content validity by data from interviews with a sample of key-persons in positions from top to bottom in the organisation.

At Nijmegen University the Stress Research Group is at present working on norm-profiles, reflecting the stress- and strain-figures as found with various samples in various types of organisations, using the same questionnaire (see Kleber, Winnubust and De Wolff, 1980).

The organisation under diagnosis may then be compared with the appropriate norm-profiles, and we are able to see whether our organisation shows more or less stress on certain aspects or subjects than the comparable norm. Should we find equal or even lesser amounts of stress it does not necessarily mean that we can sit back and rest; the norm-profiles only tell us about the average amounts of stress, they say nothing about their absolute values. And even the average amounts may be too much.

In the *Middenkader* study it appeared that stress, as middle management experience it, may be classified into three key stress factors: ambiguity, workload and poor relations with others. Each of these stress factors was shown to have important relations with psychological and physiological strains, the negative consequences of being exposed to stressors.

Classification

Once we know at which 'stress-centres' our programme should be aimed, we have to make a distinction between avoidable and non-avoidable stress. This distinction is based on the possibility or impossibility of eliminating the causes of the stress. An example of avoidable stress might be role ambiguity caused by insufficient feedback from the superior; in principle we are able to teach the superior to give more and more frequent feedback on his subordinate's functioning. As an example of non-avoidable stress I suggest long sailing periods both in the Navy and the merchant navy. Of course we might take ships out of service for longer periods, but I am afraid such action would interfere with the organisation's interests.

The classification into avoidable and non-avoidable stress is relevant at each of the four levels on which coping may take place.

(a) On the level of the structure of the organisation

A faulty or very ambiguous communications system, for example in which wrong channels of information are being used, in which people are being informed too late or not at all, and in which it may happen that subordinates get certain information before their superiors would be seen as 'avoidable'.

(b) On the level of organisation-processes

Today's much looked for 'social leadership' has advantages and disadvantages. Middle managers are often insufficiently equipped, which shows in their demand for training in social aspects of their tasks. Moreover, secondary analysis of our data revealed that sub-ordinates of more socially-orientated managers showed more absenteeism than subordinates of less socially-orientated managers.

(c) On the level of the job

Middle management's buffer position puts them under pressure from two sides of the organisation. They have to try to reconcile the con-flicting interests of (top) management and workers. We must ask if this is inevitable.

(d) On the level of the individual

Having too low an education level for the job demands, not being able to deal with people, or showing a personality characteristic that enhances vulnerability to certain stressors typical of his or her job all suggest inappropriate, and therefore avoidable, selection, placement and/or training.

Attack

Once the stress is classified into avoidable and non-avoidable stress, once the causes are more or less clear, and once we have established which causes can be altered, the third step, the attack on the stress-centres, follows. Again I want to emphasise that in a general story like this, only general examples of what might be possible can be given. So, I will simply give a list of some topics which might be worth attacking. First, regarding *avoidable stress*.

(a) Physical job-environment

A number of stressors, influencing mental and somatic well-being, are located in the physical job-environment. Dependent upon the situa-tion, we may think of reducing debilitating noise levels; reducing the possibilities of inhaling toxic substances or gasses; air-conditioning to level off the effects of extreme heat or cold; improving levels of illumination and reducing reflections from for instance, keyboards; introducing better, ergonomically designed office equipment etc.

(b) Organisational structure

We may think of altering the organisation's formal structure, for instance, by making it less bureaucratic, by 'flattening' the organisa-tion in order to shorten the chain of information; or by integrating a production department and a technical service department in order to facilitate daily maintenance.

(c) Work-structuring

It is possible to (re)structure jobs in such a way that they are optimally in accordance with the production-process. To reduce workload we may check whether tasks and competencies are optimally delegated to lower levels of management. But we may also think of job enlargement, or job enrichment, for those jobs lacking sufficient stimulation and in which the person's skills and abilities are not fully employed. We do however have to be careful not to assume that all individuals want challenging and involving experiences at work. There is evidence that enlarging an entire set of jobs may improve the fit between 'man' and 'organisation' for some, but it will also worsen fit for others, who prefer simpler job routines.

(d) Information

Information needs to be channelled and apportioned very carefully. It is important that all employees get the right information at the right time to do proper jobs; it is also important that no one 'drowns' in it. And one has to take care that addressees receive information before others or third parties; nothing is more detrimental for good relations and good motivation than, for instance, to read in the evening paper that your department will be reorganised or even closed.

(e) Clarity

Every employee should have clarity, not only regarding his or her tasks and competencies, regarding what others expect to be done, how they think of the work and what the career possibilities are, but also regarding general company policies and the company's results. Such clarity enables one to place one's own job in a broader perspective, bringing positive effects to self-esteem. And higher self-esteem usually is coupled with better performance.

(f) Management of functioning

Being prepared to look continuously for indications of employees' dysfunctioning enables us to take action at an early stage. Building up a clear picture of how someone typically fulfils his or her job, of his or her capabilities and incapabilities, gives us a chance to notice relatively minor 'deviations', or crises with more substantial impact. We may thus be prompted to discuss their functioning with employees and so work towards attacking problems and setting new goals. It might be a suggestion, if someone is exposed to stress, not to focus on what he still does, but on what he neglects. It is very probable that his problems are in this area.

(g) Support from superior and colleagues

It has appeared from our research that receiving support from superiors and colleagues softens the serious effects of stressors. Support may thus act as some kind of buffer. Management and the middle manager should discuss situations which are ambiguous for the latter. Even without the direct possibility of solving problems, the fact that problems are recognised as such may reduce uncertainty. Middle managers seem to want clear guidelines, for example with regard to disciplinary actions. Moreover, the superior should watch his own speech. Very often one thoughtlessly uses words and phrases which are in fact punitive, such as 'You are rather late with it', 'Yes, you have said that before', 'OK, but only a minute, I'm very busy'.

(h) Participation

The opportunity to exert more influence on decisions affecting the person himself or his work may lead to more clarity, less conflicts and better relations with others. In particular middle management should be used more frequently to assist in the organisation's policy making. An additional benefit of participation is that the increased control allows the employee to structure the job the better to fit his abilities and values, whatever they may be. Those who want more complex and challenging jobs can take advantage of the opportunities opened up to them. Those who prefer simpler jobs can choose to delegate decision making to others who want this job demand. Remaining tasks can be routinised in ways which minimise their demands on the worker.

So far I have presented a rather randomly chosen list of stresses which are largely avoidable. In the following section some actions regarding non-avoidable stress will be discussed.

The 'attacks' on non-avoidable stress start from the viewpoint that one is trying to equip the person better for working under stress, or to withdraw him temporarily or at the right time from stress-situations. We may think of the following.

(a) Selection

Ordinary selection routines very rarely take into account the stressful aspects of a job. Few if any tests exist to measure tolerance for ambiguity, workload or conflict. However, sometimes intake-interviews put people under stress by making them give information and solve problems, at the same time being under attack from the interviewer who makes hostile remarks and asks very personal questions. Often the candidate is put under time pressure. I don't think this stress-interview will ever win a prize for ethical behaviour! But one might argue that by being less than ethical one may prevent serious illnesses, mental as well as somatic.

(b) Training

Training may enlarge the individual's abilities to handle stress successfully. Assertiveness-training could be particularly valuable, but any training to prepare someone for a new job or novel situations in the job can play an important role. Usually the course is attended before entering the new situation. This seems logical, but putting training into practice is usually a very different, and difficult, matter. Perhaps further 'top-up' training could also be made available. For example, everybody in the organisation could be offered the possibility of spending a few days each year on a self-selected course. This might give a positive turn to the perception of stressful situations, and, thus, their negative consequences.

(c) Job-rotation

Job-rotation is almost always used as a tool for management development. However, we could also think of using it as means of letting people work in stressful situations or jobs for a shorter time, and letting them 'recreate' in easier jobs in between.

(d) Part-time jobs

It might be worth considering whether it is possible to have stressful jobs done on a part-time basis, in order to reduce the amount of time an individual is exposed to stress. This routine is followed in working with toxic substances; in the chemical industry part-time schemes are often used in jobs involving dangerous work. And the procedure may be compared with the one on board Royal Dutch Navy ships with, for example, radio-radar plotters or sonar operators. Their work requires so much attention that it can only be done for a short stretch of time.

(e) Career-planning and guidance

It appeared from our study that one out of every three middle managers has to leave the job between the ages of 55 and 60 because of mental or physical disabilities. An even greater percentage sees this age-bracket as the ideal time to stop 'middle managing' and change jobs. We will have to change the working-attitude to make it acceptable to 're-trace one or two steps' at the end of a career curve. If one gets overburdened, it should be possible to turn to an easier, but nevertheless satisfying job, in which one's knowledge and experience is of special value. We could, for example, make it company policy to keep employees for a shorter period in specialist jobs than we do now, but to reserve a number of those specialist jobs for our older employees.

This means that in specialist functions the 'practical experience in a management function' element may be brought in more strongly, while management positions in the line organisation will be occupied by more vital, younger people, more in touch with the mentality of the younger subordinates and with the technical and social developments taking place in the line departments. And it might also help to make the career-image less rigid.

At the end of this rather long list a number of topics regarding an attack on stress at the individual level will be presented, although I am not particularly fond of them myself. I think our first priority should always be to try to adapt the organisation and the job to the employee, instead of the reverse. Curing is silver, prevention might be gold. At the individual level stress may be reduced by giving the individual the opportunity to work off his tensions. This may be done in a number of ways, presented in random order.

(a) Sports

Sports may channel built-up aggression, work off tension by intense physical activity and build up a good physical condition, preventing tensions from having physical consequences too quickly.

(b) Counselling

Counselling may be a good method to work on personal problems. The client gets the opportunity to deal with his own problems creatively and to look for solutions himself. Support and guidance from professionals like psychiatric social workers and psychologists is necessary.

(c) Support from family and friends

A helpful attitude by partner and friends regarding problems gives the individual concerned the opportunity to find support and understanding in the vitally important home-situation. This means, however, that we might have to begin to build bridges between the work-place and the home, providing opportunities for the worker's wife (or, now, husband!) to understand better her husband's job, to express her views about the consequences of his work on family life, and to be involved in the work-related decision-making processes that affect all members of the family unit.

(d) Other interests

Just like sports, hobbies and all other sorts of leisure activities may give the opportunity to be taken out of oneself, and to build up new energy to resist work-problems.

(e) Relaxation techniques

Relaxation techniques are quite popular these days. And they may be good methods for physical recreation, if their usually mystical ideological elements are taken out. Physical recreation, or better relaxation, is important, because stress is accompanied by raised muscle-tension, which raises heart frequency and blood pressure by, in fact, pinching off the arteries. I refer here to the relaxation parts of techniques like Zen, yoga and transcendental meditation, but also of bio-feedback.

I have by now given you a rather long list of possible action-points and techniques, to be used on various levels in the organisation. Once again, the list is rather randomly chosen, and certainly not exhaustive, not least because coping with organisational stress is still in an experimental stage. However, it may be taken for granted that the action-points and techniques I have presented may help; to what degree, and whether that degree is sufficient, is still unknown. Nevertheless, I think we ought to start right now. Both because the level of stress in a number of jobs and organisations has become quite intolerable, and because 'practice' gives us the opportunity to learn.

Before giving you an example of how one of the companies that participated in the *Middenkader* study dealt with the results, I will mention two complicating factors. The inescapable conclusion of the 'fit' theory I mentioned before is that, in order to reduce job stress for all persons, programmes must allow individualised treatment of a worker. It must be recognised, however, that this objective can conflict with the technology associated with the job, with organisational control structures, and with the system for allocating rewards. Moreover, one has to realise that changing the organisation's structure is a time-consuming activity. Usually one is prepared to wait about two years for a change's concrete results, but two years is patience's limit. Other studies, however, have shown that it takes about five years for a major change to become really accepted and work well. Should we introduce new changes after the two years, because the old programme 'apparently' did not work, we start in fact a new five years' cycle.

An example of stress management

I think that a lot of the stress-problems in most companies can and must be solved by the organisations themselves. An assumption thereby is that these organisations do rather well, maintain reasonably good communications and have the intention to deal with issues from stress research they recognise or want their own organisation to check on. The following procedure is no manual for organisational develop- ment, nor a procedure applicable for organisations with very big problems; in those cases professional help is needed. And again, even surmountable problems take time to solve and to get solved. In fact, it is not essential which party takes the initiative to start dealing with stress-problems: it may be top management, middle management, the workers, the works-council, the personnel department, etc.; however, it is essential that top management is informed of what one plans to do according to what procedure, and that they agree with the planned action and actively support it.

One of the participating large companies intended to tackle the problems for its middle management, and top management supported actions to be taken to achieve that end. For that purpose the middle managers from the company who had participated in the study were called to follow-up meetings. (Two meetings were held, otherwise the group would have been too large to be able to communicate properly.) Apart from the middle managers, representatives from the Personnel Department, the Psychological Department and the Organisation and Development Department were present at these meetings, together with a deputation of the researchers. Before the meetings were held the participants had all received a copy of the summary of the research results, written specifically for this company.

First, one of the researchers presented the results to the meeting (using flip-over sheets), dealing with the middle manager's job as it was found in the study, and giving a detailed account of the problems the job gives. This results presentation triggered a spontaneous, lively discussion among the meeting's participants. They discussed which of the problems were recognised by each of the middle managers, what might be done to solve them and who might take the action.

The participants agreed to list the problems which, in their opinion, should be tackled, in two categories: (a) problems recognised by all middle managers, common to the job itself; and (b) problems specific to any department, and to be solved within the department itself. The Personnel Department was available to give support and to coordinate actions, only if they were asked to do so. A 'problem-list', according to the frequency of mention, was made up in both middle managers' meetings; each group was informed about the results of the other group.

A second type of meeting was held in which the participating parties were the same except for the middle managers, who were replaced by their immediate superiors, because these might play an important role in the solution of the problems. Again the results of the study were introduced by one of the researchers, and again a lively discussion resulted. The immediate superiors of the middle managers agreed with the suggested procedure; they too drew up a list of problems, important in their opinion, existing for their middle managers. One of their suggestions was to discuss a number of problems on a wider basis, for instance, in a meeting with middle managers and themselves, together with representatives of the personnel department and top management. The report of this meeting was sent to all participating middle managers.

In a subsequent meeting of researchers, the Organisation and Development Department, and the Personnel and Psychological Departments, the problem-lists of the previous three meetings were brought together into one list of action-points, and suggestions for solutions were added, stemming from the meetings and from the answers on one of the interview questions asked of middle managers: ('Do you have any ideas on what could be done at an organisational level, or in the field of education or training, to improve your job?'). With symbols, it was indicated which group (one of the two groups of middle managers and the group of their superiors) had raised a particular problem and which group brought in which solution. This 'major' list was sent to all discussion participants for approval. All agreed on its contents.

Then it was decided that another meeting should be held, this time with all middle managers from the sample, to discuss which problems should be dealt with at an organisational level, and which ones were to be solved in their own departments. Not only the middle managers from the sample, but all middle managers in the company received a copy of the list.

The list was then discussed in another meeting of middle managers and top management. The latter agreed that a lot of the problems listed were worth dealing with. The problem to be solved *now* was how the problems on the list could be tackled. All participants thought that the most efficient way to deal with most of the problems was to set up a special training course for middle managers, focused on these issues. A working-group was set up, consisting of representatives of the groups concerned (middle managers, their immediate superiors, and the Personnel, Psychological and Organisation and Development Departments) to come up with the link between the research results, the agreed-upon problems, and the training-course. At the moment this working-group has almost finished its job and very soon the special training-course can start.

I do think that the way this particular company handled the results of the research for the benefit of its middle managers (and probably also for others in the organisation) is an excellent example of how modern management can use research results in order to cope with stress at an organisational level, making full use of the 'subjects' themselves, thus creating the necessary commitment of all concerned.

The work is now nearly completed, two and a half years after it was started. This may seem a long time; however, the time it took to create the problems was much much longer. I think the fact that 'something is being done' already creates better atmosphere, and the results of all efforts will have been worth waiting for; a thorough, well-thought-out, problem-oriented course that may cure as well as prevent; and, in fact, all worked out by the company itself.

REFERENCES

R. D. Caplan, S. Cobb., J. R. P. French Jr., R. Van Harrison and S. R. Pinneau, *Job Demands and Worker Health*, HEW-publication 75–160 (Washington: HEW-NIOSH, 1975)

N. van Dijkhuizen, 'Measurement and Impact of Organisational Stress', an address given to the 4th workshop on psychosocial stress and coronary heart disease (Klinik Höhenried, LVA Oberbayern, July 1979), in M. J. Halhuber, and J. Siegrist (eds), *Psychosozialer Stress und koronare Herz-krankheit 4* (Berlin: Springer-Verlag, forthcoming)

———, 'Recognising Stress – how Stress Management Works', a paper presented at the EMAS management research conference on the management of stress (London, June 1979)

———, 'Towards a Sequential Model of Stress', a paper presented at the NIAS conference on stress and anxiety (Wassenaar, Feb. 1980)

———, 'From Stressors to Strains: Research into their Interrelationships (forthcoming)

N. van Dijkhuizen, and H. M. J. K. I. Reiche, *Het meten van organisatiestress: over de bewerking van een vragenlijst*, report A & O 001–76, 002–76 and 003–76. (Leiden, The Netherlands: Rijksuniversiteit, 1976)

N. van Dijkhuizen, and H. M. J. K. I. Reiche, 'Psychosocial Stress in Industry: a Heartache for Middle Management?' a paper presented at the symposium on the role of psychosocial factors in the pathogenesis of coronary heart disease (Maastricht: March 1979). *Journal of Psychotherapy and Psychosomatics* (forthcoming)

J. R. P. French Jr., and R. D. Caplan, 'Organizational Stress and Individual Strain', in A. J. Marrow (ed.), *The failure of success* (New York: AMACOM, 1972)

R. L. Kahn, D. M. Wolfe, R. P. Quinn, J. D. Snoek, and R. A. Rosenthal, *Organizational stress: studies in role conflict and ambiguity* (New York: John Wiley, 1964)

R. J. Kleber, J. A. M. Winnubust, and Ch. J. de Wolff, *Stressgroep Nijmegen: werkprogramma 1980* (Nijmegen, The Netherlands: K. Universiteit, report 80 A0 03, Stressgroep Nijmegen publ. no. 20, 1980)

L. H. Lofquist, and R. V. Dawis, *Adjustment to work: a psychological view of man's problems in a work-oriented society* (New York: Appleton-Century-Crofts, 1969)

H. M. J. K. I. Reiche, *Stress-management: het beheersen van stress in organisaties*, report 79 A0 11, Stressgroep Nijmegen publ. no. 16. (Nijmegen, The Netherlands: K. Universiteit, 1979)

H. M. J. K. I. Reiche, and N. van Dijkhuizen, *Vragenlijst organisatiestress: handleiding voor testafname* (forthcoming)

J. van Vucht Tijssen, A. A. J. van de Broecke, N. van Dijkhuizen, H. M. J. K. I. Reiche and Ch. J. de Wolff, *Middenkader en stress* (Den Haag: COP/SER, 1978)

Index

AA (Alcoholics Anonymous),
24, 173, 175
AAFDBI (American Association
of Fitness Directors in
Business and Industry), 82
absenteeism
causes of, 30, 154, 189
civil servants, among, 206
cost of, 80, 206
indication of stress, as, 20,
120
low at Plessey, 153
records of, 81
reduced by fitness
programme, 29
ACAS (Advisory Conciliation
and Arbitration Service),
155
ACCEPT (Alcoholism
Community Centres for
Education, Prevention and
Treatment), 163–4, 168,
170, 174–7
accidents,

alcohol a cause of, 23, 29,
166–7
change a cause of, 60
increased rate of, 113
most caused by human error,
190
proneness as sign of stress, 20
Adams, J. D., 45, 58, 63
Addiction Research Unit (of The
Institute of Psychiatry),
175
Administrative Staff College
(Henley), 43
Advisory Conciliation and
Arbitration Service
(ACAS), 155
AEC (Alcohol Education
Centre), 175
alcohol, 13–14, 89, 100
abuse of, 81, 163–80
accidents and, 23
damaging to the liver, 166
dangerous during pregnancy,
169